ONE DAY AHEAD
A Tour de France Misadventure

Richard Grady

First published in Great Britain in 2014

ISBN 9781075930621

ONE DAY AHEAD

Following a 17 year career in corporate finance, Richard Grady eventually escaped the rat race and founded a number of successful Internet businesses. During his time in the world of Internet marketing, he wrote prolifically and published several best-selling eBooks on the subject.

These days, Richard is more likely to be found writing about his adventures as an, often reluctant, traveller. You may find them amusing. Chances are, Richard didn't.

For Helen
You were right
I should've just stayed at home

Author's Note

In an adventure such as this, when a group of people are thrown together for a long period of time in close quarters, it is inevitable that tensions will arise. It was no different for the One Day Ahead team and we certainly had our ups and downs. This recollection is, obviously, told from my point of view and I am sure that others may have a different viewpoint when it comes to certain incidents.

With this in mind and as I was unable to speak to all concerned prior to publication, I have opted, as a matter of courtesy, to change the names of some individuals.

START

Germany

Belgium

Switzerland

Italy

Spain

LIÈGE
VISÉ
TOURNAI
SERAING
BOULOGNE-SUR-MER
ORCHIES
ABBEVILLE
SAINT-QUENTIN
ROUEN
METZ
TOMBLAINE
ÉPERNAY
PARIS
RAMBOUILLET
CHARTRES
BONNEVAL
LA PLANCHE
DES BELLES FILLES
BELFORT   PORRENTRUY
BESANÇON
ARC-ET-SENANS
MÂCON
BELLEGARDE
SUR-VALSERINE
ALBERTVILLE
LA TOUSSUIRE
BRIVE-LA-GAILLARDE
ANNONAY
DAVÉZIEUX
SAINT-JEAN
DE-MAURIENNE
SAINT-PAUL
TROIS-CHÂTEAUX
BLAGNAC
PAU   SAMATAN
FOIX
LE CAP D'AGDE
LIMOUX
PEYRAGUDES   BAGNÈRES
DE-LUCHON

Stage Profile

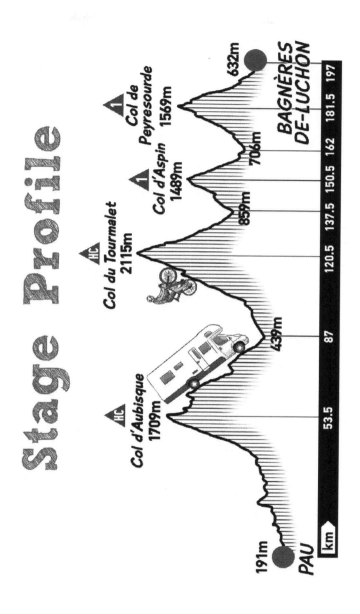

Col d'Aubisque 1709m

Col du Tourmalet 2115m

Col d'Aspin 1489m

Col de Peyresourde 1569m

191m

439m

859m

706m

632m

PAU

BAGNÈRES DE-LUCHON

km 53.5 87 120.5 137.5 150.5 162 181.5 197

PREFACE

First held in 1903, the Tour de France is a multiple stage cycle race, held over twenty one days during a three week period in July each year. Two additional days are allotted as rest days. The Tour came about as a publicity stunt designed to increase the circulation of French sporting magazine, L'Auto. Announced in January 1903 in L'Auto, the cycle race would consist of six stages starting on the 1st July 1903 and would cover 2,428 km. Sixty cyclists entered and twenty one managed to complete all six stages, which had an average distance of over 400 km. It was a gruelling and formidable event but one whose popularity continues to grow after more than a 100 years.

Competing in the modern-day Tour de France is a privilege reserved for the most elite of athletes; many consider that it is one of the most challenging sporting events anyone could face. The professional Tour de France rider is, of course, paid for putting his body through the pain of racing 3,500 km around France but even a briefcase full of cash wouldn't be enough to persuade most people to give it a go.

Most cycling fans would be happy just to ride a single stage of the Tour. The majority wouldn't dream of attempting the whole route and certainly not in the same ridiculously short time period as the professional riders. But some people don't fit into the category of 'most cycling fans' and this minority are prepared to push themselves further. I'm not one of these people. Unfortunately I have friends who are.

Richard Grady

6 MONTHS BEFORE THE TOUR

'Get a bicycle; you will certainly not regret it, if you live.'
Mark Twain - Author

'Have you seen what Mick is planning on doing next?'

The email pinged into my inbox and my first thought wasn't 'What is Mick doing?' rather 'Why is his sister-in-law telling me about it?' Usually when Mick had a new madcap scheme or challenge up his sleeve, either he, or more likely, his long-suffering wife Sara, would be the one to break the news. This would be swiftly followed up with the details of how I was to be involved in the aforementioned scheme/challenge.

So when the news came from Kim, Sara's sister, my immediate reaction was one of suspicion. I read on…

'He's found someone who is riding the entire Tour de France route and they've said he can go too.'

It transpired that Mick was in contact with a couple of amateur cyclists who were planning on riding the entire 2012 Tour de France route within the same three week timescale as the professionals complete it. To add to the pressure of the challenge, the intention was to complete this ride while the actual Tour de France was being held, riding each stage one day ahead of the main event.

The fact that Mick was planning on getting involved in something like this was not surprising. He loved riding his bike and had competed in various amateur cycling disciplines since he was 14 years old. Riding the Tour de France route would be just another thing to tick off the list. In fact, plenty of ordinary people have made it their business to ride Tour routes over the years, although the vast majority don't do it in the three week period granted to the professional Tour de France riders and the reason for this is simple. It is a very, very long way and the race goes over some very, very big mountains.

Not that any of this would bother Mick. In his head he would just be getting a three week holiday in the sun riding his bike. I turned to my partner Helen and summarised the contents of the email, expressing my concern as to why Kim was the bearer of this news and not Mick or Sara.

'Well that doesn't take a genius to work out does it?' came Helen's reply, 'You're going with them but they just haven't worked out how best to tell you.'

'That's exactly what I was scared of,' I replied.

I knew that Mick wouldn't have me in mind to actually ride the Tour with him; there was no way that would be happening. Instead I would have a far more important and quite frankly, awful job and that would be providing support. I'd been roped into Mick's challenges before in a support role, always with Sara, and they always resulted in me wondering how I had ended up in the position. Previous events had been short though, the longest being a twenty seven hour non-stop canoe race from Devizes, Wiltshire to Westminster in London. The Tour wasn't short. The Tour lasted for three weeks and that was assuming nothing went wrong. Three weeks wasn't twenty seven hours. Three weeks was considerably longer than that.

After absorbing Kim's email, I figured that the best thing to do was ignore it. I hadn't actually been asked to go along so maybe I was worrying unnecessarily. Maybe Mick just hadn't had a moment to tell me about his latest project. Yes that was it, he was just busy. I wasn't going to France, I would just hear about how much fun he had had once they got back. Yes, that was definitely it. Just me being daft and worrying over nothing.

I was due to see Sara and Mick later that week.

'Did Kim tell you?' blurted Sara as she opened the front door.

'Yes, he's mad,' I replied.

'We wanted to ask you something...' Uh oh, here it comes, why am I always right?!

'If I can't get the whole three weeks off work, will you fly out and cover for me to support Mick and drive the motorhome?'

Mmm, this was sounding a little more positive. Firstly, I wasn't required for three weeks, just whatever period of time Sara couldn't get off work and secondly, I was only required to support Mick, not any of the other riders (although at this point it seemed a little unclear as to who the other riders actually were).

'So I only have to be there when you aren't and there will definitely only be me and Mick in the motorhome, no one else?'

Sara had a habit of filling their motorhome with as many bodies as possible. I think in her head it made for a better adventure. Of course, it is always more fun to have six people squeezed into a space instead of just two. One year I went out and bought my own motorhome just so I didn't have to partake in this adult version of sardines. We all went away to France to watch that year's Tour — me in my motorhome alone and Mick, Sara and three others crammed into theirs. I know who was the most comfortable on that trip and their names didn't begin with M or S.

'No, it will just be you, Mick and possibly me for a bit depending on logistics...oh and Adnan.'

'Adnan? Who the bloody hell is Adnan?' I had known Sara and Mick for over ten years and knew most of their friends. I had never heard of Adnan.

'He's, um, he's, he's one of the cyclists doing the ride,

there isn't any room for him in the other motorhome,'

'Right, but who is he? I've never heard you talk about him before.'

'No, well, that's because we don't know him yet, he saw something on the Internet about the ride and emailed to say he'd like to do it with us. He's a doctor, it'll be fine. I'm sure he's really nice.'

This was just getting better and better. I'm not great at meeting new people, it isn't something I enjoy. I've had a close circle of friends for the past couple of decades and I don't feel the need to add to them. I struggle to talk to a stranger for longer than five minutes at the occasional social event so living with someone who could turn out to be a complete weirdo (after all we met him on the Internet) for an, as yet undefined period, in the confines of a motorhome was not up there on my list of things to do this year.

Further investigation revealed that Mick had met Adnan briefly. He confirmed that he 'seemed alright.' That was something I suppose although Mick is a man of few words. He is the sort of person who telephones you and stops talking after saying 'Hello.' This is most confusing as you know it is Mick phoning but you don't really know what he wants. I know I am not the only person who has had to ask him this very question. I'm sure that Mick's words are rationed. Only a certain number allowed each day. Once they are used up, that's it, no more talking. Telephone words count for double. It is for this reason that I knew that whatever Mick was basing his opinion of Adnan 'being alright' on, it wouldn't be very concrete as their conversation would have only lasted for two or three sentences at most.

As we talked more about Mick's Tour, or One Day Ahead, as it became known, the more I softened to the idea of going along. It would be a challenge and an adventure and as much as I might think I'd like the idea of being at home, I knew that if I were, I would feel as if I was missing out. This was just as well in the end. Sara managed to get the full three weeks off work and therefore based on our original conversation there was no requirement for me to go at all. Funnily enough, this original conversation was never mentioned again and it appeared that I was now the only one who had any recollection of it even happening. Somewhere along the line it had been forgotten by everyone else and I was going to France. For three weeks.

It was December when the above discussions took place, six months before the start of both the Tour and One Day Ahead. Once I had confirmed my intention to tag along, we arranged to meet up with Stephen and Matt. One Day Ahead was Stephen's gig; he was the one who had come up with the idea over a pint one night with his mate, Matt. Matt's dad knew Mick from his cycle racing days and it was Matt's parents who had contacted Mick to see if he would go along to keep an eye on Matt and Stephen and be the 'grown up' of the group. This amused me somewhat as, although Mick is a retired firefighter and therefore, in theory, perfectly responsible, the fact is that he is more prone to mischief than most twenty-somethings. I'm guessing that Matt's parents knew this but didn't know anyone else who was capable of cycling 3,500 km in three weeks, so if they wanted an 'adult' to go with the boys, it would have to be Mick.

Stephen had big plans for One Day Ahead although it was clear from the outset that whilst he was thinking big, he may not have been thinking practically. Getting four riders around France safely and within the timescales dictated would be no easy task. The professional Tour de France involves a small army of support staff, hundreds of vehicles and the backing of big-name sponsors, not to mention the full cooperation of every town the race visits. We had none of this. Stephen had managed to secure the backing of several corporate sponsors (as well as riding for personal enjoyment, the team were planning on raising money for charity) and had also made arrangements to hire a second motorhome. Sara and Mick's motorhome, or Motorhome One as it became known, would be crewed by Sara and me and would provide accommodation for Mick and our new friend from the Internet, Adnan. Motorhome Two, looking after Stephen and Matt, would be in the hands of their respective partners, Nicole and Jess. This all sounded fine so far, however none of the Motorhome Two crew had any experience driving a motorhome or indeed, of dealing with all the chores which go with it – emptying the toilet cassette, filling up with water and so on. These were tasks which, with that number of people on board, would need to be done daily. As we were discussing the plans further, it became clear that Stephen and Matt had invited various other friends and acquaintances to join us at different points en route for a few days holiday.

It was time to nip things in the bud and fortunately Mick had some words left over from the day before so was able to do this. He bluntly explained that there wouldn't be room in either of the motorhomes for anyone who didn't serve a specific purpose. In other words, if you weren't a rider or support, you weren't coming. As it was, four people in each motorhome would be a tight fit especially with bicycles and three weeks worth of clothing and kit. Equally, we weren't going to have time to be ferrying visitors back and forth to airports and train stations. The ideal scenario was to leave on day one with everyone and not deviate from the Tour route for the next three weeks. Stephen eventually conceded that this made sense but did insist on his brother and sister, Christian and Hannah, being able to join us part way through the trip so that they could ride some of the Tour route.

As it turned out, we also ended up with one final member of the team, who ultimately proved invaluable. Emily was a physiotherapist and Stephen and Adnan had managed to get her manager to agree that she could accompany us for the full three weeks, in return for a bit of publicity for his business. This was a major coup and having our own in-house physio would surely be a huge advantage for the cyclists. After all, the professional Tour riders all get a good going over with their physio each night so if it was good enough for the pros…

Preparations for One Day Ahead began in earnest in January as the riders started to get some training miles in their legs and the support team started to think about what lay ahead. As far as I could tell, it was Stephen and Matt who were doing most of the training rides. Mick wasn't really doing any more cycling than he would have done normally although when questioned he told me, 'I really don't see that the cycling is going to be a problem.' Of course not, why would it be?

Adnan, it turned out, was not just a doctor but also a surgeon and he was working somewhere in the region of a hundred hours a week. This left little time for training, especially in the short daylight hours of a British winter.

I did little in terms of preparation although I did have a couple of conversations with Stephen about his plans. During one such chat, he outlined an idea for a daily video diary which he wanted to upload to the Internet each evening so that people could see how we were getting on. I could feel this video diary project being, very gently, palmed off in my direction and I quickly pointed out that whilst the idea sounded great in theory, in practice it would be a nightmare to effect. How much time did he think we were going to have each evening to start editing videos? Even if we managed to find the time to put these videos together, how were we going to upload them? A mobile Internet connection would cost a fortune and the reception would be sketchy at best in some of the remote locations. McDonalds offer reliable (and free) Wi-Fi but how many branches of McDonalds were we likely to find out in the sticks or halfway up a mountain? Fortunately this idea was put to bed very quickly but it was already clear to me that few of the people embarking on this adventure had any idea how much work it was actually going to entail.

JUNE 2012

'Sometimes I ride my bike to nowhere, to see nothing, just so I can ride my bike.'
Anon

As the day of departure grew closer, preparatory work intensified. Sara and I started to collate maps and other equipment which we knew we would need. Cycling kit was sourced with our sponsors' logos proudly emblazoned; Adnan had managed to source a huge quantity of energy drinks, gels and bars, which would be vital to keep the riders energy levels up during those incredibly long days in the saddle. Stephen was busy getting the word out and managed to get articles in some high profile cycling magazines. Eurotunnel tickets for the two motorhomes had been arranged and the people at Eurotunnel had kindly discounted the tickets as the ride was being done for charity.

It felt as though things were starting to come together, although I personally felt quite apprehensive about the whole thing. This was going to be a huge undertaking and would be a pretty tough task to pull off. I don't mean the cycling – that was the easy bit! Oh no, the difficult bit was the support and logistics. Getting vehicles, bikes and riders to the right place every morning, ensuring the riders were fed and watered along the way and then collected in the evening. Then you've got to get everyone to the start point for the following day's stage – it is rare for the Tour de France to finish in one town and then start the next stage the following day from the same town. The next day's start town could be 200 km away and that's on top of the 200 km you've just ridden and driven for that day's stage. No, the cycling was the easy bit, the riders had nothing to do but concentrate on enjoying the scenery and pushing the pedals round. I and the other supporters were most definitely the ones with the raw deal on this trip.

A couple of days before we were due to leave, Mick phoned me.

'Alright?' I responded appropriately and listened to the silence buzzing on the line.

'What do you want Mick?'

It seemed there was a problem with his motorhome. The motorhome in question was brand new, having just been imported from Europe. This importation formed the basis of the problem. As the vehicle was still on European number plates, Mick's insurance company were only prepared to offer cover if the motorhome stayed in England. A problem this most definitely was. The Tour route this year did not go through England and even if it had, 90% of it would still have been in France. Fortunately, Mick and Sara still had their old motorhome and therefore this was what we would use.

Now from a purely personal point of view, this suited me much better and I was actually quite pleased that this problem had arisen. On paper (and in real life as it happens), the new motorhome was, by far, the better option. It had air conditioning, a huge garage at the back for bikes, spares and tools and three double beds. The old motorhome had none of these features and although perfectly serviceable, it had seen better days. And this was exactly the reason I was happier to use it. I knew that I would be doing a lot of the driving over the coming three weeks and quite frankly, despite the fact that I had no intention of crashing or dinging either motorhome, the 3000 odd miles we would be travelling was a long way and if an accident was going to happen,

I'd rather it didn't happen in the new, much more expensive, model. Yes it would mean driving in 40° heat without air conditioning and yes it would mean sleeping in a single bunk bed (rather than the luxurious double offered in the new motorhome) but it would certainly make my driving experience a more relaxed affair. Anyway, the old motorhome went to the Tour every year so it was used to it, it knew what was required of it and it wouldn't let us down.

One problem solved, another one comes along right behind it. The day before we left, Mick went with Jess and Nicole to collect the second motorhome, which we were hiring. The original intention was for Nicole to do most of the driving of Motorhome Two. However when they got to the hire company, there appeared to be a problem with Nicole's driving licence. I'm still not exactly sure what the issue was but the bottom line was that she couldn't drive the motorhome. This left poor Jess very much in the wrong place at the wrong time. Jess is American which means she drives on the wrong side of the road. That's a bonus if you are driving in Europe though because they drive on the wrong side of the road too. This bonus was outweighed by the fact that Jess had never driven anything the size of the motorhome before, the fact that the steering wheel was in a different place to back home, oh and of course that most cars in the USA don't have gears. I imagine Jess very quickly assimilated the situation before her and realised that her worst nightmare was coming true – she may very well be spending the next three weeks driving a huge vehicle around France despite the fact that the controls were all in the wrong (right) place.

Jess was, however, thrown a lifeline, when physio Emily stepped up to the plate and agreed to share the driving. Fortunately the hire company were happy with an email copy of Emily's driving licence and the necessary arrangements were put in place. This was the first of many occasions during the trip in which Emily went well above and beyond her original brief.

The 99th edition of the Tour de France started in Liège, Belgium on Saturday 30th June 2012 and would finish in Paris, three weeks and 3,497 km later, on Sunday 22nd July 2012. Our team would be riding the full route, one day ahead of the professionals. Thus our start day was Friday 29th June 2012.

The keen-eyed amongst you may well have spotted what appears to be a glaring error in the previous paragraph – the Tour de France starting in Belgium? Well, yes, it is actually very common for the Tour to dip into other countries along the way and it regularly starts outside of France. In 2012 it was Belgium's turn so that's where we were headed.

Although the Tour has changed considerably since it was first held in 1903, the basics are the same with the riders cycling anything up to 226 km in a single day (in this year's Tour). This sounds like a long way. Well, I suppose it is a long way but modern riders should consider themselves lucky – early Tours were far more gruelling. The longest ever Tour was in 1926. That year the Tour took place over 17 stages and covered 5,745 km. In 1920, Stage 5 was 482 km long – you'd be pretty tired after driving that distance, just imagine trying to do it on a bike. A bike from the 1920s too – not a nice modern machine which comes with a full support team, mechanics, physios, doctors, a chef and more. I was beginning to think that this challenge might be too easy for our boys – I would need to remember to tell them that if they started moaning about having hurty legs.

Thoughts of how easy this adventure might be were far from my mind as I drove up to Sara and Mick's house early on 29th June 2012. Space was going to be limited in the motorhomes so we had all agreed to bring just one kit bag of clothes and toiletries. In line with many of my male counterparts, I am not overly bothered about clothes and therefore managed to fit almost my entire wardrobe into my holdall. I also had my road bike with me as I had made it a condition of my support that I would be able to cycle myself at least every other day. I had noticed a few extra pounds creeping on in recent months and this seemed the ideal opportunity to shed a few and I had visions of spending an hour or two a day cycling in the sun in rural France. Looking back, I really have no idea where I got the idea from that I would have time for such indulgence, but I had, so the bike was coming.

At this point, I was still yet to meet the mysterious Adnan or as I called him, 'the weird bloke who emails random people online to see if he can go on holiday with them.' When I pulled up at Mick's, Adnan was already there. We were duly introduced and I realised from the outset that we had struck lucky with our funny little Internet buddy. Mick had been correct, Adnan was alright and I, in turn, was relieved.

The driveway was covered in bikes, kit, bits of bikes, food, energy products, kit bags and a variety of other items, all of which needed to somehow be crammed into two motorhomes which already looked full to bursting. As chief driver of Motorhome One, I tentatively raised the issue of weight limits. Motorhome One had a gross weight limit of 3500 kgs. In other words, the motorhome, plus equipment plus people couldn't weigh an ounce over this figure to be road legal. I'm guessing that the motorhome alone weighed about 3100 kg empty and with no fuel or water. In addition, the four passengers probably added another 300 kg. So that left 100 kg for bikes, spare parts, kit, food, clothes, tools, diesel, water etc. I pointed out this glaring insufficiency to Mick and got the response I knew I would get. I honestly don't know why I bother to open my mouth sometimes.

'The weight thing is only a guide, they only *like* you to be under it. Don't worry, we won't get put on a weighbridge, well, I never have so far.'

Perfect! What was I worried about? It did occur to me to point out that the fact that he has never been weighed before probably means that, statistically at least, he is more likely to get weighed this time. I didn't of course, I would only have been wasting my breath.

Whilst the final checks were being made to ensure we had absolutely everything we needed, I happened to walk behind Motorhome Two and had to double-take at the biggest bike I had ever seen hanging off the back of it. It was huge! It belonged to Matt, who is a tall chap, well over six feet and therefore needs a massive bike. I commented to Mick and he laughed saying that the first time he had seen it, it had reminded him of a gate with wheels. He was right, that's exactly what it looked like, a giant red gate. Needless to say, for the rest of the trip, Matt's bike was referred to as simply, 'The Gate'.

My final job before setting off was to install CB radios in both motorhomes, in order that we had a cheap and easy way to communicate. I had owned a CB radio in the early eighties when they were first legalised in the UK and had spent many hours of fun chatting to complete strangers about absolutely nothing. 'What's your handle (nickname)?', 'What's your 20?' (where are you?) and other such inane conversations. Mick also had a bit of experience on the CB but of course the youngsters in Motorhome Two wouldn't have had a clue about the old days. They were all in their twenties so grew up with mobile phones and computers. Oh what a treat we had in store for them! It didn't take too long to realise that the youngsters didn't share the same level of enthusiasm for CB radio as Mick and I. They clearly didn't get the whole handle thing and the more we tried to explain it, the dafter it sounded. Fine, forget the handle, just press this button to talk and release it to listen.

'You've got to press a button to talk? Why?' It was going to be a long three weeks.

A couple of hours later we were driving onto the Eurotunnel train, our adventure well and truly started. It was lunchtime so Sara did what she does best and set to work in the kitchen. Having owned a motorhome for many years and having toured most of the UK and Europe ferrying Mick to bike races, she has become adept at conjuring up a meal from nowhere. I've seen her cook a full pasta dinner whilst on the move so making a few sandwiches while being slightly rocked from side to side on the train was not a problem.

That was until a piercing screech echoed through the carriage and all of the lights went off. Just before we were plunged into complete darkness, we felt the motorhome shunt forward. Mick and I were sitting in the front seats of the cab and therefore we had the best view of the bonnet bouncing off the back of the caravan in front. Then it was dark. Mick and I looked at each other like naughty children wondering if they were going to get away with some dastardly deed which they had just performed. This was despite the fact that we hadn't actually done anything, it was the train which had performed some sort of emergency stop, so any damage was definitely down to the Eurotunnel people. However, we were on a time limit and didn't need to be held up in

France arguing the toss over a bit of scratched paint. No one had come out of the car in front and given the way the train had abruptly come to a halt, it was likely that the occupants hadn't felt the bump on their caravan. We therefore decided to wait until the train started to move again and then Mick would release the handbrake on the motorhome, allowing the forward momentum of the train to gently roll us back and away from the caravan. We could then inspect the damage (if any) and decide what to do next. This was not the last time on this trip that someone was heard to utter the words, 'I'm glad we didn't bring the new motorhome.'

It took about an hour before there were any signs of the train moving. We found out later in the journey that some sort of circuit breaker had gone off causing the power to be cut and the brakes applied as in an emergency situation. When we started to pull away, Mick executed our cunning plan and we rolled back somewhat more smoothly than we had rolled forward an hour previously. A quick inspection showed absolutely no damage whatsoever, not the slightest mark, which was good news all round. No need for us to get delayed and no reason to trouble the elderly couple in front and give them something to worry about on their holiday.

The main downside of this incident was that we were now behind schedule. We still had to get to Liège, find somewhere to stay for the night and the boys had to ride the first stage. It couldn't be done tomorrow as the real Tour riders would be on the course and One Day Ahead would be over before it started.

PROLOGUE
Friday 29th June 2012
LIÈGE – LIÈGE
Prologue – 6.4 km

*'Give a man a fish and feed him for a day. Teach a man to fish
and feed him for a lifetime. Teach a man to cycle and he will realise
fishing is stupid and boring.'*
The Most Reverend Desmond Tutu

It was starting to get dark as we rolled into Liège. Having
been up since dawn, I was pretty much ready for my bed,
even if it was a cramped single one. Regardless, it would
have to wait. We had to find somewhere to park up for
the night and the riders still had a 6.4 km prologue ride
to complete.

The Tour de France prologue is part race and part ceremonial event, the first opportunity for spectators to see
their favourite riders and teams in action. Along with
the riders comes all the Tour traffic – team coaches,
articulated lorries full of barriers and other equipment,
cars belonging to the teams and other officialdom and of
course, representatives from the world's media. You
could be forgiven for believing that having a Tour stage
start or finish in your town was a complete pain in the
neck but actually, you couldn't be further from the truth
and huge sums of money change hands in order to
purchase such an opportunity.

The organisers of the Tour de France, Amaury Sport
Organisation (ASO), receive around fifty thousand Euros
as the fee from a start town and around eighty thousand

if you would like your town to host the finish of an individual stage. The cost to act as the host town for the *grand départ* is considerably more and can run into the millions. Liège would have paid dearly for the spectacle they were about to host, not least because Stage 1, the day after the prologue, would also start in the town. Each year, the ASO receive over 200 applications from towns wishing to act as either a start or finish location and only a handful are lucky enough to be chosen.

And the costs don't stop with the fee. Once selected, stage towns receive a package of requirements to which they must adhere which could include anything from removing street furniture to resurfacing roads. These extra costs are likely to put the overall total of calling yourself a stage town well in excess of half a million Euros. The hope is then that the cost is recouped from the money spent by both Tour visitors and future visitors, inspired to come after seeing the town on television during the Tour coverage.

As for the riders, the prologue in Liège will give them a gentle introduction to the pain and suffering they are about to endure. This year's prologue is a 6.4 km time trial, which means that each pro rider will race the course individually and against the clock. This will give each rider a starting point, in terms of time, to which all future stage times will be added. This makes the prologue an important day for riders looking for an opportunity to wear the yellow jersey.

There are several competitions running simultaneously within the Tour de France, it is the very definition of a race within a race. The most desired prize is that of the yellow jersey or *maillot jaune* which is awarded to the rider who completes the Tour route in the fastest overall time. This yellow jersey competition is also known as the General Classification or GC. The holder of the yellow jersey can change several times during a Tour and usually does. In fact, the last time the same rider wore the yellow jersey for the entire race was in 1935, when Romain Maes had the honour. Before that, only three other riders had led the race from start to finish. Of these three, only Maurice Garin missed out on the opportunity to wear yellow. Maurice won the very first Tour de France in 1903 but unfortunately for him, the yellow jersey wasn't introduced until 1919.

Increasing your lead in the GC is a tough thing to do. Pro riders all tend to be capable of riding at a similar pace on the flat 'easy' stages. Thus the main body of riders (*peloton*) will stay together. Although most days will see a breakaway of a handful of riders, realistically most have little chance of completing the stage before being caught by the *peloton* who are highly skilled in chasing them down. For breakaway riders, the glory of leading a stage for a while and the extra media coverage their sponsors and team will receive is sufficient reward.

The stages which sort the men out from the boys are the mountain stages and the time trials. In an individual time trial, as we were about to see in Liège, there was nowhere to hide. No safe *peloton* to sit safely in, away from buffeting winds. Just you, the bike, an open road and a ticking clock. This was the time for serious contenders to pick up a few precious seconds over their rivals and maybe gain a head start towards wearing the coveted yellow jersey, even if only for a day.

Our guys had no such worries. They weren't racing and this is one of the key differences to note between their ride and the pro riders. Many people had commented prior to us leaving for Belgium that our team would never be able to complete the full Tour route in the same three week time period as the pros; after all, that's why the professionals were, well, professionals. A fairly logical conclusion to draw I agree, however the Tour riders are *racing* for the full three weeks and would be flying round France at a rate our guys could only dream of. Once a stage had started, there would be no stopping, other than for a quick call of nature; any food required would be consumed on the go and even basic medical attention would be administered on the move with the Tour doctor hanging out of a car window alongside the cyclist. Professional cyclists don't want to stop unless they absolutely have to and the last place they want to find themselves is a kilometre or two behind the charging *peloton* as riding back to it could prove an impossible task.

In contrast, the One Day Ahead team could, to a certain extent, take it easy. They would be riding at a far more relaxed pace and would be met every 60 km or so by one of the support motorhomes for a leisurely meal break. Okay, maybe not leisurely but they'd have the chance to get off their bikes, stretch their legs and enjoy a bite to eat.

But before any of that, we still had to find somewhere to park up. As might have been expected, Liège was absolutely jam-packed. It is a major city which would be playing host to the start of the Tour de France the following morning so no surprise there really. We headed out of town and about 5 km away we found a small campsite which looked as if it would serve our purpose. As we drove in, it was clearly very busy and I was immediately concerned that there wouldn't be room for us. However, luck was on our side as the friendly German owner was a big cycling fan and when I explained what we were up to, he assured me he would find us a spot.

Five minutes later and Motorhome One was parked up under a large tree at the end of a row of tents, caravans and motorhomes. Next to it and half blocking the main access route through the camp, was Motorhome Two. I am still not entirely sure how Motorhome Two managed to get stuck in the mud and I hadn't even noticed that the site was that muddy but stuck it was. It appeared that Emily had managed to find the only patch of mud on the entire site and had driven the front wheels of the motorhome well and truly into it. It was too late, too dark and we were too tired to be worried about it now, it could stay there until the morning.

Ten minutes after arriving and I was into 'support mode,' getting the bikes off the motorhome and filling some water bottles up so the team could complete the time trial course. It was 9:30 pm and dark. These days the pro Tour teams are safely massaged, fed and tucked up in bed by the time the sun goes down but in the early years, cycling at night was the norm. Stages could be over 400 km long and would start in the early hours and finish late into the night. For one night only, the One Day Ahead team would be doing it 'old school.'

It made no sense (to me at least as one of the drivers) to take the motorhomes back into town to drop the boys off and I thought it would be quicker for the riders to cycle to Liège and then ride the time trial course. Admittedly this doubled the distance of the ride but it meant that I could spend the time sitting on my backside getting tucked into one of the countless bottles of wine I had seen safely stashed in the motorhome fridge.

So with shiny bikes and perfect team lycra, the riders pedalled off to begin their epic ride. I grabbed a fold up chair, a glass and a bottle of white and Sara fired up the oven and started making some sort of pasta surprise. I was starving but apparently I had to wait until the boys got back before I could eat. Fortunately Sara sensed my disappointment and she soon had a stick of garlic bread heading my way to keep me going.

By the time the boys returned from their night-time adventure (which we were informed, was a piece of cake and hardly worth talking about), I had polished off the white and was helping Sara with her rosé. Alcohol does funny things to you and it gives you a completely different perspective on reality. I had forgotten what I was here to do and was suddenly on a lovely camping holiday. Good job I didn't have to get up early tomorrow and drive 200 km.

We all tucked into the pasta bake accompanied by a huge salad, bread and more wine. It was our first opportunity to get to know each other properly as, while Sara, Mick and I had known each other for years, I had only met some of the others for the first time that day. I was obviously not the only one who thought they were on holiday. At one point Jess asked if anyone had got any idea of which sights they wanted to see over the next three weeks. Sara and I looked at each other, both thinking the same thing, 'Sights? There won't be any time for sights.' We had one job for the next three weeks and that was to get our four cyclists around France. This was explained to Jess as politely as possible. Jess was left with a look of both surprise and disappointment on her face. Her boyfriend, Matt, had obviously sold her something completely different when he suggested a European trip.

It was also during this conversation that it became clear that both Nicole and Jess intended to ride quite a bit of the route with their respective partners. Again, Sara and I looked at each other, having simultaneously worked out the potential problems this could cause. Firstly, if they were riding, it meant that Emily would have to do most of the driving and that wasn't what she was here for. It didn't seem that the girls had asked Emily if she was happy with this arrangement, more that they had just assumed she would do it. Secondly, to my knowledge, the girls were not capable of cycling at the same speed as the boys and this would mean either that the boys would have to wait for them (I couldn't see Mick wanting to do that) or that we would effectively be supporting two groups of riders each day. This would be far from ideal and certainly not practical.

Our plan was to take it in turns to support the riders. One motorhome would follow the same route as the cyclists and stop every few hours to provide food, drink, first aid or whatever else may be required. The second motorhome would drive on ahead to the following day's start town in order to find somewhere to stay for the night. In addition, the non-support motorhome would be in charge of any food shopping required and would also take the opportunity to fill up their water supplies. We were going to need a lot of water, not only for the boys to drink while cycling but also for showers, dishwashing and the cleaning of clothes. In other words, both teams of supporters would be busy every day and adding extra duties, such as looking after additional riders, was not something I was keen on. My plan to cycle every other day was already fast becoming a distant dream and the more I thought about it, the more I realised how impractical this would be. Nicole and Jess didn't seem to have drawn the same conclusion but hopefully they would catch on once we were a few days into the trip. As far as I was concerned though, I was here to get Stephen, Matt, Mick and Adnan through this challenge and that was it. Nothing more. It was only day one but already I could see that other people had different agendas for this trip.

Sara and I tentatively suggested that perhaps it might not be reasonable for the girls to think that they would be riding most days, not least because it wouldn't be fair on Emily. Nicole, in particular, did not seem receptive to our suggestions. I suspect that, like Matt, Stephen had fed Nicole a slightly different story about how the trip would pan out and she had taken him at his word. I suppose Stephen was just trying to be fair to everyone, indeed, he said at one point that he 'wanted everyone to get something out of the trip.' That's fair enough but it was important to remember why we were all there. Riders ride. Supporters support. You don't see the Team Sky bus driver getting to ride a stage because he didn't fancy driving the bus that day.

I could see that this was going to become a bone of contention over the coming days so I decided the best course of action was to have another drink.

It did occur to me that maybe Nicole had a point. Maybe we should just leave the riders to it and enjoy a pleasant twenty one day holiday touring France. After all, did they really need supporting? Indeed, when Henri Desgrange (the 'Father' of the Tour although the original idea for a race around France was actually his assistant's, Géo Lefèvre) planned the early Tours, no mechanical support was permitted for the riders and any rider accepting assistance of this nature could expect to be punished with a hefty time penalty.

Take Eugène Christophe for example. In the 1913 Tour, he was leading the race by about 18 minutes but whilst descending the Col du Tourmalet, Christophe noticed that there appeared to be something wrong with his handlebars and he could no longer steer his bike. He came to a halt and saw that his forks were broken. Not to let a small thing like a useless bike spoil his chances of victory, he picked up his cycle and set off for St Marie de Campan, the nearest village some 10 km down the mountain. When he arrived, he was, I am sure, overjoyed to see a blacksmith in the village. Christophe obtained permission from the blacksmith to use his forge and set to work repairing his forks. A Tour official stood by to ensure that no rules were broken. Unfortunately, when Christophe asked a local boy to operate the bellows for him, he was informed by the official that this constituted assistance and he was given a time penalty of ten minutes. A touch draconian when you consider that, by this point, Christophe had already lost over four hours.

Eventually, after some protesting, the time penalty was reduced to three minutes but the time lost was already far too great for Christophe to claw back. Regardless, he still managed to finish the Tour in a very respectable seventh place, some fourteen hours behind the eventual winner, Philippe Thys. Interestingly, in the same race, Thys also suffered a broken fork and was also given a time penalty for accepting help with the repair. Thys, however, managed to find a bicycle shop to repair his fork, which I can only assume was far quicker than a do-it-yourself job at the local blacksmith.

Our day eventually started to come to an end around 1:00 am with what was to become a nightly ritual - stowing the bikes safely in or on the two motorhomes. Between us, we had some very expensive pieces of cycling kit including several carbon fibre bikes. Even the cheaper bikes were worth close to £1000 each. Sara's bike, which was only to come off the roof of the motorhome once during the whole trip, had carbon wheels worth £1000, or as she told me, 'worth more than your entire bike.' A £4000 carbon bike is an attractive thing to a bike thief and we managed to devise a way of storing the most expensive cycles within the cab area of the two motorhomes. The cheapies were chained to the cycle rack and roof of the motorhome with one of Mick's 'good chains,' which looked big enough to anchor a ship. Good luck cutting that off Mr. Bike Thief.

The rest of the campsite had headed to bed a couple of hours earlier and most of our team now did the same. After doing some basic tidying, Sara and I had a brief discussion about how we thought things were going to pan out. We both had a lot of concerns but none of them were about the boys' ability to get through this challenge. We were both confident that Mick would have no problem, he would just keep pedalling until we told him to stop. Adnan seemed more than capable and had a very small build which should help him float up the mountains. Matt had been cycling for years and seemed confident, as did Stephen. Our concerns were more to do with how helpful the other support team would actually be and how much work we would end up doing on their behalf. Sara had spent many years supporting Mick at various events and I also had some experience of supporting on similar endurance events. But neither of us had undertaken anything like this. Most of the events we had covered had lasted a day or maybe twenty four hours at most. Even Mick's mammoth canoeing expedition was over in twenty seven hours. The Tour de France lasted three weeks and was the equivalent of nineteen endurance events one after the other and yet it seemed that, other than the riders, we were the only ones who had any understanding of what this meant. It was pretty clear to us that if you thought on day one that you would be sightseeing, then you obviously had absolutely no idea of what was coming up. Equally, anyone in the support team who thought they would be spending a good percentage of the next twenty one days merrily pedalling around the French countryside enjoying a smashing holiday, were likely to be in for quite a surprise when the reality hit home.

As we sat there talking, we both realised that we sounded like the old grumps, like our parents moaning about our twenty-something selves. For the next three weeks, however, we were the adults and Motorhome Two were the kids. Motorhome Two became the 'Kids' Bus.' The name stuck although I'm not sure 'the kids' knew anything about it.

Sitting there in the dark, while everyone else was drifting off to sleep, I had a clear picture in my mind of how the next three weeks were likely to pan out. I had always thought it was going to be tough but I was beginning to think that I had severely underestimated the task ahead. My eyes were drawn to the stuck motorhome, with mud now covering a third of the front wheels. Somehow that needed to be sorted out too, no doubt this would be a job for the grown ups.

Before we could worry about the motorhome we had to get the boys through Stage 1. It was a flat stage which looped out from Liège and back to Seraing. It should be an undemanding ride for the team and indeed for Sara and me as support. It had always been the intention for the two of us, in Motorhome One, to support the first stage so that we could get a feel for the best way to run things. Given that Motorhome Two was stuck, there was now no option. This meant that the girls in Motorhome Two would be left at the campsite all day. Maybe they would work out a way of getting the motorhome unstuck. Maybe. Or more likely, maybe not.

My alcohol-fuddled brain remembered something about setting up the Garmin GPS unit for Mick's bike – he had a rather neat mini sat nav, designed specifically for cycling and I had managed to find the necessary route files online for the entire Tour route. All I had to do was get them from my laptop onto the Garmin. No doubt a straightforward task when you know how to do it and it had been my intention to sit and have a play when we originally parked up. Unfortunately a glass or three of wine had helped me to forget this important job and it was now going to have to wait until the morning. Alcohol is very good at making you think the most insurmountable task is a walk in the park (this whole trip had been conceived over beer after all). I was good with computers so it would only take a minute or two to sort the Garmin out. Probably.

Sara and I crept into the motorhome. Mick and Adnan were already sound asleep, although probably not so much once my hand had slipped on the bathroom door sending it flying into the side of Adnan's bunk, jolting him to life and waking Mick at the other end of the motorhome. Everyone likes a drunk bloke in their motorhome. Neither of them said anything although Adnan was probably wondering about the quality of his support team at this stage.

Squeezing into my bunk underneath my new roomie, it didn't seem odd at all that I still had my jeans and a thick sweatshirt on. Good old alcohol, always there to take away the ability of my brain to work in any kind of effective manner. It had seemed pointless putting the last bit of wine back in the fridge – it would only take up valuable space – so we had drunk it. How many bottles had we gone through? Two? Three? More? I couldn't work it out, which wasn't a great sign but who cared? We were on holiday so a few drinks wouldn't hurt would they? Actually, yes, quite a bit as it happens.

STAGE 1

Saturday 30th June 2012
LIÈGE – SERAING
Flat – 198 km

'If it was easy, everyone would be doing it.'
Mick - One Day Ahead Team

I woke around 7:00 am and immediately knew I had overdone it on the booze. My head was spinning, my eyes were throbbing and I felt generally dreadful. There was something else though, I felt uncomfortably damp. On the plus side, I appeared to be fully dressed so that was going to save me a job.

It was being fully dressed which explained my dampness as I now noticed how hot it was in the motorhome and how much I was sweating. Adnan was already up and stood next to my bunk grinning down at me.

'Alright? How you feeling?' he beamed.

'Terrific,' I groaned.

The boys wanted to get going about 9:00 am in order to get into town and out again before it started getting busy for the actual Tour prologue which would commence at 2:00 pm. I sat up in bed having completely forgotten that there was another bunk above me. Adnan doubled over giggling as I cracked my already throbbing head on the bottom of his bed. I swung my feet round and steadied myself. I was tempted to say, 'never again,' but what was the point?

I shuffled into the bathroom and brushed my teeth in the hope that this would remove the most unpleasant taste in my mouth. It didn't. I needed a cup of tea. Right on cue I heard Mick shout through the door, 'Tea?'

Sara had obviously been up early as the dining table was set with various breakfast options from pastries to cereal to toast. All I wanted was tea. Although I had taken my sweatshirt off, I was still incredibly hot, even sitting next to the window with a cool breeze blowing through. I could feel myself burning up. This wasn't good especially given that I was supposed to be driving the motorhome in a couple of hours. As I sat there feeling quite nauseous, I felt a particularly large wave of sickness flow over me. Weirdly, my first thought was, 'Please don't let me be sick, I only met Adnan last night, it'll be really embarrassing!'

'I feel sick,' I mumbled to no one in particular.

At this point I can only tell you what the others told me as my next recollection was coming round, lying on the motorhome bench seat, with Adnan holding my legs up in the air.

It seems that a few seconds after uttering my warning, my eyes rolled back in my head, I shook my hand a bit and then dropped my head straight down onto the table. I think this amused Mick considerably; certainly for the rest of the trip he was happy to perform his impression of 'Richard's dizzy do' to anyone who wanted to see it. Adnan was slightly more helpful although before doing anything, he had asked Mick and Sara if I was 'messing around'.

Once he had established that I was not, in fact, messing around and was, quite possibly, dying of some terrible and undiagnosed illness, he leapt into action and brought me back to life. It was very handy having a doctor on board and Adnan diagnosed low levels of sugar in my blood, or hypoglycaemia, caused by too much wine the night before. That would explain the sweating (a warning symptom of hypoglycaemia), although wearing all my clothes to bed wouldn't have helped and it was likely that I was also massively dehydrated. It was pretty scary to be honest, there have been many occasions when I have had maybe one or two too many drinks but never had I felt like this.

Once I was back in the land of the living, my new medical team went to work to bring my sugar levels back up to normal. Fortunately the one thing we had with us in plentiful supply were hundreds of energy bars and gels. I guzzled a few but honestly I was struggling to eat anything as I still felt terrible.

I went back to my bunk for a lie down and it soon became clear that I wasn't in any fit state to be driving the motorhome anywhere. As well as feeling physically lousy, I now felt dreadfully guilty. I had been brought along to do a job and here we were on day one, with me lying in bed. This meant that, today at least, Sara was going to have to drive and probably navigate too as every time I sat up, I was overcome with nausea. I apologised profusely to Sara (although I must at this point question how come she felt okay - after all, we were sharing the wine so she must have had as much as me) and promised that if she did the driving today, I would do all of the driving from tomorrow until we reached Paris. Sara didn't mind, I think she was more concerned about what would happen if I didn't pull through. Mick had already been heard to state that 'getting a stiff through Customs on the way home would be a right palaver,' and that it would be 'easier just to lose him somewhere along the way.' Nice.

Needless to say, I wasn't capable of working out how the Garmin worked so, yes, I should have done it the night before. To their credit the boys didn't make a fuss, they said they would manage without. One of the advantages of riding the Tour de France route the day before the actual Tour is that you can piggyback on the official Tour direction arrows. These direction arrows are printed on neon yellow boards and are attached to road signs, roundabouts, lamp posts and so on, every few hundred metres along the route. To watch the guys putting these signs out is quite incredible. Two vans drive in convoy and every now and then, one will stop, a man jumps out, attaches a sign to the nearest post with cable ties and jumps back in. Meanwhile the second van will be doing the same a little further up the road. Van one then overtakes van two and the operation is repeated. It takes seconds to add each sign and this is done for the entire race route. They start putting the signs up on the morning of the day before a stage is due to take place. In other words, the morning of the day which our guys would be riding the stage. If they didn't start too early, the One Day Ahead team could effortlessly follow the official Tour signage.

The chaps who put out all the direction signs are saved the hassle of having to go and collect them after the stage has been raced. These signs are something of a souvenir which means that once the Tour riders have shot past, spectators help themselves to the signs, thus providing an automatic clean up operation. What surprised me when I first saw this in action was the fact that the spectators are so disciplined and actually wait until after the race has passed by before swiping the signs. No doubt a small number do get pinched ahead of race day but in the main, they are respectfully left alone until they have done their job and guided the *peloton* onwards towards Paris.

Somewhat later than planned, the One Day Ahead team were ready to go at 11:30 am. I was all for letting them cycle into Liège in order to loosen their legs up but they didn't fancy it for some reason, lightweights. So Sara drove the motorhome and our four intrepid cyclists into the centre of town, while I continued to feel very sorry for myself in my bunk. Despite voicing our reservations in respect of the girls riding the stages with the boys, Nicole had insisted that she was going to ride today's stage. We therefore had five cyclists on board. I was too ill to protest but Sara had made it quite clear that if Nicole started dropping behind the boys, she would have to finish her ride as Sara was not prepared to support two separate groups.

Despite the fact that the Tour de France was due to start there later that day, Liège wasn't actually that busy. This meant we could get right up to tomorrow's start line. This was handy as we had anticipated that we might need to drop the team as much as a kilometre away from the start, thus adding extra distance to their ride before they got started. There wasn't anywhere to park legally though so it was a case of stop, drop the bikes off the back and go, no time for pleasantries, just a quick, 'See you at lunch, good luck,' from Sara and a moan from me.

Mick stood at the doorway of the motorhome.

'Try not to die Rich,' he called to me at the back of the motorhome, 'I do actually quite like you.'

With that, they were off. Sara had arranged to meet them at about 60 km into the ride, which would be about two hours later.

Stage 1 of the 2012 Tour de France was, according to the official Tour documentation, a flat stage. However a quick look at the stage profile in the Tour race guide magazine (which was to become our bible in the days and weeks to come) indicates five category 4 climbs. Admittedly, a cat 4 climb is the lowest grade of climb on the Tour but it is still an incline which would make the average cyclist wonder if driving might have been the better option that day.

There are a few different stories floating around to explain how the categories were first calculated. My personal favourite (which may well be based on nothing but myth and legend) goes something like this. The Tour organisers needed some way of grading the difficulty of the hills and ultimately mountain roads which made up the Tour (the mountains were first included in the Tour de France in 1910 when the Tour passed through the Pyrenees). They therefore drove an old banger of a car up each climb and recorded which gear the car was able to complete the climb in. If the car could drive up in fourth gear, the hill became a category 4 climb, if the car needed to be dropped down to third gear, the climb was a cat 3 and so on. If the car was unable to make progress, even in first gear, the climb was recorded as 'uncategorised' or *Hors Catégorie* (HC).

These days the category applied to a climb or mountain pass is a bit more arbitrary, with various factors coming into play. As well as the steepness and length of the climb, the importance of that section of the race also plays a part. The category of a climb affects the number of points available for the 'King of the Mountains' polka dot jersey so if the organisers want to award more points for a particular climb, they can notch up the category. Equally, a climb at the end of a very long and tough stage may well have its category lifted to recognise the fact that it will be harder than had it been placed earlier in the day.

From a general point of view, however, the stage profile and climb categories serve to give spectators and riders a quick visual summary of how easy or hard that day's riding should be, at least from the point of view of the steepness and length of any gradients.

So, today's challenge was to get up five category 4 climbs, each one an average of 2 km long with a gradient averaging just over 5%. The route also took in the highest point in Belgium, the Braque de Fraiture, at 606 metres. A height which, by the time the guys had reached the Alps and Pyrenees, would seem like a mere pimple. Overall, a nice easy day then.

We had arranged to meet the team between the second and third climb, approximately 60 km into the ride. I was still no use to man nor beast and lay at the far end of the motorhome willing myself to feel better. As Sara negotiated her way out of Liège, I considered the fact that I wasn't far from home. When you feel ill, regardless of whether it is self-inflicted or not, all you really want is to be safely tucked up in your own bed. For the next couple of days, we were going to be driving towards England before making a complete U-turn and driving further and further away. I convinced myself that despite the fact that I could barely stand up without feeling nauseous and lightheaded, if Sara dropped me at a train station, I would be able to struggle back to Calais and ultimately to my bed. The last thing I felt like doing was a road trip around France. Yes, going home to bed was a much better option. I tried moaning a bit more to see if the penny dropped.

It didn't. Every now and then Sara called back, 'Are you okay?' I would grunt or groan in response.

I was trying to get my groans to convey the message, 'I'm okay but could really do with being dropped off at the nearest railway station so that I can be home in time for tea' but Sara wasn't getting the translation. I suspect the main reason she kept calling back to me was to make sure I hadn't died, Mick's concern about bringing a body back through Customs fresh in her mind.

For the time being at least, I was replaced by the sat nav, which safely and accurately guided Sara, me and the motorhome out of Liège and into the countryside and extensive forests of the Ardennes. Sixty kilometres later we parked up in a dusty lay-by at the side of the road along which the pro Tour would race the following day and along which, hopefully, our boys would soon arrive.

I was starting to feel a bit more human and was beginning to feel hungry. It is a wonderful feeling when you have been ill or hungover and you start to come out the other side and you realise that you will soon be back to normal. Sara was already in action in the kitchen area, firing up the oven to heat up pizzas and buttering bread for sandwiches. I put the kettle on, a lovely cup of tea, that's what I needed first.

When I realised that I wasn't dying and that I had been suffering from nothing more than a particularly unpleasant hangover, the feelings of wanting to go home soon passed. I was a bit more optimistic about our challenge and I was starting to feel some of the excitement which comes with the Tour de France. Within minutes of our arrival, two more motorhomes had parked up beside us. The occupants came over to check that the Tour would definitely pass this way the next day. They were looking for somewhere to stay overnight which would ensure a good viewing position for the race. We confirmed that the Tour would indeed come past this spot. However we also warned them that, as the road was on a reasonable decline, the Tour riders would pass by at quite a rate of knots and therefore it was likely that the *peloton* would flash past them in a matter of seconds. They might be better off trying to find a position on a slower part of the route so that they could maximise their viewing experience. This hadn't occurred to them so armed with their newly found insider knowledge they headed off in search of a better location.

Once the food was prepared, Sara sat down to enjoy her first break of the day and joined me with a cup of tea. We had calculated that we would probably have to wait at least an hour for the boys to get to this point so we were amazed when they turned up about fifteen minutes after we had arrived. It was a pretty straight run from the starting point in Liège to our current location but the cyclists had had the luxury of being able to filter past the traffic in the city which had gained them valuable time.

They were all in good spirits and quickly started devouring the spread of food which Sara had laid out on fold up tables outside the motorhome. Dr. Adnan checked on my welfare and I confirmed that I was recovering, thanking him for his help earlier in the day.

Matt seemed to be struggling slightly with one of his shoes; it was rubbing and causing him some discomfort on the side of his foot. This wasn't an ideal situation given that they had only ridden 60 km and had over 3,400 km still to do. Adnan suggested loosening the straps a bit to give his feet more room to move. They were probably swelling up slightly because of the warm temperature.

At this point, there was no sign of Nicole; she hadn't ridden in with the boys as they had dropped her about half an hour ago according to Stephen. This is exactly what Sara and I had been afraid of because now we would have to sit around waiting for her when we could have been on the road to the next pit stop.

Stephen was keen to keep pressing on and didn't want to waste too much time hanging around. Clearly his girlfriend was now our problem. Fair enough and none of us wanted another late night, me in particular. We arranged another meeting point just before the fourth cat 4 climb and they jumped on their bikes and headed off.

After waiting for Nicole for forty minutes, we were beginning to get concerned. Was she okay? Had she had an accident? Was she even riding on the correct road?

For all we knew she could have managed to get lost and gone round us or off in a completely different direction. We could do without having to retrace our steps looking for her. Our priority, as we had explained the night before, was looking after the boys, the ones who actually had a chance of completing this immense challenge. We had no intention of repeating this little episode again as it merely served to add additional pressure to our role.

Eventually, nearly an hour after the boys had left, Nicole arrived along the road. She had struggled to keep up over the last climb and she had asked the boys to go on without her. We explained that they were now an hour ahead of us and that we had only just made it to the first meeting point ahead of them so there was every possibility that we would now be late for the next stop. The boys wouldn't wait for us if we weren't there; they would keep pushing on rather than waste time. This would mean that they could potentially be running low on food or water and unless we overtook them on the way and actually saw them, we might not know if they had passed the meeting point or not. We could try phoning them but we didn't really want to phone unless absolutely necessary because if they tried to take a call while riding, it's obviously dangerous and if they stopped, it would waste time. We needed to press on and try as best we could to make up some of the lost time.

Sara agreed to carry on driving but I moved from my bunk up to the cab. I was feeling much better now that I had eaten and it was a beautiful, sunny day which always helps to lift one's mood.

As we traversed the Belgian countryside, Sara voiced her concerns about Matt's shoe. It really wasn't good that he was suffering so early in the ride. Matt had told Sara that the shoes he had brought with him weren't the ones he would normally use and that perhaps he should have packed his others. With the benefit of hindsight, this would definitely have made sense. It didn't help that the only other male on the trip who had spare cycling shoes with him was me and despite not being particularly tall, I do have fairly large feet and take a size 12, which were too big for Matt. So basically he was stuck with what he had. That said, his mum and dad were driving out to join us for part of the trip so they could bring his other shoes with them but they weren't joining us until the mountain stages, over a week and 1,800 km away.

For much of the journey, we followed the route that the cyclists would ride. Already many of the roads were lined with spectators parked up in their motorhomes, eagerly awaiting the arrival of the pros the next day. Flags and team shirts were hung from awnings and pinned up in the windows of the motorhomes. Couples and groups sat on fold up picnic chairs enjoying beer, wine and nibbles. They had at least twenty four hours to wait but there was still plenty to see and enjoy. It had become apparent very quickly that our chaps were not the only ones who were riding the full Tour route. There were actually quite a few groups including a team of American women who were tackling it. The spectators had plenty to see and plenty of riders to cheer, '*Allez! Allez! Allez!*' being the most common shout of encouragement, which basically translates as, 'Go! Go! Go!' It didn't matter that the riders weren't pros. It didn't matter whether they were riding the whole Tour or one stage or even just a part of one stage. The enthusiasm was the same and the crowd loved it. This constant encouragement was to persist all the way round France and must have given the riders a fantastic boost, especially if their energy levels were starting to flag or they were beginning to think they had just about had enough.

Not today though, this was Stage 1, no one had had

enough yet, not even me now that I was feeling brighter and at the second meet up point, everyone was still on top form. We had overtaken our group a few kilometres from our planned stop point, which was a relief as we were starting to wonder just how much ground they had managed to make on us. With fresh legs and a keen enthusiasm, they were flying through this first stage. Mick wasn't saying much, just that all was okay. We didn't expect much more from him, no doubt one of the other riders had been chatting to him along the way and he had used all his words up for the day. Adnan and Stephen were both fine, no problems. Matt was still suffering a bit with his foot but was pushing on regardless.

After some more food and a top up of water bottles and energy gels, the riders (less Nicole) pedalled off once more and Sara and I cleared up the empty plates and drove on to the finish line in Seraing.

Arriving in Seraing, we saw that the last part of the route wove its way through a housing estate and the stage profile showed that the stage actually finished at the top of a category 4 climb. The housing estate consisted of fairly narrow one-way streets so rather than tackle them with the motorhome, we decided to park at the bottom of the climb and walk up. We had time to kill and the boys would pass us en route if they were early and the walk would give us the chance to stretch our legs after a day in the motorhome.

The stage profile indicated a 2.4 km long climb with an average gradient of 4.7%. What it didn't reveal was the rather nasty 17% gradient right at the start of the climb. After cycling 196 km, a 17% hill would look like a wall in front of you. Just walking up it was enough to get your pulse racing, cycling up it would be most unpleasant. Sara and I both found much amusement at the thought of seeing the team almost at the end of their first big ride, only to find this final hurdle.

'Serves them right,' said Sara, 'they wanted to do this silly ride.'

Nicole struggled to see the funny side and thought we were being quite cruel. I'm afraid this only made it seem even funnier.

After the initial steepness, the last part of the route settles down to a far more gentle incline and ended on a nondescript road just outside of the housing estate. It was strange to think that at that moment there was nothing to set it apart from any other road, but within twenty four hours, the place would be transformed as the Tour rode into and almost immediately afterwards, drove out of, the area.

But today there wasn't much to see at the finish, actually there was nothing to see, so we turned around and walked back towards the motorhome. Part way down the road, we saw four somewhat tired looking cyclists riding towards us. We could hear the expletives from several feet away. It appeared that they weren't best impressed with the last little climb. Mick looked unphased.

'How was it?' I asked him.

'No problem,' he replied, 'that last bit wasn't great but if it was easy, everyone would be doing it wouldn't they?'

Yes, I suppose they would.

All four of them had now stopped and for some reason had assumed that Sara, Nicole and I were standing at the finish point. Given that the official Tour signage and barriers were yet to be erected, there was nothing to indicate the actual finishing line. The boys were ever so pleased when I told them that they still had about 1 km to do and we sent them off up the road to finish the stage. Well, if you are going to do a job, you might as well do it properly.

Back at the motorhome, we loaded up the three bikes and The Gate and a weary group of cyclists settled down with protein shakes and more pizza for the short drive back to the campsite. Although they had ridden almost 200 km, they had looped round in a circle and were now only about 13 km from where they had started.

Driving back, I remembered that there were two other members of our team waiting for us back at the campsite with Motorhome Two. I had been so busy being ill and then looking after our riders that I had forgotten all about them. I also remembered that Sara and I should, in theory, get a day off from supporting the next day as it was down to the Motorhome Two team. Then I remembered that Motorhome Two was stuck in the mud and try as I might, however positively I tried to think about the situation, I just knew that Emily and Jess wouldn't have managed to get the motorhome unstuck. In fairness, it wasn't really Emily's job to get the motorhome moved and I imagine Jess would have been more interested in looking through the guide books to see which sights she wanted to visit.

We pulled into the campsite just before 9:00 pm and my fears were confirmed. Motorhome Two was still exactly where it had been when we left it that morning and the girls were sitting in deckchairs reading. It looked as though they had been there for some time.

Frustratingly it seemed that they hadn't actually made much of an attempt to get the motorhome free and even more frustrating was the fact that the lack of transport had meant they hadn't done any food shopping and therefore nothing was ready for anyone to eat. I had to bite my tongue quite hard, the city of Liège was only a few kilometres away and they had had all day. There had been plenty of time to walk there and back or failing that, get a taxi but no, sitting in the sun had obviously been the preferable option.

The result of this was that, after spending the day driving and preparing snacks, Sara was now back in the kitchen making dinner for the evening meal while Mick and I cobbled together a plan to free the second motorhome. Armed with a couple of sheets of cardboard and an improvised spade made out of a random piece of plastic, we attempted to give the wheels something to grip. Emily was in the driving seat and was following our instructions to the letter, right up to the point where we said, 'Oh just floor it and see if it pops out.'

It didn't. Instead, the engine revs rose and then, without any warning, the engine cut out and all the lights on the dashboard died. Everything was dead. No lights, no engine, no nothing. Something electrical had blown and given that nothing was working, it was clearly something fairly major. We began the task of checking every single fuse, a fiddly and time-consuming process. Emily took her leave at this point and started to set up her massage table so that she could do what she was actually there to do and pummel the boys' legs back into shape for the following day's ride.

Despite a thorough check of all the fuses, we couldn't find any that had blown. The suspicion now being that something considerably more substantial than a single fuse had died. This made sense given that all of the motorhome cab electrics were now dead, it was highly unlikely that this had been caused by the blowing of a tiny fuse. Fortunately the habitation area (the bit you live in) ran off a completely separate electrical system so all was well in the sleeping quarters.

Time was pushing on, dinner was being served and it was getting dark. With no fresh ideas and the motorhome now in a worse state than when we started, we gave up.

Someone would have to call the European equivalent of the AA in the morning and hope that they could fix the problem quickly and easily. My thoughts of a day off quickly evaporated as I realised that Sara and I would be supporting the riders again on Stage 2. Oh well, at least I was now fully recovered although I opted to give the wine a miss for a night!

Weirdly, alcohol has a close association with the Tour de France and up until 1960, when rules were introduced banning stimulants, riders would regularly have a drink both before and during the race. In 1950, Algerian rider, Abdelkader Zaaf had broken away from the main *peloton* and was pushing on in a 40° heat. It isn't clear what happened next, whether he stopped to drink a bottle of wine or whether he just drank whatever spectators were offering but regardless, he ended up slightly worse for wear and started wobbling down the road.

Zaaf eventually stopped for a sleep at the side of the road but Tour spectators woke him up and urged him to continue with the race, which he did but in the wrong direction. Before he was able to turn round an ambulance was called and Zaaf was taken off to hospital for a check up. Despite turning up at the start of the next day's stage, Zaaf was refused permission to race. Regardless, his drunken performance had ensured Zaaf celebrity status. He later claimed that he had received wine from a spectator but being Muslim, was not used to the alcohol.

Not feeling any great desire to drink alcohol and with everyone feeling weary after a long day (well, some of us at least), we all turned in at a reasonable hour. A flat, straight stage tomorrow which would see us heading towards the French/Belgian border. This would be our last day in Belgium and should, in theory, be plain sailing for the boys. As it turned out, it was to be the hardest day of the entire trip.

The 99th Tour de France started today. At 2:00 pm, 198 riders faced the 6.4 km time trial which our riders had tackled the evening before. Unlike our riders, the pros had daylight and sun to ride in. At the 3.2 km mark, Team Sky Tour favourite, Bradley Wiggins, was only in 10th position but he did what he does best and made up the time in the second half, ending the time trial in second position. Not quite good enough to take the yellow jersey on day one though, which in the end went to Fabian Cancellara of the Radioshack-Nissan team.

Tour De France 2012 Results after Prologue:

Stage Winner: Fabian Cancellara/Radioshack-Nissan

Yellow: Fabian Cancellara/Radioshack-Nissan
Green: Fabian Cancellara/Radioshack-Nissan
Polka Dot: N/A
White: Tejay Van Garderen/BMC Racing Team

STAGE 2
Sunday 1st July 2012
VISÉ – TOURNAI
Flat – 207.5 km

'Money can't buy you happiness but it can buy you a bike and that's basically the same.'
Anon

Our motorhome was the proverbial hive of activity from about 7:00 am. Sara sorting breakfast, Adnan and Mick stuffing themselves with as many calories as possible and me doing what I should have done yesterday - working out how this flipping Garmin thing works. At the same time I was trying to nab as much of the breakfast buffet as I could before it was gobbled up by everyone else. Mind you, they'd have to be quick to get in front of me, I do enjoy my food!

During our initial discussions about One Day Ahead, I recall Sara telling me that feeding the team was going to be one of the biggest challenges.

'They'll need to be eating at least six thousand calories a day just to replace what they are burning off,' she had informed me.

'Six thousand calories a day?' my eyes lit up, 'I don't think that will be any problem whatsoever, I can definitely manage that.'

'I was talking about the cyclists,' she replied.

Sara was right though; the boys would be burning off in the region of 5000 to 6000 calories a day cycling for seven hours or more. This would be in addition to the calories that they'd burn off each day just being alive, which would amount to another couple of thousand. To actually consume that much food day after day can be quite hard going. The pro teams have a chef or two travelling with them, along with nutritionists and all sorts of other experts who ensure that the riders are eating exactly what they need.

A pro rider could expect his eating day to start several hours before he started pedalling. A big breakfast of oats, fruit, eggs, maybe even rice, pasta or noodles might be the first meal of the day, eaten in time to digest before the stage starts. During the race, sports gels and energy bars help to replace burned calories and riders will also eat real food as they ride, such as paninis, cut up fruit or rice bars. The last thing a rider wants on the Tour is to suffer from the 'Bonk,' a condition caused by the rider using up all the glycogen stores in his body resulting in a sudden and extreme loss of energy. One way to avoid bonking is to load up on carbohydrates in the days leading up to a race and then continue to maintain the carb intake for the duration of the event. It was for this reason that both the Tour riders and the One Day Ahead team placed so much emphasis on eating pasta and other carb-rich products.

With the absence of a professional chef or any nutritionists, our system was a little more basic – make sure that there was a choice of food and plenty of it. It was no good trying to force someone to eat a plate of pasta if what they were really craving was a sausage roll – better they eat something than nothing.

Our rider's diets (and indeed, the support team's diet), therefore consisted of cereal, bread, pastries and cakes for breakfast; pasta, sandwiches, breads, pastries, cake, pizza and all manner of snack food for lunch and usually a hot pasta dish or similar for the evening meal. From a health point of view, it wasn't a great diet, certainly there was a lot of pizza and cake floating around and unfortunately a lot of it managed to find its way into my mouth over the three week period. The riders ate incredible quantities of food, as did I. They all lost weight on the trip, I gained over a stone.

In addition to all the food, it was also vital for the riders to keep up their fluid levels, especially as we started to get further south and into much hotter temperatures. They would need to be drinking at least a 500 ml bottle of water an hour, maybe more when we got to the mountain stages. Usually the water was mixed with a powdered supplement which helped top up carbohydrates and electrolytes.

Our job for the day was pretty simple then, keep the team fed and watered and get them safely through Stage 2 of our Tour de France. The girls had the task of getting their motorhome free and driving on to tomorrow's start town, Orchies, in order to find somewhere to park up for the night. We weren't planning to use campsites every night and actually, had no intention of using them at all if possible. Sara, Mick and I had all travelled extensively in motorhomes in France and knew that there were a multitude of places you could park up without the need to pay for a pitch on a site. Many towns and villages have areas, known as *aires* (short for *aires de service* or service area), which are specifically allocated to motorhomes and these are often free or maybe just five or ten Euros a night.

Even if a town doesn't have an *aire*, the French are incredibly accommodating when it comes to tourists parking up for the odd night and as long as you are considerate, you can get away with wild camping in all sorts of different places. This is particularly the case during the Tour de France, when almost anything goes. If we could avoid campsites for the entire trip, we would save somewhere in the region of nine hundred Euros – an amount not to be sniffed at for sure.

While we were eating breakfast, Stephen had made a phone call to the Belgian AA, membership of which was included in the motorhome hire package and they confirmed they would be along within the hour. Hopefully the problem would be something simple that could be fixed in situ and without the need for a long drawn out detour to a local garage.

Before the guys could start their 207.5 km jaunt towards France, we needed to transport them to the start point in Visé, some 15 km away. This gave the cycling team an opportunity to relax in the rear of Motorhome One, munching their way through a few more pastries.

Visé sits on the Meuse River and is a notably smaller town than the city of Liège which we had just left. For this reason, we had no trouble at all driving the motorhome right up to the stage start point and dropping the boys and their bikes at exactly the right place to get going.

As we had done the day before, we agreed a point approximately 60 km down the road and waved the pedalling foursome off. Nicole wasn't riding today, Sara and I had refused to sit around waiting for her and as it was unlikely that she would be able to keep up with the boys, there was no option but for her to sit this one out. I can't say that this decision was taken well and it was probably the start of a rift between Motorhome One and the kids' bus, which would widen as our trip lengthened.

Fully recovered and feeling full of beans (or was it *pain au chocolat?*) I was now, quite literally, in the driving seat. I do enjoy driving in Europe and have always felt that guiding a motorhome around France is much easier than doing the same in the UK. I'm not sure why, probably the main reason is that there is a lot less traffic. The country is so much bigger than England and everything is more spread out. You don't feel like you are fighting for space all the time. Europeans are also far more forgiving when they see a motorhome on the road – they aren't all in a rush to pass you as is the case in England. All in all, it's a more laid back experience and when you throw the sat nav into the mix, there really isn't anything to think about at all. Jane, as we had called the sat nav, did most of the work for us and Sara only needed the occasional glance at a map just to fine-tune our destination or to confirm that Jane wasn't having a wobble, which she was prone to on occasion.

While other things had been sent to try us during the first couple of days, one thing which had been on our side was the weather. Not too hot, not too cold and no sign of rain. Lady Luck had other ideas today though and she was off to cast her blessings on some other fortunate souls. I nodded to Sara at the road ahead, well to be more specific, at the black storm clouds sitting just above the road ahead.

'Oh dear, I wouldn't want to be out on my bike in that,' she said.

We both share a similar sense of humour and for the next ten minutes, entertained ourselves by laughing at the thought of the boys cycling along in the pouring rain. This was made even more amusing when we realised that they had left their wet weather gear in the back of the motorhome because 'it didn't look like it was going to rain.'

Reaching our first stop point, I parked up at the side of a main road and Sara hung her Union Jack flag out of the window. The wind nearly tore it out of her hands – I hadn't really noticed how stiff the breeze was as it had been blowing directly down this very straight road (which now that I thought about it, we had been travelling on for some time) and straight onto the front of the motorhome. As the wind was hitting the front of the vehicle, it wasn't as noticeable to me as if it had been buffeting the sides but now that we had stopped it was clear to me that it was blowing a gale.

By the time the boys cycled up, forty five minutes later, it was also absolutely chucking it down with rain. Sara and I stifled laughs as each of them dripped into the motorhome in search of a waterproof jacket. They definitely weren't finding things so easy today, they all looked thoroughly miserable. The headwind which we had been oblivious to had been somewhat more apparent to the cyclists as they had been fighting against it for almost the entire route. Riding into a headwind is most unpleasant. As hard as you pedal to try and get some speed up, the wind just relentlessly pushes you back as if to say, 'No, no, you're going to have to try a bit harder than that I'm afraid.'

Throw in some driving rain and you have one of the worst combinations for a cyclist. Had I been out riding in such conditions, this would be the point where I immediately headed for home or dismounted and sought sanctuary in any dry, warm building until the weather had passed. But I wasn't cycling and as much as Mick, Adnan, Stephen and Matt might want to seek shelter in the motorhome, it wasn't an option, so off you go boys, see you in 60 km!

Matt was still suffering with his foot; however I think the weather was helping to take his mind off it. As Stephen was walking down the treacherously wet steps of the motorhome, Sara called out, 'Careful of the steps Stephen, they are really slippery when they are...'

Too late, Stephen crashed down the steps as his smooth-bottomed cycling shoes slid from under him. It looked really painful and the bruise which developed on Stephen's lower back later that day confirmed that it was.

Fed and watered, our happy bunch of cyclists reluctantly remounted their steeds and pushed on. It was very apparent how much slower they were to get going, with each of them commenting, 'Come on, we really need to move now,' several times before any movement actually took place.

I suppose that's one of the advantages of the professional Tour – once they start, they don't stop until the end of the stage. If they want to eat, they do so on the move. If they want more food or drink, one of the team will collect it from the team car which travels behind the *peloton*. A rider may quickly jump off their bike to answer a call of nature but they don't hang about for fear of being left behind by the main group. If their legs are tired, they are a bit cold or if it starts raining and they fancy a little sit down, they quickly find they have chosen the wrong career. In this respect, our boys were incredibly lucky and I thought they would appreciate me telling them so as I overtook them in the motorhome.

'Stop moaning, it's only a bit of rain, just pedal faster – I need to close the window now, I think some spots of rain are coming in.'

Judging by the number of fingers which were thrown up in my direction and the shouting, I could only assume our riders didn't want to be pro-cyclists any more.

Once past the group, Sara suggested giving them a little tow in order to lift their spirits a bit so rather than rush away, I kept the motorhome at roughly the same speed as the boys were riding. This gave them the opportunity to tuck in behind the vehicle and benefit from the fact that the headwind was now being absorbed by the motorhome rather than their lead rider. Slipstreaming is something which you see in professional cycle racing all the time and it is incredibly effective. Even just with two cyclists you can notice the difference. On many occasions I have sat behind Mick on a cycle ride and pondered why he, the supposedly better cyclist, is furiously tapping away at the pedals, yet I, very much a fair weather and even then only occasional rider, am free-wheeling behind him barely breaking a sweat. My first assumption was that I was much better at this cycling lark than I thought. I believed this right up to the point where Mick suggested I have a go on the front. After a couple of miles, I was panting, this was much harder work, no wonder Mick had looked like a hamster on a wheel. When Mick shouted from behind and asked if I could speed up because, 'he was having trouble going so slowly,' I dutifully took my place behind him and let him take over the hard work.

Slipstreaming can help riders save considerable amounts of energy, with the following riders using up to 40% less effort when compared to the leading rider. This is one of the main reasons that the *peloton* is such a powerful force. A rider can sit at the front for a while and then slip back and let someone else take a turn as he benefits from a bit of a rest. The mass of the group continues forward at the same rate. Hence why it is rare for breakaway groups to succeed in reaching the finishing line first – the *peloton* knows how far away the breakaway group is and when they are ready to catch them, one of the teams will take over control at the front and work together to hunt them down. A small breakaway group rarely has a chance against a *peloton* of almost two hundred riders.

With a team of four, it is possible to take turns on the front but fewer riders means more turns and therefore it is far more tiring than having the option of sitting in the middle of a large pack of cyclists, fully protected from the wind.

So an opportunity to get out of the wind behind the motorhome would surely be appreciated. After all, Tour riders will sometimes try and slipstream the team cars if they are making their way back up to the *peloton*. The motorhome, being much larger, offered several times more wind resistance than that of a car. While discussing this comparison, it occurred to me that, under Tour de France regulations, slipstreaming the Tour vehicles is actually prohibited as it gives a rider an unfair advantage. Well far be it for me to help our guys cheat, they wouldn't be able to live with themselves knowing that they hadn't done the Tour properly. Therefore and for no other reason than to help the boys do the right thing, after about half a kilometre, I put my foot down and left them to it. What a sorry sight of dripping wet lycra they looked in the wing mirror. Ha ha ha ha!

It could have been a lot worse. In 1909, the Tour was experiencing some of the worst weather it has ever seen. One hundred and fifty riders had started the race and after six days, fifty of these had dropped out. The riders had to battle through rain, wind, snow, mud and deeply rutted and unsurfaced roads. François Faber, the eventual race winner, dominated the beginning of the Tour, winning five consecutive stages. Faber completed much of his racing alone having broken away from the rest of the bunch, so there were no opportunities to slipstream for him. In the fifth stage, Faber rode the last 62 km alone and after a day spent navigating potholes and knee high water, he rode up the Col de Porte in such a strong wind that he was blown from his bike. A short while later, he was knocked off his bike by a horse but remounted and went on to win the stage with a five minute margin. Our boys really had very little to complain about – no snow, beautifully surfaced roads and a hot meal every 60 km – luxury really. Faber would be turning in his grave.

We had been putting it off all morning but now came the time to make the phone call we had both been dreading. The call to the girls to see if they were on the move yet. I was driving so the task fell to Sara. We knew that the AA had arrived fairly promptly as we had seen the truck driving in as we left the campsite. We hadn't heard anything from the girls though as to whether the mechanic had been successful in getting Motorhome Two back on the road. The fact that we hadn't heard anything had us fearing the worst.

Sara made the call and as it turned out, it was good news. Our diagnosis had been correct, it was a blown fuse but it was a rather larger one than the ones we had inspected. The fuse was hidden away under the seats, near to the motorhome battery. The mechanic seemed surprised that it had blown; this was not a common problem. Needless to say, he didn't have the correct part with him to replace it and wouldn't be able to obtain said part for a couple of days but he had managed to effect a temporary repair, which would be 'good enough until you can get to a garage.' I imagine this meant he had fashioned a fuse out of some tin foil and a bit of coat hanger – rather like the old days when a fuse went in your house and you tried to repair it by ramming just about anything metallic between the contact points. He had impressed quite strongly the need to get the motorhome to a garage quickly so that it could be repaired correctly. In other words, his repair was maybe not the sort you would have received from a main dealer and was, quite possibly, dangerous and a fire risk. Of course, he didn't actually say this, it was just my interpretation but I suspect it was, nonetheless, an accurate summary of the situation. Needless to say, given that this was the kids' bus and not the adults' bus, the temporary repair remained exactly that until the motorhome was returned to the hire company three weeks later.

Motorhome Two were currently on their way to Orchies, with full instructions on how to find the perfect location to stop overnight. Now that they were up and running again, they were also in charge of making dinner for everyone this evening and they were just on their way to the supermarket to pick something up. Let's hope that the kids weren't really as kid-like as maybe we were making them out to be or it would be fizzy pop and bags of Haribo all round.

Knowing that Motorhome Two was back on the road was a massive relief. It meant that we could go back to our original plan of supporting every other day and sharing the workload. Trying to support the cyclists and fit in shopping, cooking and all of the other mundane tasks which needed to be done would have been next to impossible on our own and may well have brought the trip to an early conclusion. That said, in a few days time we would both have been very pleased if this had been the outcome but for the time being, we were happy and keen to get the job done.

By the time we met up with the boys again, they were completely fed up. Although the rain had let up, the wind was still driving against them. There wasn't much talking going on and it was clear that they just wanted to get to the end and forget about this stage. Towards the end of the Tour, I asked each of them which had been the worst stage and I fully expected them to answer one of the gruelling mountain stages but they didn't. They all said it was this stage purely because of the relentless wind. The route was also very straight which meant you could see right along the road and the scenery was completely unchanging, making it quite monotonous. Who would have thought that a flat stage in Belgium could have been the hardest stage in a Tour de France?

Seven hours and forty minutes after dropping them off in Visé, we picked the boys up in Tournai. The sun was now out and the team had dried off but it was obvious that they were absolutely shattered and very pleased to get off their bikes. We now had a 20 km drive to Orchies, where we would meet up with the other half of our group in Motorhome Two.

Nicole had telephoned an hour or so earlier to say that they had arrived in Orchies and were trying to find somewhere to park up. I was starving hungry and was really hoping that they had found somewhere suitable as I was not really in the mood to be driving round looking for camping spots. All I really wanted to do was park the motorhome and relax before getting back into my bunk.

As we were entering Orchies, the phone rang. It was Nicole. They had found a car park next to a cycling club and when they explained what we were up to, the club had confirmed that they were happy for us to camp there for the night. Perfect.

We had the car park to ourselves so we parked the motorhomes side by side, with an area between for tables and chairs. Something with pasta and garlic bread smelt delicious so obviously we weren't getting Haribo and within half an hour, we were all sitting down enjoying a meal as the sun started to dip behind the trees. With bikes and various bits of kit spread out all over the place, I dread to think what we looked like but the locals didn't bat an eyelid. This was either the norm or they were far more tolerant than us English folk when it comes to things like this.

Emily had already done a decent day's work by the time we settled down to eat as she had carefully navigated Motorhome Two from Liège to Orchies, a distance of 194 km, plus a stop en route for a bit of food shopping. But her real job began just as the sun was starting to set. Emily set up her physio table in the car park (it seemed odd setting up our mobile massage parlour out in the open at first but everyone soon got used to it and in the end, we hardly noticed how weird it must look to passers-by) and Mick was the first customer. I hadn't been paying a lot of attention to the physio event when it took place the evening before but today was a different matter. I was first drawn by a rather unusual sound coming from Mick's mouth, it was the sound of pain and wasn't something I was used to. Mick is very much a grin and bear it bloke, he isn't one to moan about something as trifling as a bit of pain. So when I saw him grimacing, I knew I had to investigate further. Taking a folding chair and a can of beer, I plonked myself down in front of the massage bench and took in the view. It was obvious that Mick was in some discomfort as Emily dug her fingers into his thighs and calves. This was most amusing and very entertaining.

'Oh dear, is the little lady hurting your legs with her big strong fingers?' I cooed at Mick,

'Why don't you go and find something else to do?' is a loose translation of his very sweary reply.

If Emily's pain-inflicting digits were causing Mick to roll around like a little girl, I couldn't wait to see what a fuss the others would make. Sure enough, Stephen and Matt were both almost crying once Emily got started. She delighted in telling them that she was only applying about three levels of pressure when she could go up to ten. I delighted in that too because it meant that I had lots more entertainment to come. This was going to be a long and stressful trip; I had to get some enjoyment where I could.

Only Adnan didn't act like a complete wuss during his time on the bench. He kept a completely straight face, continued his conversation as normal and was, quite frankly, a big disappointment in terms of entertainment value. Not to worry, three out of four wasn't too bad and the other three were hilarious. Sara missed out on the show as she was busy doing more important jobs but when I relayed the story to her, she was keen not to miss the follow-up performance the next night.

After dinner, our ideal scenario would have been to settle down and watch the highlights of the actual Tour on TV. Sara and Mick's new motorhome was fully kitted out with the latest Sky TV set-up, which meant we should be able to pick up the Tour from anywhere we chose to park. Unfortunately, the new motorhome was on their driveway in England and we were in the old motorhome which had no Sky TV. It did however have a small portable TV along with a fairly antiquated rooftop aerial. This was more than Motorhome Two had but after messing around with it for half an hour, it became clear that we had more chance of getting a bus to the moon than successfully locating a TV signal.

Had we managed to pick up the local sports channel, we would have seen 198 riders sign on for Stage 1. Immediately racing began, Nicholas Edet attacked, taking with him six other riders and by the 11 km mark, they had a lead of three minutes on the main group. At the 24 km mark the barriers of a level crossing came down and held the lead group up for 45 seconds or so. In the early days of the Tour, it is unlikely that the riders would have waited for the train to pass and ducking under the barrier in order to gain some advantage would have been more likely. Health and safety is more of a concern these days and no doubt any such behaviour would now be rewarded with a stiff penalty. Despite this delay, the breakaway group had pushed their lead up to 3.5 minutes by the 30 km point.

When the escapees had managed to put almost 5 minutes between them and the main field, the Radioshack-Nissan team decided that enough was enough and put their boys to the front of the *peloton* to bring the leaders back in. With 70 km to go, they had reduced the gap by just under a minute and at the 45 km to go mark, the advance group were a minute and twenty five seconds ahead. Having let Radioshack-Nissan do the hard work, some other teams took their turn on the front and with 20 km left to ride, the breakaway group had an advantage of just 25 seconds. The lead group were caught with 8 km left to race and the teams started to sort themselves out for the upcoming sprint which was won by Peter Sagan of the Liquigas-Cannondale team, after battling his way up that nasty little 17% incline.

Peter Sagan is a good all round rider with a particular talent for sprinting and he would have his sights on the second main jersey up for grabs in the Tour, the green jersey (*maillot vert*), also known as the points jersey or the sprinter's jersey.

Points for the green jersey can be won in two ways. Firstly, the winner of any given stage will pick up a number of points, as will the next fourteen riders, the amount of points reducing depending upon the rider's position across the line. Secondly, each stage will have one or two intermediate sprints, basically the first fifteen riders through the intermediate sprint pick up points, the higher your place in the group, the more points you get. At the end of the Tour, the rider with the most points wins the green jersey. Simple!

Actually, not that simple. It used to be that the intermediate sprints were given a far lower priority than the final sprint for the finish line. However in 2011, this changed and the number of points awarded in the intermediate sprints was greatly increased. It was now not possible for a rider in contention for the green jersey to just sit in the *peloton* and be carried to the end and then brought out to do their thing. Now they had to make a decision about whether they would expend energy getting to the intermediate sprints first by getting into a breakaway group or just battle it out with the other sprinters in the *peloton* at each sprint point. It gave the sprinters a lot more to think about and consider and this in turn made it more entertaining for the spectators.

Most sprinters won't ever be in contention for the overall general classification win as sprinters don't tend to be very good at climbing mountains and vice versa. Sprinters tend to fall back on the mountain stages and actually, run a very real risk of being disqualified if they don't make the formal cut-off finishing time. This time is calculated as a percentage of the winner's finishing time for each stage and everyone must cross the line within this calculated time or that's the end of their race and they are disqualified from the Tour.

Isle of Man sprinter and winner of the green jersey competition in 2011, Mark Cavendish, has made it perfectly clear on a number of occasions that he enjoys racing over mountains not one jot. The mountain days are days which he just has to get through. He knows he has no chance of winning the stage; it's just a case of getting to the end before the cut-off. Put him on a flat stage though and Cav is hard to beat. Cavendish had moved to Team Sky at the start of the season and I couldn't help but feel that this was going to be a difficult Tour for him. Sky's main aim was to bring home the yellow jersey with

Bradley Wiggins and it would be nigh on impossible for them to target the green jersey at the same time. A successful Tour rider needs the support of their team and if the team were going to be supporting Wiggo, then Cav would be left out in the cold and would actually be part of Wiggins' support rather than being the main man as he had been used to.

Maybe this was Peter Sagan's year for green. He certainly had some incentive as, in addition to the jersey and prize money, a few days before the Tour had started, Sagan had asked the Liquigas team boss, Paulo Zani, if he would buy him a Porsche if he won the points competition. Zani had agreed but only on the condition that Sagan won at least two stages along the way. He'd already won one stage; it would be interesting to see how far he could go.

I'm sure if our boys had been given the incentive of a Porsche each to carry them along, then the pain they had suffered that day (both cycling and at the hands of Emily) would have seemed worthwhile. As it was, there were no Porsches, only further days of pain to look forward to. As I helpfully reminded them, these are the easy stages and we weren't even close to the mountains yet. A couple of stinking socks and a cycling shoe flew towards me. I don't know what the problem was, as Mick had said only the day before, if it was easy, every man and his dog would be at it.

Once the boys had finished their dinner and physio and enjoyed a hot shower each, the long and arduous ride of earlier in the day was soon forgotten and the riders could look forward to the next stage. As for Sara and me, well we were looking forward to a day off from supporting, although we were soon to learn that this was to be a trip without any real days off.

Tour positions at end of Stage 1

Stage Winner: Peter Sagan/Liquigas-Cannondale

Yellow: Fabian Cancellara/Radioshack-Nissan
Green: Fabian Cancellara/Radioshack-Nissan
Polka Dot: Michael Morkov/Team Saxo Bank-Tinkoff
White: Tejay Van Garderen/BMC Racing Team

STAGE 3
Monday 2nd July 2012
ORCHIES – BOULOGNE-SUR-MER
Hilly – 197 km

'It is by riding a bicycle that you learn the contours of a country best, since you have to sweat up the hills and can coast down them. Thus you remember them as they actually are, while in a motorcar only a high hill impresses you, and you have no such accurate remembrance of country you have driven through as you gain by riding a bicycle.'
Ernest Hemingway – Author

Today's route would see the team heading west once again and everyone was relieved to wake to a fine and more importantly, windless day. The stage would start in the small town of Orchies which, for the first time in Tour history, had put in a joint proposal to host a stage with yesterday's finish town, Tournai. Orchies also had a second 'first' claim as in 1982, the team time trial stage was cancelled due to a strike by local steel workers. There was no sign of that happening today and as was becoming the norm, our little pop-up campsite was bustling with activity.

Stephen stuck his head into our motorhome.

'Ready to go in ten?' he asked.

Adnan had only just got up and hadn't even had chance for a cup of tea yet and Mick was wandering about in a state of undress which, had Stephen taken any notice, would have confirmed that he would not be ready in ten.

'Yup,' they both replied without any urgency or indeed any intention of being ready to go until it suited them.

Sara caught my eye as we both wondered whether tensions were forming in the riding group as well as the support groups.

Mick and Adnan sat down and began to tuck into some breakfast.

'I'll go when I'm ready to go,' said Adnan. Mick nodded his concurrence.

Orchies is only a small town, with a population of just under 8000. For this reason and due to the hospitality of the local cycling club the evening before, there was no need to transport the riders to their start point. It was only round the corner so they could just ride there. I confirmed this with Mick as I programmed the Garmin with the day's stage and calculated that the start point was about 400 metres away.

I picked up what was already a well-thumbed race guide to inspect the stage profile for the day. 197 km with four cat 4 climbs and two graded at category 3. Things were starting to get a bit more interesting. Not that Sara and I would see any of the riding today as we had our first 'rest' day. This meant stocking up on food, finding somewhere to fill the motorhome up with water and the toilet cassette needed emptying too. Too many days like this and it wouldn't be the drink causing me to keel over but the excitement.

'Ready to go?' said Stephen as he appeared at the door for a second time.

Mick still wasn't dressed and Adnan was sitting eating a bowl of cereal, so no, neither were ready to go.

'You said ten minutes,' said Adnan, obviously trying to wind Stephen up.

'That was fifteen minutes ago,' came Stephen's reply.

Adnan just looked at him blankly before bursting into a giggling fit when he turned back to his own motorhome.

Half an hour later the team were ready to move. Just a

couple of days in and I could already see that the enthusiasm to set off was waning very, very slightly. I knew the feeling. I had no intention of moving anywhere fast that morning and I was planning on at least three or four cups of tea before Sara and I hit the road.

The Motorhome Two team didn't have that option as they had to get to the first meeting point. We had briefed them about what they would need to do and also impressed upon them the importance of not hanging about as there was every possibility that the boys would cover ground faster than they would. They left the car park ten minutes after the boys, as Sara boiled the kettle.

Our first priority for the day was to find water and empty the motorhome toilet cassette. We had been slightly spoilt for the first couple of days as the campsite had easy access to water and of course, a chemical waste disposal point. These two jobs would dominate our lives over the next three weeks as both were vital to the smooth running of our support vehicle.

Living in a motorhome with limited water onboard gives you a real sense of respect for this valuable resource. At home, with water quite literally on tap, it is easy to be wasteful and one doesn't really give a second thought as to how many times the toilet is flushed or leaving the tap running while you brush your teeth. In a motorhome, especially a motorhome with four people living in it, you have to think about every drop. The motorhome held enough water for two adults to live normally for two, maybe three days. Double the number of people and you halve the length of time the water will last. In addition to the main tank of water, we also had a separate, portable container which held a further 23 litres. Once fully loaded with water, we had enough on board for all of our needs for about twenty four hours, maybe thirty six at a push. The toilet cassette would last about a day but fortunately we had two so we were able to rotate them.

Showers were prioritised for Adnan and Mick given that they would have been riding all day. This was as much for Sara's and my benefit – we didn't want to be sharing the motorhome with those two stinking up the place. Sara and I usually managed to get a quick shower each day but in order to conserve water it was a case of turning the shower on to get wet, turning it off to soap up and then rinsing off as quickly as possible. On days where we had managed to park near to a water supply, we would reward ourselves with 'luxury' showers – showers where we just left the stream of hot water running with no care as to whether it ran out. A luxury shower was a real treat.

Aires were the ideal place to locate fresh water and it was usually possible to hook a hose up to a tap and fill the motorhome tank directly from the service point. You would also find a chemical toilet emptying point at the vast majority of *aires*. Two birds, one stone.

In the event that there wasn't a conveniently located *aire*, there were plenty of toilet blocks on the motorways. These would always have water but no option to connect a hose. Therefore it was necessary to fill the motorhome tank by going back and forth with the portable container. It took about five trips to fill the tank and this could take over half an hour to complete. The taps didn't tend to have a very high pressure so filling the container was an arduously slow process. These motorway toilet blocks were also an ideal option if you needed to empty a toilet cassette. Not quite as easy as dumping it all down a specially made hole in the ground and it had to be done with great care as they were prone to being a bit splashy, but if you took your time, it was a relatively straightforward task to empty a cassette into a normal toilet with no mess.

The final option for fresh water was something which I discovered about halfway through our trip. France is littered with small towns, villages and hamlets and most of these have their own cemeteries and guess what they have in cemeteries? They have taps for topping up the flower vases. Again, no chance of hooking up a hose but there is usually enough room to squeeze the portable container under the tap thus granting you access to the precious water.

So, our first job was to find water and all being well, we could sort the toilet out at the same time. Then we needed to find a supermarket and do some shopping; no problem there as Jane the sat nav would find somewhere to shop. Finally we had to get down to Abbeville to find somewhere to park up for the night and prepare the evening meal. It was gone 11:00 am and I was beginning to wonder what was happening to our rest day.

We managed to fill up with water almost immediately after coming across a suitable tap behind a petrol filling station. We had stopped to fill up with diesel (something else which we would need to do at least every other day). Stephen had given us his American Express card to use, as his employer had agreed to pay for our fuel by way of sponsorship. I filled up the tank and Sara went to pay, only for Stephen's card to be declined. She paid for it on her own card, cursing as she returned to the motorhome and probably calculating how much this little adventure of Mick's was now going to cost in fuel alone.

There was nowhere to empty the toilet cassette but we still had the spare one, which was empty, so this wasn't an urgent job. Food, however, was urgent so we got Jane to point us in the direction of the nearest Carrefour super-market. Carrefour, as well as having over 13,000 stores in

Europe, have also been the sponsor of the Tour de France King of the Mountains competition since 2009. The King of the Mountains competition is, as the name suggests, won by the best climber in the Tour de France. The first riders over the top of a climb receive points, with the highest number of points being awarded for the tougher climbs. For a small cat 4 climb, only the first rider over the top gets a point, but for an HC mountain, the first ten riders will be rewarded. The rider at the end of the Tour with the most points is the winner and receives the polka dot jersey (*maillot à pois rouges*) which is white with red dots.

Given the association of Carrefour with the Tour, it seemed only right that we use their supermarkets wherever possible so we started as we meant to go on. Now, in common with the majority of the male species, I really cannot stand shopping. Shopping for clothes is definitely the worst but food shopping is up there in second place. When I go to the supermarket, I can do a full shop in about ten minutes, absolute maximum. Admittedly I might come out with less than five items but that's fine, as long as I've got enough to eat for that day, then I'm happy. One thing I can't abide is walking up and down every single aisle, looking at offers and deals. A lot of women love all that but fortunately Sara isn't one of them. She hates shopping almost as much as I do so I was greatly relieved when she agreed that we needed to be in and out in as short a time as possible.

We stocked up on the basics - pasta, meat, snacks etc and threw in some treats to keep the boys happy. St. Michel, one of the leading bakery brands in France, sell a range of cakes and biscuits and we found some bags of bite-size cakes which Sara picked up for Mick and Adnan to munch on. We noticed over the course of the Tour that Adnan couldn't get enough of these little cakes and they were soon being referred to as 'Adnan Cakes.' Sara even took to leaving a couple on his pillow at night. And this was about as close to a 'boutique hotel experience' as our accommodation ever got!

As planned, thirty minutes and a couple of hundred Euros later and we were pushing a substantial quantity of food back to the motorhome, already wondering if we had bought enough. As we wandered across the car park, we noticed several office workers, clearly on their lunch breaks, leaving the supermarket with enormous pastries. These things must have been fifteen inches across and we laughed as we imagined the conversation back at the office, 'Just nipping out for lunch, I'm having a MASSIVE cake again today.' For a race of people who really love their cakes and pastry products, you have to ask why they don't seem to have anywhere near as many larger folk as we do in England.

Abbeville was a two hour drive away and with the important jobs done, we decided to have lunch in the Carrefour car park. That's the beauty of motorhoming – you can stop anywhere you like to eat and you get to enjoy some wonderful, scenic locations. The view from this particular Carrefour car park included not only a petrol station but also a car wash and a Mr. Bricolage store (the French equivalent of B & Q).

While we were pondering whether we should have a third cup of tea before making our way down to Abbeville, Sara's phone rang. It was Nicole and there had been an accident. It was inevitable I guess that, at some point, one of the riders would fall off their bike during this mammoth endeavour. The details were a bit unclear but the gist was that Matt and Stephen had crashed but both were okay.

Picking through the bones of the story later, it seems that the group were negotiating a roundabout and

Stephen made a mistake in respect of which exit they needed to take. Rather than continue round with the group, he pulled off sharply towards the wrong exit and rode straight into Matt who was alongside him. The pair then ended up on the ground. It sounded as though the incident was completely avoidable and a case of particularly careless riding but we were just grateful for the fact that no one was seriously hurt and that no damage had been done to the bikes. Put this one down to experience and hope that it was the first and last time that anyone would make contact with the tarmac.

A couple of hours later, we pulled into Abbeville and began to search for a convenient parking spot. As ultimately turned out to be the case nearly every day, we got lucky and found the perfect position within minutes of arriving. In the centre of the town there was a large park and judging by the stage which was in the process of being erected, it seemed likely that this was going to mark the start of the professional Tour in two days time. Along one side of the park was a one-way street with a line of parking spaces. I manoeuvred the motorhome into one of the spaces and we blocked up a second space with chairs, ready for the Motorhome Two to arrive.

Sara got the dinner on and it wasn't long before we were joined by the second half of the team. It became apparent that Matt was suffering with quite a sore shoulder and the reason was obvious when he took his shirt off as he had a nasty graze and a rather large patch of missing skin. Our motorhome was equipped, thanks to Sara, with a first aid kit with which I am sure Adnan could have performed minor surgery, had it been necessary. Matt was soon patched up but this shoulder injury was to be something which would bother him for several days to come. Still, as I helpfully commented, it would take his mind off his foot.

We ate dinner *al fresco* while watching the activities of the locals enjoying the last of the sun in the park. Children and their parents gave way to dog walkers and ultimately teenagers on their mopeds who sat in groups chatting. In the UK we would have expected the teenagers to be rowdy and unruly but it wasn't the case here. They were quiet and seemed respectful. At 10:00 pm they all got up and headed off, leaving the area as they had found it and rather peaceful given its town centre location.

Some of the locals had paused to watch Emily's physio session, which they appeared to find most amusing. I laughed along with them as the boys winced in pain, something of which I would never tire. The French made various comments, I have no idea what they were saying but they ended with laughter so I joined in and that seemed to be sufficient.

The last task of the day was kit washing. The boys essentially had two lots of cycling kit each and therefore, every night, one set needed to be washed and then dried. In addition, the water bottles which had been used during the day also needed to be carefully washed up. Having clean water bottles was absolutely vital as the hot conditions and sticky energy drink made for an ideal environment for bacteria and other nasties to grow. An upset stomach was not something which any rider wanted so it was essential that the bottles were given a good scrub every night. Each rider had four bottles which they used in rotation each day, thus there were sixteen bottles to clean every night and which would also have already been washed at least once during that day's ride. This was one more little job which sucked time and fast became a complete drag. Sara noted that on the one night she had let the bottle washing task out of her hands, the cleaning hadn't been to her high standard and there was still residue from the energy drink in the mouthpieces. After this, she insisted on taking control of the bottle washing every day. Sometimes it was easier just to do these jobs yourself.

It would have been nice to have done as the professionals did and just not bothered with bottle washing. They simply chucked their bottles away once they were empty. If you watch the Tour you will see the riders launching their empty bottles towards the roadside when they have drunk them dry. Spectators then rush to pick them up so they can take them home as a souvenir of the day. Unfortunately we didn't have the levels of cash support behind us that the pro teams do and chucking away perfectly good bottles was not an option. Bottles cost about £3.00 each, so working on the basis that each rider used up to eight clean bottles a day, over a twenty one day period, fresh bottles for four riders would have cost over £2,000. I dread to think what the pro Tour spends on bottles – they get through something like 40,000 of them!

As for the cycling kit, we took the washing of this in turns, with the support team on their day off having the honour of washing the dirty kit from that day's ride. In fairness, I got out of this as Sara did the washing every day. The closest I got to a pair of stinking lycra shorts was hanging them out to dry and that was plenty close enough for me.

Stephen, Matt, Jess and Nicole retreated to their motorhome soon after dinner, leaving Emily sitting with us. As the temperature started to drop, we all went back to our motorhome for a last glass of wine. We asked Emily how she had got on today and discovered that as well as doing all the driving, she had also had to do most of the navigation and had made the bulk of the food for the boys along the route. It sounded as though she was getting the raw end of the deal, with Nicole and Jess happy to load her up with as much work as they could get away with. Emily wasn't complaining and she was happy to go with the flow. As she pointed out, she was the only one being paid to be there but it didn't seem fair to us. She was being paid to do the physio each day, not to be a general dogsbody to be taken advantage of at every opportunity.

We called it a night shortly after 10:30 pm and felt quite sorry for Emily as she made the short journey back to her bed in Motorhome Two. All the lights were off now, the others had obviously gone straight to bed and she had to creep in like a naughty teenager coming back from a night out.

Stage 2 of the pro Tour saw all 198 riders signing on and starting their ride to Tournai. No early attacks formed and it wasn't until 22 km into the race that Anthony Roux (FDJ-Bigmat Team) made a bid for freedom, closely followed by two other riders. By the 29 km point, these three riders had gained an advantage of 3 minutes and 40 seconds over the main group and by 42 km they had pushed this up to 8 minutes.

Roux decided to try and put some distance between himself and his two fellow escapees with 31 km to go but despite this, he was eventually caught by the *peloton* 14 km before the finish. Time for the sprint teams to get themselves in order and it was Lotto-Belisol who dominated the closing kilometre in an attempt to set things up for their man, André Greipel. Greipel was perfectly lined up but couldn't manage to beat the incredible power of Team Sky's Mark Cavendish, who took the stage victory. Peter Sagan claimed sixth place and now leads in the points competition and he will wear the green jersey tomorrow.

Tour positions at end of STAGE 2

Stage Winner: Mark Cavendish/Sky Procycling

Yellow: Fabian Cancellara/Radioshack-Nissan
Green: Peter Sagan/Liquigas-Cannondale
Polka Dot: Michael Morkov/Team Saxo Bank-Tinkoff
White: Tejay Van Garderen/BMC Racing Team

STAGE 4

Tuesday 3rd July 2012
ABBEVILLE – ROUEN
Flat – 214.5 km

'Nothing compares to the simple pleasure of a bike ride.'
John F Kennedy – 35th President of the United States of America

'We're going to have to cut back on food,' said Stephen.

'Mmm,' I thought, 'this should be an interesting conversation.' Sara had presented Stephen with the bill for our food shopping the previous evening, along with an estimate for the total food costs for the rest of the trip. From this figure we could work out what each of us needed to pay towards the food bill, with a slightly larger sum being paid by each of the cyclists given that they were eating quite a bit more than the rest of us. Stephen had passed this information back to his colleagues in Motorhome Two and for some reason, the fact that they would be expected to contribute to the food expenditure had come as a bit of a surprise to Matt and Jess, who were travelling very much on a budget.

Jess, as an American citizen, wasn't able to work in the UK. Jess and Matt had met some months earlier and she hadn't worked since, other than a bit of casual work whilst travelling. Matt had been working in a cycle shop prior to starting the One Day Ahead trip but as he was unable to take three weeks leave, he had resigned rather than miss out on the opportunity. The result of this was that neither of them had much in the way of spare cash and neither had expected to pay for food.

In fact, although everyone in Motorhome One had expected to pay for their food, it appeared to be the case that Stephen had told Matt, Jess and Nicole that this cost would somehow be covered by sponsorship. Matt and Jess had therefore come along with the expectation of paying next to nothing during the trip and were now, quite understandably, baulking at the prospect of having to shell out a couple of hundred Euros for food.

'There is absolutely no way we are cutting back on food,' was Sara's response, 'the riders need to be eating properly or there is no way they will get round the whole route. You can't be trying to do something like this half-heartedly.'

I suspect that this put Stephen in an awkward position. He was the one who had told Matt and Jess that there would be no requirement for them to contribute to the food bill so really it was his problem to sort out. Adnan and I looked at each other suitably amazed - who comes on a trip like this without money? Our view was that you would have to pay for food if you were at home so what was the difference? The difference was, of course, that Matt and Jess lived with their parents and therefore buying food was not their responsibility. This was just another example of the generation gap between Motorhome One and Motorhome Two.

No immediate solution was offered to the food issue but our position couldn't have been clearer. Whatever food we needed would be purchased and we expected everyone eating it to contribute towards it. The only person who it had been agreed did not have to chip in was Emily, on the basis that she was here in a professional capacity, rather than because she was a friend or partner of one of the riders. This had also been the original agreement with her employer when it was agreed that she could join us.

I could see that this was going to be an issue which would raise its head a few more times before our journey through France was over, just one of several bones of contention which would start to gnaw away at Sara's and my patience.

Still, for the time being at least, we had plenty of food in the cupboards so we all fell into our morning pre-ride routines. Sara making breakfast, Mick and Adnan getting dressed and sorting their bikes out, me programming the Garmin and assisting as required, the others no doubt doing similar things in their motorhome.

I went to have a chat with Jess. She had mentioned yesterday that they were low on water and they hadn't managed to top up since we left the campsite two days ago. In addition, their toilet cassette was full and therefore out of use. There were some portaloos on the other side of the park in Abbeville which they could use this morning but both of these issues needed resolving sooner rather than later.

Jess had expressed concern as to how and where they could get water. The only option they had to fill their tank with water was with a hose – they didn't have a handy portable container like we did, which meant that filling up from a stand alone tap wouldn't be a quick or simple process. I suggested that if they couldn't find an *aire*, then maybe they could go into a campsite and offer them a few Euros to fill up and empty their cassette. Alternatively, they needed to buy some sort of container or even just a bucket with which they could transport water from a service station tap to the motorhome. It wasn't ideal but it was a solution. The bottom line was that they needed to get on top of these basic tasks and get a system in place. Sorting the water and toilet out should be fairly straightforward up here in Northern France but it certainly wasn't going to get any easier once we got down into the mountains of the Alps and the Pyrenees.

For the time being, I emptied our reserve container of water into their main tank in order that they had some water onboard. This now left us short and meant that as well as handling rider support, we also had to find somewhere to top up our own water. I told Jess that they should prioritise sorting the water and toilet out above all else today. They had nothing else to do except pick up a bit of shopping and then get to Rouen, which as well as today's finishing town, was also the start town for the next day. Rouen was only about an hour or so away. The reality was therefore, that they had nearly a whole day to devote to resolving these issues.

As had been the case the day before, we were parked within half a kilometre of the official start point of the day's stage. No need for me to drive the guys anywhere and within half an hour of finishing breakfast they were saddled up and heading off towards Rouen. Today's route would take the team south west along the coast of northern France before turning roughly south east to Rouen. From the point that they turned inland, we would be heading away from England for the next thirteen days, at which point we would be in southern France and would eventually turn sharply north and head for home.

The stage profile didn't look anything to be concerned about, a handful of category 4 climbs and a flat finish. I'm sure the boys were not impressed at how easily their support team were already dismissing these lower category climbs as being hardly worthy of mention. Maybe if Sara and I had had to cycle over them we would have had a bit more respect.

We had now slipped into a routine on our support days and we had managed to get things running as close to like clockwork as was possible. Once the riders were on the road, all we needed to do was get to the first checkpoint. We'd park up and I would set up tables and chairs, while Sara made lunch and laid it all out. The kettle would go on and we'd treat ourselves to one, maybe two cups of tea, while watching out for Team One Day Ahead. When they arrived, I would remove all of their water bottles and top them up with water or energy drink depending on the individual rider's preference. The boys would take about twenty minutes to eat, use the toilet and generally stretch their legs, at which point we would agree a rough meeting place for their next stop and they would mount up and continue their ride. Sara and I would tidy away the tables, do the washing up, maybe have another brew and then set off behind them.

It was pretty monotonous. Drive, park, tables, food, bottles, wash up, drive and repeat. It was day five and I was already starting to get a bit fed up with this game. I had noticed that Sara had been getting a bit more sweary over the past couple of days. A sure sign that she was also losing interest.

We tried to keep our spirits up by moaning. This might seem odd but it helped and boy, did we have plenty to moan about. Why do we get drawn into these stupid ideas of Mick's? Who comes on holiday with no money? How can you not find water in a country the size of France? Who gets a motorhome stuck in a field which isn't even muddy? What do you mean, cut back on food? Gosh what a fantastic holiday we were having, the hours just flew by.

The boys on the other hand, were having a brilliant time. Now that the wind and rain of Stage 2 was well behind them, they were enjoying a three week holiday cycling around France in the summer sun. For a cyclist, there really was no better way to spend July and the biggest thing they had to worry about was how often they needed to stop to apply sun tan cream. The tan lines competition was in full swing and Adnan had taken an early lead although he did have the advantage of starting with darker skin in the first place. It was quite surprising how much of a tan he actually gained and his fingerless gloves caused him to develop a most unusual monochrome design on his hands and fingers.

The scenery along the coast had been stunning and the boys had met up with some Dutch cyclists who were also riding the stage. As they approached the intermediate sprint section of the stage, the Dutch pointed it out and they all raced for the sprinter's points. Unfortunately it wasn't clear where the finish line was so Mick had to settle for second place. No green jersey for you Mick – no one remembers who came second.

Our final food stop of the day was located just after the last cat 4 climb and left the cyclists with approximately 60 km to ride to the end of the stage. Before we set off to the finish, we phoned Nicole to see if they had found anywhere to park up for the night. We thought it might be a bit harder to find somewhere suitable in Rouen as it is a reasonably large city and indeed this was proving to be the case.

Despite having circumnavigated the city several times, the girls hadn't managed to find anywhere suitable to pull up but they had found the road where the riders were due to finish. Therefore, we suggested that they park close to the finish so that they could pick up the boys once they arrived and Sara and I would get to Rouen as fast as we could and find somewhere to camp.

It was obvious as we entered Rouen that we would be hard pushed to find somewhere in the city centre or even close to it which would be suitable to stay overnight. We had no option therefore but to head towards the outskirts of the city. Our first possible overnight location was the car park of a Carrefour hypermarket. Not ideal but a definite maybe. We might not have much choice.

If you believe in good omens, what happened next was surely one. About 3 km outside of Rouen, we spotted a sign to the Jacques Anquetil Gymnasium. Anquetil was an incredible Tour rider in the fifties and sixties and the first to ever win the Tour de France five times. Anquetil hailed from the Rouen area, hence the connection to the city. He first entered and won the Tour in 1957 and he went on to win in 1961, 1962, 1963 and 1964. Anquetil was also the first rider to ever win all three of the Grand Tours, the Tour de France, the Giro d'Italia (twice) and the Vuelta a España. A truly exceptional cyclist.

After winning four consecutive Tours, Anquetil opted not to enter the 1965 race, explaining,

'My contracts won't increase if I win a sixth Tour. And if I fail, I have everything to lose.'

Anquetil, we felt sure, would be more than happy for us to camp in the car park of 'his' gym and when I told Sara that, when asked by a young boy how he prepared for the Tour, Anquetil had once replied, 'With a good woman and a bottle of champagne,' we felt sure it was the ideal place for us.

The car park was empty as we pulled in and we selected a prime position, taking up about three parking bays. There was enough room for Motorhome Two to squeeze in to the front of us but there was plenty of space in the car park so we didn't anticipate any problems.

We texted the details of our location to Nicole and stuck the kettle on. They wouldn't be here for another hour at least and I decided that now might be a good opportunity to have my first shave of the trip. I had brought along a rechargeable shaver. However as it needed a 240 volt connection to recharge and as you needed to be on a campsite for such a luxury, I wasn't sure how many times I would be able to charge it, if any. I knew the shaver was good for about three uses from full charge so I had to carefully spread these out over the duration of the trip. I sat on the steps of the motorhome and set about shaving off almost a week's worth of stubble. If I had witnessed the same scene at home, I would have thought we had been invaded by my Big Fat Gypsy Cyclists. We only needed a handful of kids, a few dogs and a pile of old car tyres to complete the picture.

While I was shaving, Sara was hanging out yesterday's washing to dry – this was the first chance we had had to do it so we were desperately hoping the last few rays of sun would dry out the lycra before the morning or the boys would be starting their next ride wearing damp kit. With the washing out, Sara started to make some dinner.

It wasn't long before Motorhome Two arrived and parked up in the space we had saved. I went to enquire as to whether they had sorted their water issue. I was absolutely astounded to learn that, despite having had the whole day, they hadn't managed to get any water and would be most grateful if they could have our spare container again. I bit my lip and reluctantly handed over the container, knowing that once again, we were now short of water. I didn't dare ask about the toilet cassette but I had a pretty good idea that it would still be full. Fortunately the gym had toilets so, for this evening at least, the toilet cassette wasn't a priority.

Shortly after sitting down to eat dinner in our car park restaurant, the police turned up. It was now about 8:00 pm and I suspected that we were about to be kicked out of the car park to who knew where. A stern looking French Officer exited his car and came over to us.

As it turned out, he wasn't bothered by the fact that we

were in the car park or that we were obviously planning to stay there for the night. His concern was that the rear of the second motorhome was hanging about a foot over a disabled parking bay. We apologised and moved the motorhome forward and a smile appeared on his face. He wished us '*Bonne chance*' and returned to his car, happy that another misdemeanour had been avoided.

Around 10:00 pm, a few of the local elder folk wandered over from their houses to see what we were up to. I think we managed to get the message across to them that some of us were riding the entire Tour de France route. They seemed impressed and did lots of nodding and made lots of '*Oui, oui c'est bon*' comments. I suspect that the thing which impressed them most however was that this rabble of English scruff bags would be gone from their doorsteps the following morning.

As the pro Tour moves into France for the first time, once again all 198 riders turned up for signing on and racing. I can guarantee that no one on the Team Sky bus has suggested cutting back on food and I know for a fact that they won't be running out of water or having to use the local gymnasium's toilet facilities.

A breakout of five men formed after 5 km and after 15 km they had a lead of 5 minutes and 40 seconds over the *peloton*, which was as far ahead as they managed to get all day. Two teams, Liquigas-Cannondale and Radioshack-Nissan worked together to chip away at the gap and with

95 km to go, the leaders were 5 minutes ahead. With 38 km to go, the advantage was down to 2 minutes 30 seconds and the lead group were down to four men, who were eventually caught one by one before the 7 km to go point was reached. The fight for the stage win ended with Peter Sagan crossing the line first to increase his lead in the points competition. Cancellara finished in fourth position and so continues to wear the yellow jersey.

The Tour saw a couple of crashes today which will undoubtedly result in some riders dropping out. Just how many, we shall see in the morning.

Tour positions at end of STAGE 3

Stage Winner: Peter Sagan/Liquigas-Cannondale

Yellow: Fabian Cancellara/Radioshack-Nissan
Green: Peter Sagan/Liquigas-Cannondale
Polka Dot: Michael Morkov/Team Saxo Bank-Tinkoff
White: Tejay Van Garderen/BMC Racing Team

STAGE 5
Wednesday 4th July 2012
ROUEN – SAINT-QUENTIN
Flat – 196.5 km

'Bicycling is a big part of the future. It has to be. There's something wrong with a society that drives a car to work out in a gym.'
Bill Nye – Scientist

The first thing I do when I wake is open the window next to my bunk. The motorhome gets very hot and stuffy with four people cooped up inside. The waft of chilling, morning air is most welcome and I can see that the car park is starting to fill up with French folk arriving for their pre-work workout.

No one gave us a second look. Perhaps the car park is a regular spot for motorhomers or maybe the locals were just taking the view that it's the Tour, so anything goes. Regardless, we were happy to be ignored and left alone to get on with our morning duties; breakfast, tea, bikes, kit, water bottles, Garmin. We could almost do it without thinking now but this didn't make it any less monotonous.

Although we were technically on a day off, Sara and I knew it would be a busy one. As well as our usual rest day jobs of shopping/water/toilet/diesel, we had to cover over 300 km to tomorrow's start town, Épernay. You wouldn't catch Sara complaining today though, as we were about to head to her most favourite part of France, the Champagne region. Whilst the region's rolling slopes of acre upon acre of vineyards are a sight to behold, Sara's fondness for the area is purely down to the fizzy stuff and no trip to France would be complete without a visit to champagne country. In the past, Mick has been forced to make several hundred kilometre diversions just to satisfy Sara's desire to visit her second home. He knows better than to try to argue, it is a waste of words, something Mick doesn't have a surplus of.

Everyone seemed more subdued in the mornings now. The enthusiasm and excitement from the first couple of days had long since passed and for me at least, the trip was starting to feel like a job. A very full-time job. A full-time job for which there was no pay. I was never very good at full-time jobs when I had them; I was discovering that I found voluntary full-time jobs even harder. No surprise there then. I send a few texts to Helen and my mum. Helen responds with her usual comment saved for days when I am fed up because I am doing something I don't want to, 'Sometimes in life we have to do things we don't want to'. Thanks, that really helps. Mum tells me to think of the money we are raising for charity. She's right; we are raising money for good causes. Stephen has been in charge of the charity money and we have raised a few thousand pounds so far, so yes, at least the charities are benefitting from our efforts. Oh and the cyclists of course, they are having a smashing time. So in reality, perhaps it was only me who was fed up? That would be about right, I was beginning to think that it was my default state or maybe I was just getting old and grumpy.

The boys set off at around 10:00 am. We were a couple of kilometres from the official start line but the weather was fine and they opted to ride rather than get a lift. This was probably just as well as the girls in Motorhome Two didn't seem anywhere near ready to leave. I suspect the boys had made the same observation as I had and figured it would be quicker to make their own way to the start rather than waiting for a lift in Motorhome Two.

Sara and I were ready to go and neither of us had any desire to hang around chatting. Sara only had one thing on her mind – champagne – and I had woken in a grumpy mood and just wanted to get on the road.

A couple of hours or so out of Rouen and with the water and shopping chores sorted, I was feeling a bit more cheery. The rest of the day should be relatively stress free. Our jobs were done; all we had to do was find an overnight spot close to Épernay for the following day's start. Actually, we didn't need to find a spot at all as we knew exactly where we were going. The same spot that we always used when visiting Champagne, one which we had found several years before and which had served us well ever since.

Our attention was first drawn to the Champagne region by a television programme presented by Oz Clarke and James May. The concept of the show was that the pair would travel across France, visiting various wine regions, while Oz tried to educate James, a committed beer drinker, about the wonders of wine. In one episode, they found themselves in a village in the Champagne region called Louvois and we see them visiting what basically looks like someone's house, to taste and buy champagne.

The 'someone' in question turns out to be Pierre Boever and indeed, it was his house. Monsieur Boever, it seems, produces a few thousand bottles of bubbly each year and punts it out at a bargain price. At the time he was charging eight Euros for a bottle of Grand Cru. This compared to something like ten times the amount for a known brand.

For Sara, the idea which ended up being inspired by this programme must have been heaven; champagne and motorhoming all wrapped up in one wonderful trip. It doesn't get any better! A few months later, I found myself heading to Louvois in search of cheap champagne and of a more immediate requirement, somewhere to park for the night.

The Champagne region is dotted with small villages and hamlets. It wasn't long before we found a dusty road which ran alongside a small river. It didn't seem to lead anywhere in particular so we drove down until it opened into a slightly wider bit of wasteland and Mick parked up.

'This'll do,' he announced and it did.

Right up until the following morning when we awoke to find that we were parked next to a rubbish skip and that the dusty road which didn't lead anywhere, actually led to the local gypsy site. Having already attracted the attention of several of the youngsters from the site, who appeared to be considering whether or not to start throwing rocks at the motorhome, we decided that maybe we ought to consider looking for alternative accommodation that night.

We didn't have to look far, just across the river in fact. Mick spotted a clearing almost directly opposite our current position which looked about as perfect as you could get for wild camping in a motorhome. All we had to do was work out how to get to it. A bit of exploring and a couple of dead ends later and we had found the single track path which led to our new pitch. The spot was actually quite a bit larger than it had looked from across the river and it was well away from everyone and everything. Perfect.

The following morning we had driven into Louvois village to seek out Pierre Boever and his cavern of bargain priced bubbles. It didn't take long to find as Louvois consists of just a handful of roads and the house was recognisable from the television show. Also, just in case we were struggling, there was a big sign outside which says, 'Pierre Boever – Champagne.' Unfortunately the gates to the Boever residence were tightly closed and no amount of ringing the doorbell had any effect. How could he be closed? We had come all the way from England! We had seen other houses in the area offering free tastings but we didn't want to risk it – if Oz Clarke thought Boever Champagne was the best, then that was good enough for us. We ended up going away and coming back two or three times that day, each time finding the same, no one home. You could be forgiven for thinking that maybe we were just unlucky with our choice of day but we have actually been back to Pierre's on numerous occasions since and he never seems to be open. Maybe he doesn't have to bother after getting the Oz Clarke seal of approval.

In the end, we decided that rather than go home with nothing, we would have to investigate one of the other suppliers, so we picked one at random and drove into a cluttered farmyard surrounded by outbuildings and a small French cottage. We were greeted by the sight of a large bearded man driving a tractor and wearing nothing but a big pair of grubby white Y-fronts. It turned out that this was the owner and would, from that day forward, be known as Monsieur Le Pants. He also gave his name to our river parking spot, which became Pants' River.

Monsieur Le Pants jumped from his tractor and called to his wife, Madame Pants, who ushered us into their kitchen and instructed us to sit down. It became immediately apparent that they didn't speak a word of English and, as far as I was aware, the language skills held by our group were equally lacking. Still, some things don't need translating and when Madame Pants opened her oversize American fridge, which contained nothing but bottles of unlabelled champagne and said, *'Champagne oui?'* we knew exactly what she meant.

A fresh bottle of champagne was opened and glasses passed round.

Sara turned to Mick and said, 'Ask her how much it is and what different types do they have.'

Why was she asking Mick to converse with this non-English speaking woman? We all knew that Mick was a man of few words at the best of times, so why does his wife think he can speak French?

Mick babbled off a sentence in what, to be perfectly honest, did sound quite Frenchy. Okay, I'll give him that, he sounded quite convincing but the true test would be when Madame Pants replied. She responded and Mick translated, 'She says that the Grand Cru is twelve Euros a bottle, rosé is thirteen and they come in cases of six.'

Sara had her next set of questions lined up but I butted in before she could reel them off.

'Hang on, when did Mick learn to speak French?' I asked, stunned at what I was witnessing, 'He can't speak English properly, where did the French come from?'

I had known Mick for a number of years at that point but no one had told me that his mum used to be a French teacher and some of her ability had clearly been passed down to Mick. I later learnt that the more alcohol Mick drinks, the better his French becomes. Unfortunately he was driving on this specific day so Madame Pants would have to manage with basic conversational.

Since that first visit, I have been back to the Pants' residence on a number of occasions. Sara and Mick go there every time they enter France, which is quite a lot. The Pants must rub their hands together every time they see their motorhome pull into the farmyard, as Sara is quite unable to resist buying numerous cases from them on every visit. Mind you, they did tell us that they only produce about 10,000 bottles a year so perhaps Sara is worried that they might run out.

As we continued towards Épernay, Sara picked up the phone to call Motorhome Two in order to check on their progress. The boys were flying today. A strong tailwind was pushing them along at a rate of knots and the support team were struggling to keep up. Apparently, after we had left Rouen, they continued faffing around for another hour before setting off after the boys and ended up missing their first meeting point. The boys had to wait until the girls had caught up with them for their first pit stop, something which, I am sure, they wouldn't have been overly impressed with.

Still, at least the tailwind would keep the boys' spirits riding high and the lack of any categorised climbs in today's stage would mean that it was as close to a rest day as they were going to get (other than the actual rest days of course). Mick told me later that he had seen a speed camera indicate his speed at 91 km/h although it quickly corrected to 56 km/h, which I suspect was the more accurate figure.

While the girls were racing to keep up with our little *peloton*, Sara and I were parking up next to the river. We had time to kill for a change so we put the kettle on and sat in the afternoon sun. It was the stereotypical idyllic setting. A meadow behind us, the July sunlight glinting off the river in front of us, the steady hum coming from the electricity pylon and cables strung above our heads. Okay, maybe not the perfect idyll but close.

It was in this very spot that I had first realised just how serious about cycling Mick was. Mick had suggested that I bring my bike on our first trip to Champagne, just in case I fancied a ride. At the time, my one bicycle was a heavy, rusty mountain bike, some twenty years old. Mick told me some time later that he thought the motorhome would tip up when he hung it on the bike rack at the rear. Shortly after arriving at the river, Mick announced that he was going to do a quick training ride before dinner. I told him I would join him and it was my intention to do so, right up to the point where I saw him pulling on lycra shorts and attaching electronic gadgetry to his chest, 'You've got a costume!' I blurted out.

Fortunately I am good at weighing up situations and I weighed this one up almost instantly and came to the conclusion that if I were to continue with my plan to ride with Mick, then I would almost certainly regret it. I quickly suggested that it might make more sense if I stayed behind and got the barbeque going. This was the right decision. A few minutes later and Mick was flying past the motorhome every fifteen minutes at a rate which I would have normally associated with a small motorbike. He had found a circuit to ride and he was pelting round it. He continued to do this for forty five minutes by which time I was exhausted and into my second cider.

Still, there was no likelihood of Mick wanting a quick training ride tonight, the 196.5 km from Rouen should suffice. As expected, the team were in a very positive mood when they turned up for dinner. The stage had been completed in super-fast time and apart from the small issue of the delayed first feed stop, there had been no problems. Matt's shoulder was still giving him a bit of trouble but Sara was reapplying the dressing each day and it was starting to heal. His foot didn't seem to be bothering him so much but maybe he was just getting used to the pain.

Statistically, there was probably a good chance that one of our riders might not make it to the finish. Every year numerous riders in the pro Tour have to drop out because of injury or sickness. It is probably the one race in the cycling calendar where the riders will do anything they can though to make it to the finish line and there are an abundance of stories of hero riders who just refused to give up. One of the most common cycling injuries is a broken collarbone, which is easily sustained after a crash. In 2003, Tyler Hamilton experienced such a crash and broke his collarbone on the first stage of the Tour. Normally this would mean a month's rest to recover. Not so with Hamilton who insisted on having it strapped up and continued to the finish, where he finished fourth overall. The year before, Hamilton had ridden the Giro d'Italia with a broken shoulder and the pain had caused him to grind his teeth so much, that he had to have eleven of them capped or replaced after the race.

Hamilton isn't unique. Just the year before our Tour de France attempt, Dutch cyclist, Johnny Hoogerland was involved in a crash when he and fellow rider, Juan Antonio Flecha, were knocked from their bikes by a French television car which was trying to squeeze past them. Flecha ended up on the road but Hoogerland was thrown into a barbed wire fence and suffered multiple lacerations to his legs. Once he had unpicked himself from the wire, he got back on his bike and continued with the stage. The Tour doctor gave him temporary medical attention as he rode along and Hoogerland finished the stage, claimed the polka dot jersey in the process and then stepped up to the podium to collect it before being taken to hospital to receive thirty three stitches. This would have been reason enough for most people to pack their bike up and head for home. Not Hoogerland, he held onto the polka dot jersey for another couple of stages and then continued with the Tour all the way to Paris, winning plenty of new fans in the process.

Continuing to ride for a three week stage race is one thing but in 2006 an American rider, Floyd Landis, pulled off a move which surely puts him in the top five when it comes to the competition for riding whilst in pain. Landis shockingly revealed that immediately after he had finished riding in that year's Tour, he would be booking himself into hospital for a hip replacement. Following a crash in 2002, one of his hip joints was so degenerated that the bone was effectively dead. He had been riding in severe pain for close to a year!

Maybe it was riders such as Hamilton, Hoogerland and Landis who were inspiring Matt to keep on pedalling.

After dinner, Emily set up her physio table and as the riders took it in turn to have their muscles prodded about, the rest of us sat chatting and enjoying a few drinks. It was suggested that as I was clearly enjoying the torture which the riders were suffering each night and as I was of the opinion that 'it couldn't hurt that much surely,' that maybe I should have a go on Emily's bench of extreme pain.

'No problem,' I said, 'but not tonight. Maybe after I've had a ride one day, just so I get the full benefit of it.'

It couldn't hurt that much could it? Regardless, I was fairly confident that this was something I wouldn't have to experience in a hurry – the chances of me finding time to ride my bike on this trip were slim to say the least.

Stephen was making a particularly large fuss over his massage tonight and Sara shouted across to him, 'I thought you used to be a Marine, Stephen? Surely a Marine wouldn't be complaining that a little girl was making his legs a bit sore?'

Stephen had indeed told us that he had been a Royal Marine, although we had our doubts, he just didn't come across as Marine material. I certainly wouldn't have expected a Marine to make as much fuss over a bit of physio as Stephen was.

'Er, yeah, I was a Marine, well I was in the reserves, I trained in America,' came Stephen's vague reply.

'Oh right, you mean you went on holiday and you *saw* a Marine?!' snorted Sara.

Being back at Pants' River cheered me up no end. I had good memories of the area and I was happy to be back. From waking up in a fairly miserable, grumpy mood, I went to bed rather more upbeat and contented. It helped to know that we had another day off from supporting the next day as Sara and I had a prior engagement. We were off to see Monsieur and Madame Pants so that Sara could stock up.

Stage 4 of the pro Tour saw 195 riders signing on, three down on yesterday. An immediate attack, led by Yukiya Arashiro (Team Europcar), saw three riders break free and build an advantage of 8 minutes and 40 seconds by the 20 km mark. By this point, Lotto-Belisol and Radioshack-Nissan had had enough and started to wind them back in. With 15 km to go, the leaders were just 50 seconds ahead and by the 8.5 km to go mark, the three were back with the rest of the group.

As the sprint teams were arranging themselves for the final part of the stage, there was a crash at 2.6 km to go and a number of riders ended up on the floor. Most notably, one of the favourites for this stage, Mark Cavendish, was involved in the altercation and was subsequently relieved of the opportunity to take the win.

This honour went to André Greipel of Lotto-Belisol, his second Tour de France stage win.

Sometimes, being a good rider isn't enough, you need to keep out of trouble too. That's half the battle on the Tour, if one goes down, there's a very good chance that several more will follow. Isn't that right Stephen/Matt?

When interviewed afterwards, a reporter commented to Greipel that riding in the Tour was a 'dangerous job.' Greipel smiled and replied, 'But I love my job.'

Tour positions at end of STAGE 4

Stage Winner: André Greipel/Lotto-Belisol

Yellow: Fabian Cancellara/Radioshack-Nissan
Green: Peter Sagan/Liquigas-Cannondale
Polka Dot: Michael Morkov/Team Saxo Bank-Tinkoff
White: Tejay Van Garderen/BMC Racing Team

STAGE 6
Thursday 5th July 2012
ÉPERNAY – METZ
Flat – 205 km

'As a kid I had a dream – I wanted to own my own bicycle. When I got the bike I must have been the happiest boy in Liverpool, maybe the world. I lived for that bike. Most kids left their bike in the backyard at night. Not me. I insisted on taking mine indoors and the first night I even kept it in my bed.'
John Lennon – Musician, singer, songwriter

Over breakfast I chatted to Mick and Adnan about how things were going in the riders' camp. Despite the size of the challenge they were attempting, everything seemed to be going to plan and neither had any worries at this stage about not completing the ride. Sitting, as we were, in Épernay, we were only about 100 km away from our ultimate finish in Paris but the route we were taking was much longer and would wind its way through the Alps and the Pyrenees before turning back to the capital. It was good to know that the boys were still confident of finishing though and while our expectation had been that they would start to feel tired after a few days in the saddle, it seemed that quite the opposite was the case. They were actually feeling stronger and their bodies were getting used to riding 200 km a day. This was a good sign and I was only jealous that my body wasn't getting used to working a twelve or more hour day.

Obviously the excellent support they were receiving was what was really pushing them on and both Adnan and Mick agreed that the food Sara and I provided during the days which we supported them was better than the offerings they received from Motorhome Two. No doubt they were telling the other support team exactly the same thing.

The girls seemed to have sorted out their early issues with keeping Motorhome Two topped up with water and I hadn't been asked for our spare container for two days which was a positive sign. Jess explained that at one point they were having to fill their main tank up by transporting water from a tap in a public toilet back to the motorhome using water bottles and saucepans. This must have taken an absolute age but they had now purchased a more suitable container on one of their shopping expeditions and so were now able to fill up with water in about half an hour.

Emptying of the toilet cassette appeared to be giving the girls more of a problem, although what irritated me slightly was the fact that, once again, this task seemed to be being left to Emily to sort out. It was bad enough that Emily was doing all of the driving, most of the shopping and helping with cooking but now she had to deal with the toilet because no one else wanted to. In our motorhome, toilet duties were very much a man's job – you wouldn't catch Sara anywhere near the toilet cassette hatch. I once asked her if she actually knew how to empty it and it was obvious from her expression that she didn't have a clue (and clearly had no intention of finding out either). I voiced this concern to the inhabitants of Motorhome Two and suggested that, at the very least, they should take it in turns to empty the cassette. A reluctant agreement was reached that going forward this is what they would do.

The riders had another comparatively easy day ahead of them today – 205 km of almost flat cycling, just a single category 4 climb to crack after about 145 km. It was another bright, sunny day too which meant they could enjoy riding through some of the 30,000 acres of vineyards surrounding Épernay. Motorhome Two were in support, leaving Sara and me to enjoy a last quick cup of tea at Pants' River, before making a visit to Monsieur Pants himself.

Pants' River is located approximately 16 km from the centre of Épernay where today's stage would start. This meant a transfer by motorhome for the boys and once three bikes and The Gate had been loaded up, Emily executed a three (or five) point turn so that she could make her way back to the main road. Sara and I stood at the front of the other motorhome to wave them off and we watched as Emily reversed back towards Sara's motorhome. Neither of us said anything, I think we were both too stunned but I'm sure we were both wondering the same thing, 'When is she going to stop?' Emily had taken to the task of driving the motorhome very well, it was a large vehicle to get the hang of when you weren't used to the size. However we realised at that moment that she hadn't quite got the hang of how long it was. The rear of Motorhome Two clumped Sara's wing mirror as Emily reversed it back and then stopped a few inches from the side of the motorhome body. With first gear selected, Emily pulled forward and gave the wing mirror another whack just for good measure as she drove off, waving out of the window.

Sara and I looked at each other, 'Do you think she even realised that she hit it?' asked Sara,

'Nope,' I replied.

'I'm glad we aren't in the new motorhome.'

Fortunately, despite being on the receiving end of not one but two clonks from a three and a half ton motorhome, no damage was caused and there didn't appear to be any marks on the hire motorhome as it drove off either. I made a mental note to have a quiet word with Emily later on and to suggest that someone should watch the back end for her when reversing in future.

Within thirty minutes of Motorhome Two leaving, we were also on our way. No hanging around today, we were on a mission. On previous visits to the Pants', we had found that it was a bit hit and miss as to whether there was anyone at home. Therefore, as we didn't have time to wait today, Mick had phoned ahead to tell them we were coming. No danger of them not being there now as they knew that Sara was good for a few cases so they would be looking forward to relieving her of some of her holiday Euros.

Madame Pants came out to greet us as soon as we pulled into their yard.

'Bonjour, bonjour!' she exclaimed, planting double kisses on both of us.

We were led into the kitchen and the first thing we noticed was that it was in the process of being refitted. Gone was the old traditional farmhouse-style kitchen, which had probably been there for generations and it was being replaced with a sleek modern kitchen complete with granite worktops.

'I expect I've paid for most of this kitchen from buying champagne,' Sara remarked.

She was probably right although our hosts still didn't speak any English so they were unable to confirm or deny this assumption.

We were slightly disadvantaged on this visit as our translator, Mick, was unavailable. Sara and I did our best to explain that he was riding the Tour de France route. Our route guide magazine was helpful in this respect and Monsieur Pants was particularly interested in the profiles of some of the mountain stages. He was amazed at the size and number of mountain passes and the fact that anyone would even consider cycling over them and he took the magazine to show the kitchen fitter. It seemed that this was the first time he had ever been aware of the fact that there were mountains of this size in his country. We tried, in our most basic French, to ask if they had ever visited that part of France. They hadn't. In fact, they hadn't even seen the Tour de France when it had visited the area on numerous previous occasions. It was strange to think that we had driven hundreds of kilometres to see something which the locals wouldn't bother driving 10 km to see.

It was still well before noon but that didn't stop Madame Pants cracking open a bottle of bubbly for tasting. She had told us on our first visit that they drank champagne every day and from what we had seen, it didn't matter what time of the day it was, it was never too early to start!

On our first trip to Champagne, we had visited some of the bigger champagne houses who all offer the chance to view their cellars or caves. Naturally these cave tours are part of an overall commercial operation and as well as being expensive, it does feel as though you are being shown the 'tourist' bit of champagne making rather than the actual production line. When we told Madame Pants that we had done the champagne tours bit, she offered to show us their caves. We jumped at the chance and enjoyed a very interesting time being shown their entire production operation – exactly the same as the big producers but on a much smaller scale. We subsequently learnt that the Pants' vines are situated right next to the vineyards of Bollinger, which would account for the fact that the two champagnes are almost identical in taste. Where they differ considerably however, is in price. Pants' Grand Cru is, at the time of writing, fifteen Euros a bottle. Bollinger is closer to one hundred Euros.

In addition, Bollinger don't give you freebies but if you buy enough champagne, you always get freebies from the Pants' Champagne House! A bottle or two of champagne liqueur is a common gift to get thrown in and this time we also got a magnum of, what appeared to be, champagne but which didn't have a label. Monsieur Pants motioned to us that we should keep it hidden and we assumed he meant that this bottle was, in some way, illegal. Most likely it hadn't been declared for tax or something but regardless, it would almost certainly be empty within the next twelve hours so he had no worries about it being picked up by French Customs as we boarded the train home.

Despite the fact that the motorhome was already overloaded, Sara still managed to squirrel several cases of champagne into little hidey-holes. She had obviously done this before. Cash changed hands and we were even able to fill up with water and empty our toilet cassettes.

As for our riders, well they had continued to make good progress. Some of the road surfaces were a bit on the rough side today which made the going a wee bit harder than they would have liked but other than that, nothing to report. I think even they were having to come up with little games to amuse themselves as they pedalled their way round France. Mick had told me about one such game which was more a set of rules that they had devised among themselves. The rules were simple; they were not allowed to be outridden by anyone who fell into one of the following four categories: a woman, anyone with hairy legs, anyone wearing knee high compression socks (or long sockers as they were referred to) and anyone with chain oil on their legs. I think the female American cycling team were giving the chaps a good run for their money but so far, our guys were still in the lead.

I wonder if the pro Tour riders have to think up similar ways of passing the time. I can't help but think that much of the time during a typical stage is taken up with riders sitting in the *peloton* having a chat with their mates. Perhaps not but it must get boring at times to spend days in a row cycling along numerous different roads without really seeing anything. We had travelled over 1,000 km since we started and all of the scenery was blurring into one. I couldn't really tell you anything about any of the towns we had stayed in as we hadn't had the time or inclination to do any exploring. Maybe we should have taken more notice of Jess when she had asked what sights we wanted to see and actually come up with a list.

Part way to Tomblaine and we pulled over in a Carrefour car park for some lunch. I was quite content to sit here for a couple of hours so Sara took the opportunity to give the motorhome a good clean. It doesn't take long for it to start getting grubby when there are four people living in such a confined space. The bathroom got a good going over and the floor was swept. The kitchen area was wiped down and our temporary house was soon clean enough to be messed up once again. As Sara worked, I wondered if there was any mileage in publishing a guide book to the Carrefour car parks of France. How could it not be a bestseller?

It's the smallest of things that keep you going on a trip like this and knowing that the water tank was full and the toilet cassettes were both empty were what kept me smiling. For Sara, it was knowing that there was food in the fridge and that the bathroom was clean. A quick dash around Carrefour and we were both as happy as Larry. Although I'm betting that Larry has never had to provide support for a three week cycling trip or he wouldn't have been half as happy as he apparently was.

Onwards to Tomblaine and hopefully a decent place to stop for the night. We had seen on the map that the town of Tomblaine has a river running through it. Rivers are always a good place to start looking when it comes to finding a random overnight parking spot, so this is where we started. Picking our way through a bit of industrial land, we came across a large piece of wasteland which sat a few metres back from the edge of the river. Between the wasteland and the river was a path along which people were jogging and cycling. A few hundred metres along the path was a rowing club and several people were launching canoes in preparation for an early evening paddle. The spot was well away from any houses and we doubted that we would be bothering anyone here so it was an ideal spot to pitch camp.

It was another superb evening and this was one of the best times of the day for me. All the driving was done for the day and there was nothing really to do until the team returned. Sara had dinner under control so I was able to sit outside the motorhome with a beer soaking up the atmosphere. A group of teenagers were riding BMX bikes along the footpath by the river when one of them decided to ride down the slipway and pull off a 180° skid just before reaching the water line. Unfortunately, whilst he had the confidence, he didn't have the skill. I burst out laughing, along with his friends, when he skidded straight into the river, bike and all.

'Shall we open a bottle of Pants'?' asked Sara. She had been dying to open a bottle since we had left Louvois earlier that morning. So we did and when Motorhome Two turned up, we were sitting by the river quaffing champagne without a care in the world.

Emily parked the motorhome behind ours and disappeared up onto the roof – they were short of storage space inside so some of their kit had been strapped to the top of the motorhome. From her vantage point, she shouted down to me, 'Rich, when I pulled off this morning, how close was I to the other motorhome?'

It had been my intention to have a quiet word with Emily rather than cause her any embarrassment in front of the others but now everyone had heard her question so I answered in the only way I could, after all, I didn't want to lie!

'Pretty close, you hit it…twice,' I responded.

Silence and a very red face.

'Could've been worse,' I added, 'it could've been the new motorhome.'

Actually it could have been a lot worse. For starters Emily only suffered the embarrassment of bumping the motorhome in front of our small team. At the following year's Tour de France, one of the drivers of the Orica Greenedge team bus was embarrassed in front of the whole world. The driver, Garikoitz 'Gary' Atxa was driving the bus for the first time and was slightly late arriving at the finish of the first stage. He needed to guide the bus under the finish line gantry and into the reserved parking area. As he approached the gantry, he thought that it looked a bit on the low side but as the other buses had made it through and as there were officials waving him forward, he assumed there was enough room for his bus to fit.

What he hadn't realised was that the gantry is lowered once all the vehicular traffic has passed through in order that the sponsors' names, which appear along the top, can be seen by the television cameras when the cyclists cross the finish line. Atxa's lateness meant that the gantry had already been lowered and as he edged forward, he got stuck fast underneath. Unable to move forward or backwards for fear of causing more damage, Atxa had no choice but to bury his head in his hands, an image which was broadcast around the world for all to see.

To make matters worse, the race was, by now, only a few kilometres from the finish, which added even more urgency to the task of moving the bus. Teams were told that the finish line had been moved forward by 3 km and utter chaos was created as everyone tried to get the message out to the riders. With minutes to spare, Axta managed to reverse the bus out after the tyres had been deflated. Even more confusion ensued as the riders were now told that the finish line was back to where it had started. It certainly added to the drama of the stage but I'm sure it is a day that Atxa would be pleased to forget. Orica Greenedge were fined 2000 Swiss Francs for not respecting the timetable put in place for auxiliary vehicles arriving at the stage finish. Fortunately the team didn't blame Axta for the mishap and he was back driving the bus the following day. There certainly wasn't any danger of removing Emily from her post as driver – no one else was prepared to do it so it didn't really matter how bad her driving was.

At one point during the evening, Mick came over to proudly show me that the Garmin was declaring that he had burnt off 7,750 calories on the ride today. This seemed an awful lot. Perhaps the Garmin circuitry was designed by the same bloke who built the speed camera which told him he was doing 91 km/h yesterday?

Someone in the group calculated that we had, at some point today, passed a significant milestone (or should that be kilometre stone?) and our team had already covered over a third of the total distance of the Tour. Excellent progress we all agreed and it was nice to have something positive to concentrate on given that the first category 1 climb was coming up the next day and just to make things interesting, it would be right at the end of the 199 km stage. Ha, ha, ha, that should give them something to think about while they try to sleep.

With no further retirements, the pro Tour saw 195 riders sign on for Stage 5 this morning and as soon as racing started, Matthieu Ladagnous, FDJ-Bigmat, went on the attack and was joined by four other riders. Despite efforts by Lotto-Belisol and Radioshack-Nissan, the lead group were out by 5 minutes and 40 seconds at the 52 km point. Things didn't run to the normal plan today and with 3 km to go, the escapees were still 20 seconds in front. I'm sure there would have been some panic in the sprint teams as they saw the opportunity to win the stage disappearing and ultimately the final breakaway rider wasn't caught until the last 400 metres. The sprint trains were already charging towards the line and the end result was another win for André Greipel. No changes today to the jersey wearers.

Tour positions at end of STAGE 5

Stage Winner: André Greipel/ Lotto-Belisol

Yellow: Fabian Cancellara/Radioshack-Nissan
Green: Peter Sagan/Liquigas-Cannondale
Polka Dot: Michael Morkov/Team Saxo Bank-Tinkoff
White: Tejay Van Garderen/BMC Racing Team

STAGE 7

Friday 6th July 2012
TOMBLAINE – LA PLANCHE DES BELLES FILLES
Hilly – 199 km

'The ideal Tour would be a Tour in which only one rider survived the ordeal.'
Henri Desgrange - 'Father' of the Tour

It was usually Stephen who was keen to get off on time each morning, but today for some reason, he didn't appear to be in much of a hurry. In fact, whilst Matt, Mick and Adnan were all on the ball and ready to go at 9:00 am, Stephen decided that this would be a good time to start stripping his bike down for a bit of a service. This was completely out of character to what we had experienced all week and the reason soon became clear.

I think it was Adnan who first noticed that Nicole was missing and that's when everything started to fall into place. Nicole had decided that she was going to ride today, a decision made without any reference to the support team for the day, i.e. myself and Sara. I suspect that Nicole had got fed up with being ferried around in the motorhome and having to work every day with no reward and whilst I could kind of see her point of view, it wasn't fair to assume that everyone would fall in with her plans.

Knowing full well that Sara and I would not want to be delayed waiting for her anywhere along the route, Nicole had left early, at around 7:00 am, to give herself a head start and now Stephen was doing his best to slow the team down to give her the opportunity to get further along the route. With Stephen's bike in pieces and Stephen in no obvious rush to put it back together, the rest of the team had little option but to wait. In the end, Mick was the one who got fed up sitting around and told Stephen to get a move on so that they could get off. Stephen's plan had succeeded in buying Nicole another hour of time.

As the boys left, we told Stephen to pass the message on to Nicole that we would not be waiting for her anywhere along the route and that she needed to arrange to meet up with the boys and once they were together, we would be picking her up as there was no way she would be able to keep up with their pace.

The pro Tour has its own method for dealing with stragglers. Since 1910 the 'broom wagon' or '*voiture balai*' has followed the race collecting any riders who are no longer able to continue or who have just had enough and want to retire. The broom wagon effectively sweeps up these stragglers, although most high profile riders are far more likely to hitch a ride in the back of their own team cars as this is a slightly less embarrassing option.

Today's stage was described in the Tour guide as 'hilly.' 199 km and a couple of category 3 climbs, culminating in a summit finish at the top of La Planche Des Belles Filles. The summit was listed as a category 1 – the first of the Tour and an indication of what was to come.

We met the boys about 30 km before the first cat 3 climb. They had enjoyed another morning's cycle through the countryside and continued to cover the kilometres without anything seeming to hinder their progress. They'd had a couple of hairy leggers pass them but they had soon reeled them back in and finished them off on a small hill. They had also suffered a couple of punctures today, which were the first all week. In total, the team only had to deal with half a dozen punctures during the whole trip, which is quite remarkable given the distances the riders were covering each day. As it was to turn out, Sara and I were going to have more trouble with the motorhome tyres than the boys had with theirs.

Nicole was caught and overtaken by the boys as she was making her way up the first category 3 climb. We spotted her as we were driving along and pulled over to pick her up. I tried to impress how fortunate it was that we had spotted her as, had we not, we would have ended up sitting at the next food stop waiting for her. She didn't seem overly bothered and clearly felt that she had as much right to ride as anyone else did.

When we reached the next stop, the boys had picked up a friend. Frode was also cycling the entire Tour route but he was planning on completing the ride alone. He did have a friend with him who was driving a hired motorhome but the cycling was down to Frode. The boys had picked him up somewhere in the previous few kilometres and he had stuck with them, probably grateful for the company. There was no sign of his support motorhome so Frode ate with our team, enjoying a can of Coke and a plate of pizza and pasta. This was to become a regular thing as the boys would see Frode most days going forwards and he would often stop for a bite to eat.

I'm not sure where in Europe Frode was from but he was able to speak reasonably good English and in one conversation he revealed that he was paying his friend one hundred Euros a day to support him. Sara and I immediately realised we had been done - we should be picking up a couple of thousand Euros each for our work on this little jaunt!

Whilst it is an achievement for anyone to ride the full route of the Tour de France, doing it alone really is a tough thing to take on. If our boys were suffering periods of boredom as they pedalled around France, what was Frode going through? On some days, Frode was in the saddle for more than ten hours, cycling into the night. With no teammates to keep him motivated it was impressive that he had got this far. He was a nice guy and I really hoped he would make it to the end.

I'm sure the boys had already looked at the stage profile for the day in some detail and seen that their ride would finish in fine style. Although the average gradient of Les Planche Des Belles Filles is 8.5%, the last few metres consist of a nasty 14% incline.

As we got closer to the finish, the roads started to narrow and Jane the sat nav decided that maybe we would like a challenge of our own. One of Jane's problems was that she had no appreciation for the fact that we were in a motorhome and not a smaller vehicle. Ideally she would have had an option which allowed us to tell her to stick to decent size roads but she didn't. Usually by the time you realised that a road wasn't ideally suited for a motorhome, it was too late.

We found ourselves driving into a dense forest. The road was rapidly shrinking in width and I noticed that the scenery in front of us was only heading one way – up. Jane had opted to take us the quickest route (probably due to the fact that I had set her up to do exactly that) and today, the quickest way was over some fairly substantial hills. I would have described them as mountains but as I knew that we would soon be driving over real mountains, it doesn't seem appropriate.

Looking in the wing mirror as we rounded a corner, I saw three vehicles behind us. With nowhere to turn off and nowhere to turn round, we only had one option and that was to keep going. I hoped the cars behind us weren't in a rush because as the road started to head skywards, the slower we got. As I changed down through the gears just to keep moving, Mick's earlier comment that the weight limit was only a guide was ringing in my ears. If we needed to offload stuff to get up this road, it would be Mick's kit first!

The motorhome was really starting to struggle and I was running out of gears. Eventually I was in first gear and even with the accelerator to the floor we were barely managing 5 mph. The burning smell coming from the clutch wasn't great either and I was genuinely worried that we were about to kill the old motorhome. Sara remained confident.

'It's okay, the motorhome does this every year, it loves the Tour and knows what it needs to do.'

Really? Well how come it is complaining so much? The motorhome huffed and puffed its way to the peak of the climb by which time the temperature gauge was well into the red zone and my eyes were watering from the stench of burning clutch. As we rolled over the top, it was a complete relief to get back up to fifth gear and watch the temperature needle return to the centre of the gauge as we started to descend the other side.

Sara had been right, the old motorhome knew exactly how to deal with these ridiculous French roads but for the first time on the trip, I wished we had been in the new motorhome.

Upon our arrival at the foot of La Planche Des Belle Filles we encountered a queue of traffic. We weren't particularly surprised as it is commonplace for spectators to position themselves on the steep climbs as this is often the best place to see the Tour pass by. You need to get to the popular spots early and this usually means a day or two in advance of the Tour (or up to a week ahead of the race on the more popular mountains).

Unfortunately for the drivers in this queue of traffic, they had left it too late. The road leading up to the summit was narrow with limited parking places and these had all been taken days before. The result of this was that all the traffic was now being turned around by the local police. This was a time consuming process as each vehicle, mostly motorhomes, executed a three point turn one after the other.

Our team would have to pass by this traffic queue so even if they didn't spot us on the way up, they would realise that we wouldn't have been able to make it to the top and would simply turn around and come back down to find us.

We managed to pull in just before the start of the final climb about 7 km from the finish. A police officer stopped and informed us that we couldn't park there because the Tour de France was coming through the next day. Really? Gosh, we had no idea – we thought that the thousands of people and motorhomes were here to look at the trees. We explained that we would be leaving within an hour and weren't staying overnight. He seemed happy with this and wandered off to move the next motorhome on.

Sara and I were sitting in the motorhome enjoying yet another cup of tea when the door opened. It was Adnan. He was a few hundred metres ahead of the others and they were just about to start the climb to the summit finish. He topped up his water, grabbed an energy gel and rejoined the others who had now caught up.

'See you in twenty minutes,' I called after him.

It was actually nearer to half an hour when the chaps returned to the motorhome. They looked absolutely done in. Turns out that a category 1 climb at the end of a 199 km stage was hard work.

'Awww dear, are your poor little leggies all hurty?' I enquired. Apparently they were.

Mick's description of the last 6 km was 'way harder than Alpe d'Huez.' This was some claim. I had ridden up Alpe d'Huez the year before. Situated in the Alps, Alpe d'Huez regularly features in the Tour after first appearing in 1952. It is a formidable climb and one of the most famous Tour mountains. Probably best known for its 21 hairpin bends, the climb starts in the village of Bourg d'Oisans and continues for 13.8 km to the summit, some 1800 metres higher. The average gradient is just over 8% but the start of the climb is noticeably steeper at 10.5%. It would take a half-decent amateur cyclist around an hour and a half to conquer Alpe d'Huez.

In 2011, Mick, Sara and I, along with a handful of other friends, had travelled to Alpe d'Huez to watch the Tour ascend this mountain stage. We had arrived five days before the Tour was due and claimed the last two places on the mountain which were large enough for our two motorhomes. Anything goes at the Tour and the police are extremely accommodating in terms of allowing people to park up pretty much anywhere as long as they deem it safe. There was an incredible number of motorhomes on the mountain that year and every available space was filled with all manner of temporary living accommodation from huge American RVs to individual tents pitched on the grass verges.

Whilst I did have my bike stowed away in my motor-home, I didn't really have any idea just how big a big mountain was and therefore wasn't sure whether the bike would actually be seeing the light of day or not. When we got to Alpe d'Huez, it was dark but it was immediately obvious that getting up here on a bike was not going to be an easy task for me. I had barely ridden that year and was carrying a few extra pounds, on top of the few extra pounds I normally carried. I had pretty much made the decision as I negotiated my motorhome round the first few hairpins that there was absolutely no way on Earth, no way, definitely no way, that I would be cycling up this ridiculously long and steep climb. No way, it just wasn't happening.

Two days later and after making the mistake of listening to words that had emanated from Mick's mouth, I found myself sitting in Bourg d'Oisans with my bike and a couple of bottles of water, looking up at the enormous lump of rock in front of me. I knew that my motorhome was about three quarters of the way up the rock and there was only one way back to it.

Mick had probably said things like, 'It's not that hard once you get going,' or 'You might as well give it a go, even if it takes all day, at least you will have done it.' It will have been comments like these, which seemed perfectly reasonable while sitting in the motorhome drinking tea, which were responsible for the position I now found myself in.

At least I wasn't the only one. There were hundreds of other cyclists attempting to pedal up this monster of a mountain. All different ages and abilities riding all types of bicycles. At least I looked the part, with a reasonable road bike and proper cycling lycra. All the gear and no idea springs to mind.

I had never ridden up anything of this size and I didn't really have any idea how I should go about it. Sara had said I just needed to take it easy and find my own pace. What did that mean? I could probably walk up it faster. In the end, I decided to hit the bottom slopes as fast as I could, in the hope that I could somehow hold on to some of the initial momentum to keep me going at a decent speed. If I could keep up a pace of just 10 km/h, the pain would be over in slightly more than an hour.

Anyone who knows anything about cycling will know that this plan was doomed to fail and before I had even made it to the second hairpin, I was gasping for breath and my head felt like it was about to explode. The sun had now decided to come out and I was burning up. I'd already drunk half of one of my two bottles of water and my legs felt like lead. It was going to be a long morning.

To help you along/make you feel even worse, every bend is numbered so you can count down your way to the top. This didn't help me one bit. If you are struggling in the knowledge that you have eighteen hairpins left, knowing that there are now only seventeen won't be something which will lift your spirits. I cursed Mick most of the way up and remembered that Sara had long since warned me never to listen to anything that comes out of his mouth. She was right.

There are some stunning views as you make your way up Alpe d'Huez. I didn't notice any of them. I was too busy concentrating on keeping my bike upright and not disappearing off the road and down one of the hundred foot vertical drops. Helpfully there were large concrete blocks marking the edge of the road and I judged that these were just the right height to ensure that if you did hit one on a bike, you would be safely catapulted over your handlebars and onwards over the concrete to certain death somewhere down the mountainside.

Doing as Sara had suggested, I found my own pace. My pace involved cycling from one hairpin to the next, then getting off and sitting in the curve of the bend with other, similarly exhausted fools whilst hoping that I could control my breathing sufficiently to ensure that I didn't cause my lungs to explode. I ran out of water long before I got back to my motorhome so when I eventually made it back, I was very pleased to be able to pop inside and top up. The temptation to climb into bed was huge but I knew that I wasn't quite at the top so I had to resist the lure of my duvet and push onwards.

There were two things I wanted out of my ride up Alpe d'Huez: one of the t-shirts I had seen for sale in the souvenir shops which proudly proclaimed, 'I've done it!' and a photograph of me 'doing it' from one of the photographers located in strategic locations along the route. I wasn't going to buy a t-shirt unless I managed to finish the ride, that would be cheating and I was determined to get a decent picture from one of the photographers.

On the ride down to the start point, I had noted the location of two photographers, which meant I was able to put my best 'teeth gritting' look on my face and stand up out of the saddle as I passed them for the ultimate action shot. Photo taken and the photographer's assistant handed me a little card detailing a number which would enable me to retrieve my photo later. I barely had the energy to take it from her and collapsed over my handlebars just in time for another little rest.

The last couple of kilometres already had barriers erected in preparation for the Tour later in the week. These barriers were clearly to keep spectators back from the riders however they served a different purpose for me. They gave me something to cling on to every now and then in order that I could have a rest without having to get off my bike. At one point I was barely pedalling, just pulling myself along on the barriers.

As I neared the top, I could see Sara, Mick and the others outside a bar, cheering and willing me on. I certainly didn't deserve the cheers, the time I had taken to get up was shocking and even with the end in sight, my legs were still resisting. A small boy of about ten years old was sitting on his miniature road bike just ahead of me, crying his eyes out. Aha, I thought, an excuse for a rest. I stopped and enquired as to whether the lad was okay. Clearly not, given the amount of bawling he was doing. His dad appeared and shouted at the boy in German. I didn't understand a word but if I was to take a guess, a rough translation would have been, 'Stop crying and finish the ride! I know you've had to cycle up this massive mountain on your own because I am too fat/old/lazy to do it with you but that's no excuse, now get to the finish line!' This poor lad had, it appeared, ridden up the entire climb alone and now, within a short distance of the finish, his dad was clearly not impressed.

Well, if he could do it, so could I. I got back on my bike and pushed on to where the others were standing and I'd done it, I'd ridden up Alpe d'Huez. My celebrations were short-lived though as I was quickly informed that the official Tour finish was actually about 1 km further on.

'Oh fiddlesticks!' (Or words to that effect), I said as I remounted and wobbled off to the finish line.

When the Tour riders rode up Alpe d'Huez a few days later, they did so after racing over 100 km which included both a category 1 and an HC climb, Alpe d'Huez being the second HC climb of the day. The fastest riders shot up Alpe d'Huez in about forty five minutes. I am quite ashamed to say that it took me nearer three hours to make it from bottom to top. However, what I would say is that I doubt I was cycling for more than one hour – the rest of the time I was sitting at the side of the road trying to stay alive. So, I suppose you could say it took me an hour to ride up, not including rest stops.

Annoyingly Mick decided to beat my time the following day and conquered Alpe d'Huez in one hour and seventeen minutes. The fact that he managed to halve my time was bad enough but things were made a whole lot worse by the fact that he completed his ride on a 1971 Mk I Raleigh Chopper. It's fair to say that our cycling abilities are at opposite ends of the scale.

Still, I got my t-shirt and I got my photograph. A reminder of two things. Firstly, that I hated every minute of it and never want to do it again and secondly, that I could definitely do it quicker and if I am ever down that way again, I will have another crack at it. Ah, the dilemmas of a cyclist.

Given that La Planche Des Belles Filles was only a 6 km or so ride, it must have been a dreadful climb for Mick to compare it to Alpe d'Huez. Or maybe it only felt that bad because it was the first serious climb of the week and they had already covered so many kilometres. Regardless of which it was, I wasn't risking it, there was no way I was going anywhere near it with my bike.

I helped get the bikes and the boys loaded up before anyone suggested I go for a little spin and got out of there sharpish. The team had some pre-dinner Adnan Cakes and their protein shakes and drifted off to sleep on the motorhome floor while I drove us on to the next day's start town in Belfort, a few kilometres away.

Motorhome Two had arrived in Belfort a couple of hours before us and had found a brilliant spot in which to overnight. Following our advice to check rivers first, they had found a rowing club on the side of a lake with a large car park and had commandeered two large spaces at the back. We manoeuvred ourselves next to Motorhome Two and were quickly tucking into our evening meal and once again enjoying watching the French mess around in boats as the sun went down.

Stephen and Matt wandered over to the rowing club after dinner and discovered that there was a modern toilet block which we were able to use to refresh our water supplies and deal with the toilet cassettes. Given our conversation about taking turns a couple of days ago, we suggested that maybe Stephen should empty the cassette today. He reluctantly agreed but made such a fuss that Emily ended up taking the cassette from him, saying, 'Oh just give it to me, I'll do it!' I don't think he was asked again.

The boaters and other locals who had been enjoying the lake drifted home as it was starting to get dark and we were left alone by 10:00 pm. The next day was going to be a tough one both for the cyclists and the support team. Although the stage was only 157.5 km long, there were a lot of lumps and bumps on the way – seven categorised climbs in total. The mountains were most definitely coming...

If you ever find yourself talking to someone about the Tour de France and you know nothing about what it involves, you can always get yourself out of a hole by saying, 'It'll all be decided in the mountains.' Because it will. The mountains sort the men out from the boys and if anyone was going to struggle on this trip, we were about to find out about it.

The pro Tour saw one more rider retire as 194 signed on for the start in Épernay. Dave Zabriskie of the Garmin-Sharp team pulled away first and soon had another three riders with him. By the 72 km mark, this small group were almost 7 minutes ahead of the pack and the Orica-Greenedge and Lotto-Belisol teams started to reel them back in. By 130 km the lead was down to 3 minutes and 20 seconds.

At 26 km to go, there was a large crash in the main group and many big names were involved including Mark Cavendish once again. Zabriskie, the last of the escapees, was caught with 2 km to go and Peter Sagan, having avoided the earlier crash, pedalled home to take the stage win. Fabian Cancellara finished with the main group thus retaining the yellow jersey for another day. No changes to the other jerseys either but for how long? We now know that tomorrow's stage finishes on an evil climb and with the bigger ascents looming, it could be all change in the wardrobe department.

Tour positions at end of STAGE 6

Stage Winner: Peter Sagan/Liquigas-Cannondale

Yellow: Fabian Cancellara/Radioshack-Nissan
Green: Peter Sagan/Liquigas-Cannondale
Polka Dot: Michael Morkov/Team Saxo Bank-Tinkoff
White: Tejay Van Garderen/BMC Racing Team

STAGE 8

Saturday 7th July 2012
BELFORT – PORRENTRUY
Hilly – 157.5 km

'The bicycle is a curious vehicle; its passenger is its engine.'
John Howard - Olympic cyclist

No sooner had my head hit the pillow and the sun was already peeking through the motorhome blinds. That's what it felt like although I had actually had about eight hours of uninterrupted sleep. Even Adnan hadn't woken me on one of his trips to the bathroom. To get to the toilet, Adnan had to make a choice, jump from his bunk thus landing with a heavy thump on the floor, waking all of us or climb down by using my bunk as a step ladder, potentially waking just me. Most nights he chose the latter, partly out of consideration for Mick and Sara but mainly because he thought it was funny.

For whatever reason, last night I had been rewarded with a great night's sleep and on top of this, it was another clear, sunny day and we weren't supporting. To add to the bonuses of the day, the motorhome was full of water and both toilet cassettes were empty (thank you rowing club). Our only jobs for the day were to do a bit of shopping and to make our way to Arc-et-Senans, 130 km away. Ambling to the breakfast table, I was looking forward to a stress free and possibly even enjoyable day.

As I programmed the Garmin, I took a look at the stage profile. It looked absolutely horrendous; no wonder the boys were quiet. Seven categorised climbs consisting of one cat 4, one cat 3, four cat 2s and a final cat 1 to finish with. The individual climb profiles made even worse reading, in particular the final cat 1 which had an average gradient of 9.2% over 3.7 km and some sections of between 13% and 17% in steepness. Mark Cavendish, Team Sky, had already described this stage as 'one of two which have me nervous.' Yeah, I bet, I'd be nervous too. I wondered if our riders had actually seen the profiles of the individual climbs or whether they had decided not to look – sometimes knowing makes it worse, if you just know there's a big hill, this can be better than knowing how big. Still, not one to miss an opportunity for my own amusement, I let Mick and Adnan into my most recent discovery, 'Ooooh, that's a nasty looking bump at the end isn't it.' The unimpressed faces glaring at me told me that they had indeed taken a look at the profiles and knew exactly what to expect.

Motorhome Two and the riders had left by 9:30 am, leaving Sara and me sitting in the sun drinking tea. We wondered whether Nicole would be wanting to cycle now that we were getting into mountain territory. We thought probably not.

While we debated whose turn it was to boil the kettle next, Sara suddenly exclaimed, 'Oh no, look at the front tyre of the motorhome!'

Turning around, I immediately saw exactly what she was referring to – there was a split in the tyre right across the tread and it actually looked as though it could have been slashed with a knife. I went round to the other side of the motorhome only to find similar splits on the nearside tyre too. Surely no one would have slashed the tyres here or indeed anywhere that we had parked. The tyres did look quite low in the tread department and a quick phone call to Mick confirmed that yes, he knew the tyres were low but as the original plan had been to use the new motorhome, he hadn't really given it any thought. And now he didn't need to give it any thought, because now it was our problem.

The cuts on the tyres were fairly deep and I was very concerned about driving any great distance on them, especially given the amount of weight we were carrying. I certainly didn't fancy driving through the Alps and the Pyrenees and however many thousand kilometres it was to get home. My opinion was that we needed to sort out new tyres today and Sara agreed.

Had we been back in England, in a car and close to any town, buying tyres wouldn't have been a problem. But we weren't in England and we weren't in a car but it occurred to me that it should be easy to buy some motorhome tyres because there are so many motorhomes in France at any one time.

'True,' agreed Sara, 'but it's Saturday and you know the French don't like working on a Saturday.'

She was right, most businesses were either shut for half a day or didn't even bother opening. We needed to get a move on if we were to stand any chance of finding some new *'pneus.'*

Heading into the town of Belfort, we immediately spotted two tyre garages practically next to each other. This is going to be a piece of cake, I thought. Between us we had worked out that the following cobbled together French should give the tyre fitter a basic idea of what we needed: *'Avez vous deux pneus pour le camping car?'* (Actually, I've just stuck this into Google Translate and we were almost spot on, just omitting one word, the *'des'* between *vous* and *deux*).

The first tyre fitter looked confused when I rolled out my well-practised question. I pointed at a picture of a tyre on the wall. This clarified things for him, it seemed that my pronunciation of the word *'pneus'* was a fraction off. I do wonder sometimes if the Europeans do this sort of thing for fun, just to make us Brits work a bit harder. I think it is generally accepted that our language skills are shocking compared to the rest of the Continent but come on, at least I was having a go.

Anyway, once he had given me a quick French lesson, he was happy to confirm that he didn't have any tyres suitable for the motorhome but he could get them in for Tuesday. We tried to explain that this was no good as we would be on some other stage of the Tour de France by Tuesday but I doubt this is actually what I said. He probably still tells people about the day a mad, slightly overweight Englishman came in for a couple of tyres but couldn't have them fitted on Tuesday because he would be riding in the Tour de France.

We continued on to the tyre place next door. The owner understood my French perfectly, thank you tyre fitter number one. Unfortunately I didn't understand a word of his reply. I was rather hoping for a simple, *'Oui'* or *'Non.'* I got neither and when he stopped talking and Sara and I just looked at each other, I think he got the message, revising his original answer to *'Non!'*

We sat in the car park studying the map. There were several towns between Belfort and our final destination so the most sensible thing seemed to be to drive towards Arc-et-Senans and investigate each town on the way. Someone must have tyres surely?

A few kilometres out of Belfort and we came across another tyre garage. We pulled up and went into the tiny reception. There was a man behind the desk chatting in an animated way to another man on our side of the desk. We assumed that he was a customer being served so we waited our turn. The time was now 11:50 am and if businesses were going to close for lunch or a half day, it was likely that they would be doing so very shortly. We waited for ten minutes while the conversation continued and I began to wonder if they were talking about tyres or just friends having a bit of a chat.

At dead on 12:00 noon, the man behind the desk turned to me, *'Oui?'* He asked. I gave him my best French accent and looked at him pleadingly. He recognised me as an English imposter immediately, even with the benefit of my insider pronunciation tips and pointed at the clock on the wall as he stated one word, *'Fermé'* (closed). Turned out that the garage shut at 12:00 noon and our arrival at 11:50 am meant he didn't have time/couldn't be bothered to assist. No further words were spoken as he glanced towards the door. It was obviously time for us to leave. Thank you for your help, sorry to have interrupted your chat!

We were to experience several more versions of the same scenario being played out in tyre shops all the way from Belfort to Besançon, the last decent sized town before our final destination of the day. The answers were always the same, the size of tyre we required wasn't kept in stock and the earliest they could get some in would be the beginning of the following week.

After visiting two more garages in Besançon, we had just about given up and figured we had little option but to deal with the problem on Monday, when hopefully we would have better luck. As we were leaving the town, we saw a fairly large tyre garage on the opposite side of the road. 'I suppose it's worth a try,' said Sara.

I turned off the main road at the next set of lights, swung the motorhome round and pointed it back towards *La Maison de Pneu Mariotte.* Let's hope it really was a house of tyres and let's hope that some of the tyres were motorhome tyres.

A very smiley lady on the front desk greeted us and I delivered my, now word perfect, question and received back the following reply, 'Yup sure, we can do that, bring the motorhome up to the first bay.'

Amazing, not only did they have the tyres but this wonderful receptionist spoke perfect English. She went on to explain that although she was French, she had lived in England for several years while studying. Within ten minutes the motorhome was jacked up and both wheels were off and being inspected. I asked the mechanic if he thought the tyres had been slashed (when I say I asked him, what I actually mean is I made slashing motions across the tyre, since, unlike the lady on the front desk, he hadn't spent years in England being educated in our great language). He shook his head, no not slashed, just very, very worn out.

It was such a relief and Sara was so pleased to have found some tyres that she started to lose control of her mind and wanted to give the tyre fitters a fifty Euro tip – this was on top of the two hundred Euros she was going to have to pay for the tyres. I quickly jumped in and gave her a metaphorical slap round the face to bring her back to her senses. Mick wasn't going to be too chipper about having to shell out two hundred Euros on tyres for a motorhome that he was going to sell when he got home, he'd be even less ecstatic about dropping the fitters an extra fifty!

The service and assistance we received at *La Maison de Pneu Mariotte* were, however, superb so I hope I can make up in some small way for putting the kybosh on their tip by recommending them here and stating that if you ever find yourself in Besançon in need of tyres, then you know where to go.

Happy in the knowledge that our front tyres were no longer at risk of bursting open at any moment, we drove on to Arc-et-Senans. The town was already busy with Tour spectators and there were a number of signs directing motorhomes to parking areas. We followed them and were pleasantly surprised to find a large field which had been set aside purely for motorhomes. We were one of the first on site (given that we were effectively two days early for the actual Tour) so we had our pick of spots. Not that it was going to get too crowded; you could probably get a couple of hundred motorhomes in the field without too much trouble.

The icing on the cake was that the charge to stay in this prime position (which was located right on the route the Tour would take) was absolutely nothing. Just another example of how much the French love their cycling and how much they want to encourage people to visit the stage towns. In the UK this would have been seen as a huge money-grabbing opportunity, a chance to take £20 or more from each motorhome, but not here.

While we felt we had had a tough day visiting all the tyre dealerships in the area, the cyclists were having a slightly tougher one riding over a few of the local hills. We received news that it was going to be a late one and that they would probably get food on the way back as it would be too late to eat by the time they made it to Arc-et-Senans.

Today's stage had taken the riders into Switzerland to pay a token visit and this is actually where the stage had ended in Porrentruy. It had been a brutal day of riding and whilst the team had gritted their teeth and held on all the way to the end, they were now 160 km away from where they needed to be. Motorhome Two hadn't even started the two hour journey to our field at 8:00 pm and with no dinner to cook, other than for ourselves, there was nothing much to do but catch up on phone calls and drink some wine.

By the time the rest of the group arrived, I was on the

way to being quite merry and wasn't in the mood for doing any work. Fortunately, there wasn't really anything to do. The boys were exhausted and the girls had had a tiring day too. They had been required to meet up with the riders far more regularly than normal as the boys needed more water and food to get over the bigger climbs. Progress in the motorhome was slow due to the sheer volume of traffic going over the climbs trying to find good vantage points for tomorrow's race. Ideally the motorhome would have avoided the climbs altogether but to go round the bottom often meant a diversion of many kilometres which meant they would fall behind the riders. All in all, not an ideal situation and we had obviously been spoilt with the simplicity of the previous flat stages.

There was quite a party atmosphere in the field that night, with most people sitting out to eat and enjoy a few drinks. Hot air balloons were being launched from the field next to ours, which gave us some entertainment but by 10:30 pm, everyone was ready for bed.

Six stages down and things were hotting up in the pro Tour. Several retirements yesterday saw 182 riders sign on for duty this morning. The main breakaway of the day started after 15 km with Cyril Gautier, Team Europcar, making a break for freedom and taking another six riders with him. The maximum gain these riders managed was just under 6 minutes over the *peloton* at 76 km. Time to start closing the gap and several teams worked together to decrease the leaders' advantage and ultimately see them slip back into the main group with around 15 km left to race.

Team Sky started to apply some serious pressure on the horrible climb that is La Planche Des Belles Filles and their efforts saw almost all riders dropped, including Cancellara who can now say goodbye to the yellow jersey. Only five riders ended up out front, two of whom were Team Sky riders – Bradley Wiggins and Chris Froome. Froome won the stage with an advantage of 2 seconds. Wiggins was third but gained enough time to take the yellow jersey.

It was clearly changeover day with the jerseys today as the polka dot and white jerseys also swapped hands. The white jersey (*maillot blanc*), is worn by the leading young rider, that is, a rider aged 25 or less. Rein Taaramae took the white jersey from Tejay Van Garderen who had worn it since the prologue in Belgium. Chris Froome's stage win also gave him sufficient points to move into the King of the Mountains jersey.

Things were getting exciting in the pro Tour now, would Wiggins be able to hold on to yellow until Paris and bring this coveted prize back to England for the first time in Tour history? There was an awfully long way still to ride.

Tour positions at end of STAGE 7

Stage Winner: Chris Froome/Sky Procycling

Yellow: Bradley Wiggins/Sky Procycling
Green: Peter Sagan/Liquigas-Cannondale
Polka Dot: Chris Froome/Sky Procycling
White: Rein Taaramae/Cofidis Le Credit En Ligne

STAGE 9
Sunday 8th July 2012
ARC-ET-SENANS - BESANÇON
Individual time trial – 41.5 km

'If you want to go faster, just push the pedals harder.'
Mick – One Day Ahead team

Another day, another random town in France. I was beginning to lose track of where we actually were on the map but I was vaguely aware that we were still heading away from England and would be for a few days yet. I calculated that I had another thirteen nights to go in the motorhome and immediately wished I hadn't bothered to work it out, we weren't even halfway yet.

Adnan interrupted my thoughts, 'Did you hear the storm last night?'

I hadn't and told him as much. Apparently, at about 4:00 am, we were in the centre of an almighty storm and both he and Mick had had to jump out of bed to go and rescue our chairs and tables and to wind in the awning, which was in danger of being ripped from the side of the motorhome. Given that the awning had already been ripped from the side of the motorhome by strong winds on a previous trip, this was something which Mick didn't want to see repeated. I hadn't been even vaguely aware of any commotion.

Something was obviously tickling Adnan though because he was having one of his giggling fits. Eventually he managed to get the words out. While he and Mick were rescuing our equipment, Nicole had stuck her head out of the window of Motorhome Two and, clearly in a blind panic, had asked if we needed to move to safety. Adnan, finding the whole thing very amusing (after all, it was only a bit of wind and rain, hardly a tornado) had replied, 'YES, RUN, SAVE YOURSELVES! JUST GO!!!!'

The look on Nicole's face was sufficiently terrified that Adnan had half expected to see Motorhome Two wheel-spinning its way out of the field. I imagine that what had actually happened was that Nicole woke up the rest of the motorhome with her screams and they had promptly told her to stop being so ridiculous and to go back to sleep.

There was no sign of any storm when I made my way out of my bunk, just another bright, sunny day. Looking out at the field I could see some evidence of a bit of upheaval during the night, with chairs, tables and other camping bits and pieces scattered liberally about the place. Thanks to Mick and Adnan's quick reactions however, all of our gear was safely stowed underneath the motorhome so no need for me to wander round the field looking for any of it. Instead I could sit back with a brew and watch all the other campers looking for their stuff.

Despite my keenness to go home, today was actually one of the days I had been looking forward to. There were a couple of reasons for this. First, today's ride was a short time trial, only 41.5 km in length, so no long, drawn out day supporting and second, tomorrow was the first rest day of the official Tour, which meant we could stay here again overnight so no driving to do this evening. Given that the One Day Ahead riders would easily be able to cycle 41.5 km without any support, I had pencilled in today as a day which I would like to ride. My bike had, so far, enjoyed a very pleasant trip around France on the roof of the motorhome but to date, its wheels hadn't touched French soil. In addition, I had done no exercise for a week but I had probably been consuming almost as many calories as our riders so a bit of physical activity certainly wouldn't go amiss.

Nicole and Jess also wanted to ride today and we suggested that Sara should also take the opportunity to pedal. She was reluctant, it takes a bit of coaxing to get Sara on her bike these days but eventually she agreed as long as Mick promised to ride with her and not go racing off. This meant that the only member of the team not riding was Emily, which would have been difficult to resolve as she didn't have a bike. As if she hadn't already done enough, Emily offered to drive to the finish point of the stage and pick all eight of us up and transport us back to the field in Arc-et-Senans. Sounded good to me – I was happy with a little 41.5 km jaunt in the sun but I didn't fancy having to cycle back again as well, that would have taken all the fun out of it.

It was a real treat to be able to enjoy a leisurely breakfast with absolutely no time pressure on any of us. We had spent over a week rushing from one point to another and filling in any waiting time with one of the many jobs which needed to be completed every day just to keep us moving forward. There was a far more relaxed atmosphere in our little camp and I was in danger of starting to enjoy myself.

Around midday, we pushed our bikes across the field to the roadside, which was, as near as damn it, the start point of the stage. We looked quite the professional cycling team, as we set off in our matching sponsored team tops. There were hundreds of people riding the stage, probably one of the easiest of the whole Tour and the Tour arrows had been put out so it would be child's play to follow the route. Mick kept to his promise to accompany Sara for about a kilometre before declaring that he 'couldn't ride this slowly', as he disappeared into the distance. Sara, Adnan and I continued on together.

No one was in any great hurry. Sara commented to Adnan that when she went on a ride, she liked to take her time and her favourite type of ride would include stopping to feed ponies along the way. Adnan agreed that this would be a perfect way to improve an already good cycle ride. Almost as soon as he had spoken, we rode round a corner to find a rather sad and manky looking donkey in a field looking somewhat forlorn. I don't know whether it was Sara or Adnan who had brought the apples with them but I do know that we spent the next ten minutes feeding them to the very appreciative donkey.

We pedalled on. The stage profile for this part of the race showed no significant hills or climbs whatsoever. I was to discover that the stage profile sometimes lies. About 16 km into the stage, we found ourselves at the bottom of a fairly short but viciously steep incline. Now, I suspect that the actual gradient was only about 10%, if that, so my description of it being viciously steep may well be considered an exaggeration when compared to other inclines we had seen along the way. But the difference with this one was that I had to cycle up it.

Adnan soon left Sara and me, saying he would wait at the top. The thing with climbing, as any cyclist will know, is that you have to get up at whatever pace you are comfortable with. It would have been as awkward for Adnan to ride at our slow pace as it would have been for me to try and keep up with his quicker pace. For the same reason, Sara and I soon split up. Towards the top of the hill, I looked back to see Sara off her bike and walking. My legs were on fire and I took the opportunity to hop off and grab a rest whilst making it look as though I was waiting for her. I wasn't, I was just knackered and this was a convenient excuse.

As Sara plodded towards me, the air was turning

distinctly blue. I had seen this before, usually after Mick had persuaded her to do something which she hadn't originally wanted to do (ride up a hill, ski down a black run etc). There was a lot of swearing coming out of Sara's mouth by the time she joined me. As she paused for breath, a French cyclist, who was riding down the hill, cheerfully called out to Sara, 'Ha ha, you should be on the bike *non?*'

It was just his way of being friendly, perhaps tinged with a little sarcasm. Either way, I wouldn't like to put Sara's response into print and I just hope he was far enough down the hill that he didn't quite hear it.

The rest of the group were waiting at the top and Mick, seeing that Sara wasn't having as much fun as maybe he thought she should, dropped back to ride with her. Going forward, the route was either completely flat or downhill, with just a couple of small bumps along the way. I pushed on ahead and rode with Matt for a while. This was probably the first time I had had a chance to have a proper conversation with him. He was thoroughly enjoying himself and even though he was still suffering a bit with his foot, it wasn't spoiling his trip. His shoulder was healing nicely and his mum and dad were coming out to join us in a couple of day's time. They were driving over with the intention of offering some additional support for the boys. I asked what they were doing in respect of accommodation and Matt told me that they were bringing a tent. They were also bringing his other pair of cycling shoes, so any pain he was currently experiencing would hopefully soon be a distant memory.

Stephen was riding a few hundred metres ahead of us and I watched as he weaved from one side of the lane to another. At one point he was riding on the wrong side of the road altogether. Adnan had already told me that his riding style was a little erratic but this was, frankly, dangerous. A British cyclist drew up alongside me.

'Your mates going to get himself killed riding like that,' he said.

'Yup, probably but he is a Marine.' I replied, not really knowing what else to say.

Matt didn't pass any comment. A bit further up the road and I noticed Motorhome Two parked in a lay-by. Emily had followed the route and pulled up to see if anyone wanted any extra water. Very thoughtful given that we were cycling in temperatures of around 30°. I topped up and pushed on, riding with Adnan for a few kilometres.

We were riding two abreast, something which in England would have infuriated any car drivers behind but not so in France. Everything is a bit more laid back and no one seems to be in much of a hurry, particularly during the Tour when you can't move for cyclists. The French are more accepting of cyclists than English drivers, maybe because there is just a lot more space for everyone to spread out. I have lost count of the number of times an English motorist has tried to kill me when I've been on my bike, just because he wants to save himself a few seconds. And that's literally all these drivers usually have to gain, a few seconds. Often I have been overtaken by a car only to catch up with it again at the next set of lights. I know many cyclists who would, in that position, filter to the front of the traffic and make the motorist overtake them again just to illustrate the point. Personally I would rather be behind an impatient driver than in his sights and it made a nice change to be cycling along without having to tense up every time you heard a car.

We heard a car coming up behind us and Adnan, who was riding on the outside and therefore in the centre of the traffic lane, started to adjust his riding position so that he could slot in behind me to let the car pass. I can only assume the driver had learnt to drive in the UK as he revved his engine and sounded his horn for about five seconds in one continuous blast. Adnan resumed his position next to me.

'I was just about to move for him, I won't bother now,' he said.

It seemed we had found the one cycle-hating idiot in France but for once, we held the Ace card and his impatience caused him a delay of about a minute while he waited for somewhere to overtake. Eventually he found a big enough gap to squeeze past and he shouted something at us in French as he drove off.

'I think he said you had a nice bike,' I said to Adnan.

Riding into Besançon it became apparent that we weren't going to be able to follow the Tour route exactly because it went down some one-way roads the wrong way. The roads would be closed the next day but they weren't today and no one fancied cycling against the stream of traffic so we skirted round this part of the course and ended up in a large car park which seemed to be where the stage ended.

Emily was already there and we all finished within a few minutes of each other. I had thoroughly enjoyed the ride and it was certainly an improvement on every other day that week. I could see why the boys were having such a good time, this really was a fantastic holiday for them. No wonder they didn't understand when Sara and I started moaning about what a rubbish time we were having.

Time to see how you get nine people and eight bikes into a motorhome designed for four. It was a bit of a tight fit but everyone squeezed in and I somehow managed to bag the passenger seat at the front which meant I was perfectly comfortable. Looking behind, there was just a mass of bodies and bikes.

Irritated perhaps that I had the best seat in the house, Stephen called out, 'How are your legs Rich? Maybe they need a bit of physio?'

The rest of the group didn't need further encouragement and they all joined in, agreeing that today I should be on the receiving end of some of Emily's torture. I wasn't really bothered, my legs weren't aching and I couldn't see that a bit of a massage was going to hurt. To be fair, my neck and shoulders had been aching from all the driving so I'd rather some attention be paid to these areas. Emily said she would try and sort my neck and shoulders out with some acupuncture but only if I let her loose on my legs first. No problem, that sounded like a perfectly fair plan to me.

My God physio hurts! No wonder the boys made such a fuss. I thought my leg muscles were okay but as soon as Emily got her fingers into them, I realised how sore they actually were. Physio is a most uncomfortable pain. As well as hurting like hell, it felt as though the pressure being applied was going to cause my muscles to cramp up. They didn't but that's what it felt like. It was really, really unpleasant. I did my best not to squirm, especially when Emily said she was only on about level five of the pressure range. The rest of the team sat with beers cheering her on.

'Give him level ten!' shouted some smart arse.

Emily complied. I grimaced.

After about twenty minutes, the torture was over and I'm not really sure if my legs felt better or worse. I turned on to my stomach and Emily fetched her box of acupuncture needles. I'd never had acupuncture before so I wasn't really sure what to expect. I didn't really feel much of a sensation at all, maybe just the slightest prick as the needles went in. Even when Emily wiggled them, I didn't really register them as being stuck in my back. Fifteen minutes of poking around later and after Emily had played her funny joke of pretending she had got a needle stuck in the wrong place which was definitely going to paralyse me or cause my head to drop off, I was done. My neck still hurt.

As usual, Emily had set up her physio studio outside, next to the motorhomes. Her work attracted the attention of a number of cyclists who were also camped in the field. It wasn't long before she had a queue of them requesting physio treatment. On a normal day, there was no way that Emily would have had the time to start taking on new clients. But this wasn't a normal day so after sorting our team out, Emily duly obliged and began working her way through a few more shaved legs. I think she did quite well out of this little sideline in the end and earned herself a bit of pocket money and why not?

When it comes to shaved legs, most semi-serious cyclists will happily admit to removing every last hair from below the line of their lycra. I never have but I was very much in the minority on this trip. In fact, everyone else on the trip had shaved legs (although in fairness almost half the group were females). Cyclists will cite a number of reasons for going hairless, none of which have ever convinced me.

I originally thought that the removal of hair was an aerodynamics thing but the more I think about it, how can a bit of hair make that much difference? Unless you are racing at a top level, the extra milliseconds to be gained from removing your leg hair are surely unmeasurable.

Many cyclists say that smooth legs make a post-race massage less painful and having now spent half an hour at the hands of our on board sadist, I can confirm that this is probably very true. I'm sure that a good percentage of my suffering during my physio session was caused by my leg hairs being pulled. Also, having a load of massage oil sticking to your hairy legs after the physio isn't a great look and had me running straight to the shower.

Cyclists fall off their bikes from time to time, that's a fact and the treatment of wounds is easier if they aren't full of hair. Again, this reason for bald pins makes perfect sense to me.

Other justifications for the streamlined look include: it looks better (does it?), women like it (do they?), it's tradition. I'm not convinced but then, I'm not really a serious cyclist and certainly not a racer. I'll stick to being a hairy-legger I think.

After showers, we decided to try and find somewhere to watch the end of that day's pro Tour stage. The town wasn't huge but we had seen a couple of bars on the main road so we headed to the nearest one. Everywhere was buzzing with anticipation for the start of the stage the next day. This is probably the busiest the town had ever been, with hundreds of fans milling around. We expected that all of the bars would be showing the Tour on plasma screens, given that this was what everyone was in the town for in the first place. The first bar we entered was almost empty, just two people sitting in the corner, quietly enjoying a bottle of wine.

The French barkeeper took our drinks order and we asked if there was anywhere to watch the Tour. He stared back at us with an incredulous look on his face, 'You want to watch the Tour?' it seemed to say, 'Are you quite mad?'

When he had recovered from the shock of our preposterous suggestion, he shrugged his shoulders and led us through a door into, what appeared to be at least, his living room. There were a couple of settees and a decent sized television in a cabinet, which he turned on and then left us to it.

Perfect timing as we joined the race in the closing kilometres of the stage, as the riders raced their way to the finish line in Porrentruy, Switzerland. Out in front was French rider, Thibaut Pinot, riding for the FDJ-Bigmat team. At 22 years old, Pinot was the youngest rider in this Tour and he broke away from the leading riders' group on the final climb.

If you want to know how much the winning of a stage means to anyone in the Tour, take a look on YouTube at the clips of FDJ-Bigmat *Directuer Sportif*, Marc Madiot, hanging out of the window of the team car as Pinot pedals himself to victory. Madiot, an ex-professional cyclist himself, is hanging out of the car, banging on the side and screaming his lungs out at Pinot. I guess he is shouting at him to keep going, don't look back, just keep pedalling! It was very funny and gave us all a laugh but it just shows how serious a business a stage win really is.

Pinot himself was slightly more reserved, stating, 'I will remember this day my entire life. I can't yet get my mind around it.'

Our next treat for the day was for everyone to have a night off from cooking and washing up. We had decided to go out for a meal. We had booked a table earlier at one of the few restaurants in the town and after the racing had finished, we ambled along the main street to take our seats.

Surprisingly, the restaurant wasn't that busy and we were shown to our table straight away. Due to the size of our group, we had been placed in a side room, which we had to ourselves. If it had been my decision, I would have been happy to have eaten out every night of the Tour and actually this would probably have made it far more enjoyable. From a practical point of view however, this wasn't possible and knowing the earlier discussions about money and the need to cut back on basic shopping, it wouldn't have been an option even if we had had the time.

With full bellies and slightly fuzzy heads from the wine, we made our way back to the motorhomes. Today had felt like a rest day but tomorrow was even better – it was an actual rest day. There are two official rest days in the Tour de France. No racing occurs on these days and the riders get a complete break from cycling. Except for the fact that they don't. Even on rest days, the riders will be out for a ride of at least two or three hours, just to keep their legs moving. Our boys would be doing the same but I wouldn't. Tomorrow I didn't have to do anything. The pro Tour would be arriving in the town later that night in preparation for the individual time trial the next day. We were staying put so that we could see at least some of the racing up close and personal. To date, we had been following the route of the Tour (or rather they had been following us) for ten days but we hadn't seen any of the actual racing.

A couple of additional retirements saw 180 riders start Stage 8 of the 99th Tour de France. This stage saw the largest breakaway of the race so far with eleven riders clear at the 8 km point. The oldest man in the Tour, Jens Voigt pushed on harder and he led the race over the first two climbs. By the third climb Voigt was joined by six other riders. These leaders were caught at 47 km by a further twenty four riders. The attacks continued to come but by the top of the final climb, Pinot had raced into the lead with 17 km to go. We already know what happened next and Pinot rode to victory, assisted in no small way I am sure by the encouraging screams of Marc Madiot.

Just one change in the jersey competition today, with Fredrik Kessiakoff of Astana Pro Team relieving Chris Froome of the polka dot jersey he had won the day before. No great issue for Froome, whose main job on this Tour is supporting Bradley Wiggins and protecting that all-important yellow jersey.

Tour positions at end of STAGE 8

Stage Winner: Thibaut Pinot/FDJ-Bigmat

Yellow: Bradley Wiggins/Sky Procycling
Green: Peter Sagan/Liquigas-Cannondale
Polka Dot: Fredrik Kessiakoff/Astana Pro Team
White: Rein Taaramae/Cofidis Le Credit En Ligne

REST DAY
ARC-ET-SENANS
Monday 9th July 2012

'Consider a man riding a bicycle. Whoever he is, we can say three things about him. We know he got on the bicycle and started to move. We know that at some point he will stop and get off. Most important of all, we know that if at any point between the beginning and the end of his journey he stops moving and does not get off the bicycle he will fall off it. That is a metaphor for the journey through life of any living thing, and I think of any society of living things.'
William Golding – Novelist

'THE CARAVAN, THE CARAVAN, MICK, MOVE!!!'

Sara's shouting jolted me awake. What time was it? It felt early. I was vaguely aware of some circusy music playing somewhere outside. The motorhome door flew open and Sara shot out in her pyjamas.

Minutes later she was back, panic seemingly over. Sara's speedy exit from the motorhome was driven by an absolute desire not to miss the Caravan. The Caravan is a fundamental part of the Tour de France and although it never seems to be shown on British TV (well not on ITV4 at any rate), you haven't seen the Tour if you haven't seen the Caravan.

The Publicity Caravan, to give it its full name, was created in 1930 and came about due to a change in Tour rules by Henri Desgrange. Desgrange was becoming irritated by the fact that the Tour was being dominated by teams run by cycling brands and decided to change the format of the Tour completely in order to relax their grip on the race. He decided that the event was to be ridden by National teams and the riders would all ride exactly the same bicycles, which would be supplied by the organisers. It was an attractive plan but it would be expensive. Desgrange had the solution to the expense and he offered the major brands of France the opportunity to take part in a publicity caravan in return for a sponsorship fee. It was an immediate success and one which has formed an integral part of the Tour ever since. A survey a couple of years ago revealed that 47% of visitors to the Tour come primarily to see the Caravan.

The Caravan consists of a variety of floats and vehicles in a parade which lasts about forty five minutes. It travels the full route of the Tour and usually passes by about an hour ahead of the actual racers. The main attraction of the Caravan, other than to enjoy the spectacle, is the clamouring for the free gifts (tat) which the participants throw out to the crowds.

Having witnessed the Caravan a few times in my life, I can say that if you like complete tat, you will love the Caravan. If you want to see grown men on the verge of fighting just so one of them can grab a flimsy baseball cap or key ring with the name of one of the Tour sponsors printed on it, the Caravan is for you.

Sara loved the Caravan and this explained her rapid departure. She was premature though as the Caravan wasn't due to pass our position for another thirty minutes so she had returned for a cup of tea and a chair.

Mick and I accompanied her back to the side of the road with our morning brews. Mick was laughing about how excited the French get when one of the main partners of the Tour, Cochonou, pass by in the Caravan. Cochonou manufacture a type of salami sausage which is very popular in France and they would often give away small sample packs of their main product from the Caravan. Mick had been at the Tour one year when suddenly a French chap at the side of the road pushed his way to the front of the crowd and started leaping up and down waving and shouting, *'LE COCHONOU!! LE COCHONOU!!'* Clearly this was his favourite part of the Caravan and he wanted everyone to know it.

Ever since then, Mick watches out for the Cochonou float and when he sees it, he starts jumping around like the crazy French chap, repeating his shouts of *'LE COCHONOU!! LE COCHONOU!!'* This usually results in great amusement in the crowd, I suspect because they have all witnessed a similar thing to us at some point.

The crowds were starting to build, all anticipating the start of the Caravan. Part of the attraction of the Caravan is really how bad it is. It always reminds me of something straight out of the 1970s but they are obviously doing something right if the number of people standing at the roadside were anything to go by.

Bang on time and the floats started coming down the road. Vittel water usually have a decent sized float loaded up with student workers armed with water pistols to spray the spectators (surely this is one of the best summer jobs ever). Mick was ready for them one year and stood on the steps of the motorhome with two of his cycling water bottles filled and ready to squirt. His attack was met with the entire Vittel team returning fire resulting in one very wet Mick and one very unhappy Sara as much of the water from the Vittel truck had ended up inside their motorhome.

Suddenly Mick was jumping around like a mad man, *'LE COCHONOU!! LE COCHONOU!!'* he shouted.

We were falling about laughing, as were most of the other spectators. However from across the road, a very serious voice boomed to Mick, *'Il n'est pas le Cochonou! C'est la Banette!'*

Mick had made a grave and obvious mistake. It was not the Cochonou float; it was the bakery company, Banette's float. Similar colours and an easy mistake to make but our friend across the street was clearly not impressed with Mick's *faux pas*. Call yourself a Tour fan? How could you make such an error? Must be English, huh! This made the whole situation even funnier, not just for us but also for the other people who had heard Mick's reprimand.

Shortly afterwards the actual Cochonou float arrived.

'Voici le Cochonou!' shouted the man across the street.

We nodded our thanks, grateful to have been educated by the master.

The choice of tat was particularly poor this year and I came away with five promotional inflatable pillows and a key ring. I gave the inflatable pillows to some children who hadn't managed to grab any of their own tat. Once the last float had passed by, we returned to the motorhome for some breakfast.

As today's professional stage was an individual time trial, the riders would be set off at intervals, to ride the route we had covered the day before, on their own. The first rider was due to leave the town at 9:45 am and the remainder of the field would then follow at two minute intervals until the last rider, yellow jersey holder, Bradley Wiggins, who was due to start his ride at 4:39 pm.

The riders would leave in the reverse order of their position in the general classification. The first rider to ride the time trial would be the *'Lanterne Rouge,'* the rider currently in last position. The term *'Lanterne Rouge,'* meaning red lantern, comes from the name given to the red light which was hung on the last carriage of a railway train, which conductors would look for to make sure that no carriages had become decoupled. Coming last overall and 'winning' the title of *Lanterne Rouge* is actually a challenge in itself. It isn't sufficient to just hang back at the rear of the field as a rider must ensure that, not only is he the last one but also that he manages to make the time cut-off set for each stage to ensure he isn't disqualified altogether. There have been occasions when riders have competed to come last on the basis that they were likely to get more attention from being the very last rider than being, say, second to last. As Mick might say, no one remembers who came second and equally, no one remembers who came second to last.

After breakfast, Sara, Mick, Adnan and I took a stroll into the town and went for a nose around the preparation area which had been set up for the pro teams. The team buses were arranged with small fenced off areas in front of them, each set up with training rollers and bikes for the riders to warm up on. This was the time to catch sight of your favourite rider and almost be in touching distance. As you might expect, there were also many merchandise stalls selling all manner of Tour-branded products. I bought a t-shirt with a map of this year's route on, something to remind me of how far we had travelled (as if I would need reminding).

We then went back to the spot we had occupied earlier that morning when the Caravan passed by so that we could watch Mark Cavendish start his time trial ride. Our timing was spot on and we arrived just as he was about to start. He flew past, head down and tucked close to the bike, his team car following closely behind.

Today was very much a day of rest for us and we took full advantage of it. The boys took the opportunity to give their bikes a thorough clean and general check over. At one point, Sara and I were relaxing in the front of the motorhome doing what we do best – drinking tea – when we spotted Matt cleaning his wheel in front of the windscreen. He would clean a bit, then spin the wheel in his hands and clean a bit more. For some reason however, between every spin, he would bounce the wheel off the bonnet of the motorhome. I was watching this, somewhat stunned really at what I was seeing and I noticed that Sara had stopped talking and was also mesmerised by Matt's process of wiping the wheel and then thudding it off her motorhome. I wondered how he would feel if I started bouncing a wheel off the bonnet of his car (did he even have a car?). I was amazed at the lack of respect for someone else's property and didn't really know what to say.

Sara broke the silence, 'I'm glad we aren't in the new motorhome.'

After lunch, our riding team picked their way through the crowds and found a road which led out of town and which wasn't closed for the Tour. They went for an hour's spin just to keep their legs fresh and on their return Emily gave the boys a bonus physio session. I declined. I'd had enough the day before thank you very much. Sara spent time tidying and cleaning the motorhome. I looked through my bag of clothes and worked out how many days I would have to wear each t-shirt so that I didn't run out before I got back home. This was always going to be an issue. I simply don't own that many clothes and have never had much of an interest in fashion. Even if I had packed everything in my wardrobe, I would still have run out of clobber after about ten days. As it was, I hadn't brought everything I owned and we were on day eleven. A few quick calculations and I worked out that t-shirts needed to be worn for three days minimum each and shorts/jeans no less than five days each. Normally I wouldn't dream of wearing a t-shirt for more than one day before washing it but on this trip, I was beyond caring. There was always the option of washing some clothes but then I would have to hope that I could get them dry and I just couldn't be bothered with the extra work.

While pondering the clothes situation, Sara came along and stripped both my bunk bed and Adnan's. She had had the foresight to bring fresh bedding and today was changeover day. It takes a woman to think of these things – it hadn't even occurred to me and I would have happily used the same bedding for the whole trip. Still, if I've got the option of clean bedding, why not?

At the allotted time we took up a position close to the start ramp to see Bradley Wiggins off on his time trial ride. You couldn't really miss him in a bright yellow skin suit but we all commented on how skinny he was.

With Wiggo off down the ramp and on his way to his first stage win of the Tour, we had to think about getting across to Mâcon, 150 km away, for the start of tomorrow's stage. Sat nav Jane estimated that it would take about an hour and a half and then we'd have to find somewhere to stop. As soon as Wiggo was out of sight, the Tour traffic started to move and workers sprang into action collecting up barriers and generally clearing up. Motorhomes and spectators were also now queuing up to leave the field which had been our home for the last couple of nights. It made more sense to sit tight for a few hours and have some dinner as leaving now would only mean we would sit in the queue of traffic all trying to exit the town at the same time. I had seen this before. When we left Alpe d'Huez the year before, we had actually waited until the morning after the Tour had come through to leave the mountain. It still took us nearly three hours to travel the 13 km from top to bottom. It was 7:30 pm before we got on the road to Mâcon but by this time the worst of the traffic had cleared and we had definitely made the right choice.

As we got closer to our destination, Sara got the map book out and announced that Mâcon was located on a river so this would be the first place we would look for an overnight stop.

It was dark as we got into town but someone was looking down on us and no sooner had we come alongside the river, than we spotted what looked to be a suitable place to park up on the opposite bank. A short distance ahead and we found a bridge, so we crossed the river and pulled on to a large grassy verge on the roadside, looking across at the town. It was the sort of spot that you wouldn't dream of parking in at any other time of the year, as you would definitely have been moved on by the local police. But in Tour week, we knew it would be fine and that we would almost certainly wake up the following morning to find we had been joined by half a dozen other motorhomes.

A quick look at the Garmin route for the following day confirmed that we were only about a kilometre from the stage start point so the boys wouldn't need a lift in the morning. Sara and I were supporting the next day so it would save us a job. To save me another job, I programmed the Garmin with the next set of stage details and called it a night, snuggling up in my lovely fresh bedding.

Bradley Wiggins won today's time trial stage and retained the yellow jersey for another day, extending his lead over Cadel Evans, BMC Racing Team, in second place by 1 minute and 53 seconds. As much as we all wanted Wiggins to hold on to that jersey, we also all knew it was a loooong way between here and Paris. Chris Froome's efforts in the time trial were rewarded and he now moves up to third position in the General Classification.

Rein Taaramae returned the white jersey to Tejay Van Garderen, having enjoyed wearing it for the past couple of days.

Tour positions at end of STAGE 9

Stage Winner: Bradley Wiggins/Sky Procycling

Yellow: Bradley Wiggins/Sky Procycling
Green: Peter Sagan/Liquigas-Cannondale
Polka Dot: Fredrik Kessiakoff/Astana Pro Team
White: Tejay Van Garderen/BMC Racing Team

STAGE 10
Tuesday 10th July 2012
MÂCON – BELLEGARDE-SUR-VALSERINE
Mountain – 194.5 km

'When I see an adult on a bicycle, I do not despair for the future of the human race.'
H G Wells – Novelist

It was always going to be a struggle to get back into the swing of things after a day off and if someone had suggested driving back to Calais and going home, I would have jumped at the chance. I was tired, irritable, felt grubby and was getting fed up working my backside off while everyone else (the cyclists) had a great time. They were supposed to be doing the hard work in aid of charity but I genuinely felt that it was Sara and me and the other support team who were doing the real suffering. I admit that the cyclists might have had sore legs each night but they were enjoying themselves. I had experienced brief moments of enjoyment but on the whole, I can't really say I was having much fun.

I knew Sara felt the same; she had told me. Several times. Several times a day in fact. To be honest, we had both told each other how much of a miserable time we were having at any given opportunity, which, when you are stuck in a motorhome driving for hours a day, was a lot of opportunities. When I told Sara that I was writing this book, she said that if I ever couldn't remember what had happened on any given day, all I needed to write was, 'It was shit.' This was exactly how I was feeling now. I'd had the luxury of a day off, a day to remind myself what it was like to have my life back and to do what I wanted to do instead of what I had to do. I have never been very good at doing things I didn't want to and the more I thought about it and the more Sara and I moaned about it, the worse I felt.

Moaning wasn't going to get the job done though and we still had goodness knows how many stages to get through and a similar number of mountains to climb (real ones, not metaphorical ones).

Fresh after their rest day, the boys were raring to go and were soon on their way on Stage 10. 194.5 km to cover and the first *hors categorie* climb of this year's race. They would reach the Col du Grand Columbier after about 140 km and if the stage profile image was anything to go by, would then ride vertically into the sky for about a kilometre and a half. The mountain road would actually wind its way up over 17.4 km and there were a couple of nice, steep 12% gradient sections just to keep the chaps on their toes. If that wasn't hard enough, the Tour organisers had also thrown in a cat 2 and a cat 3 climb to keep them busy.

The early Tour riders were fortunate in that there were no true mountain passes included in their route, only less significant 'cols' (the French term for a pass between two mountain peaks). Mind you, I would rather tackle a full on mountain pass on a modern, geared bike than attempt to ride up an unmade road on the single-speed lump of pig iron they would have used in the early 1900s. The first mountain passes were seen in the 1910 Tour when the riders rode (and walked) their way through the Pyrenees and up over the Col d'Aubisque and the Tourmalet, both of which our boys would be visiting in a few days time. In 1910, the roads would have been little more than mule tracks and, as well as heavy bikes, the racers would have been carrying spare tyres, tools, food, clothing and who knows what else. The One Day Ahead team really had nothing to complain about.

Our day progressed with the normal exciting array of jobs. We met the boys about 60 km into the ride and Sara fed them. I rinsed and refilled eight water bottles with their chosen refreshment and arranged to meet them at the foot of the Col du Grand Colombier. All of these climbs were blurring into one now and I wasn't giving a second thought as to how hard it must be to keep cycling over a seemingly endless number of lumps in the road. Cat 4? Easy, not worth mentioning. Cat 3 or 2? Pointless, no discussion required. Cat 1/HC? Might take a bit longer but nothing you can't deal with, chop chop. I struggled to get myself into gear each morning just to drive along the route. If I had awoken to study yet another stage profile telling me I was going to be cycling upwards for the next eight hours, I shudder to think how I would be feeling.

It is when you get into the mountains that you really start to experience 'Tour Fever.' Much of the action occurs on these mammoth climbs and it is also only here that the professional cyclists slow down a bit which gives spectators a better chance of seeing their favourites. As such, a good vantage point on a mountain pass is a prized thing indeed and you need to be there early if you want to have your pick of the viewing spots. The majority of the decent positions will be taken up with motorhomes as these spectators have the option of arriving up to a week (or more) in advance to bag the best locations.

When we had visited Alpe d'Huez the previous year, we arrived several days before the Tour came through and we claimed pretty much the last spot on the mountain road. This was partly because of the fact that most people probably wouldn't have wanted to try and get their motorhome into the position that we ended up in as it did require some 'off-road' work to get our two vehicles clear of the main road. If you imagine two wheels on the tarmac and two halfway up the steep grass embankment, partially balanced on some wooden blocks, you'll get the idea. We decided that it would *probably* be okay. As it happens it was, but if pushed, I would agree that it could have gone either way.

Mountain stage Tour fans come ready for a party and the celebrations start the moment the motorhome engine is switched off and continue until the last Tour rider has passed through. For many, this will mean four days of drinking and partying, much of which will take place in the road. Not that the road isn't busy, right up to the day before the Tour it will be heaving with vehicles looking for somewhere to park and cyclists testing themselves against the might of the mountain. There is a continuous stream up and down from first light until late at night.

The Dutch have got the Tour party thing down to a tee. On Alpe d'Huez, they had taken over an entire hairpin bend. And I do mean, taken over. This wasn't just a case of parking up a few motorhomes and sticking some flags out. Oh no, that wouldn't have been anywhere near adequate for a nation to mark their territory. These guys had arrived two weeks before the Tour was due to pass by and the first thing they had done was paint the entire road orange. French authorities do tend to turn a blind eye to road painting, particularly on the big climbs, but usually it will be the name of a favourite rider or team which gets daubed onto the tarmac rather than a complete colour change. Not satisfied with their almost luminous road, the Dutchies had then set up a 15 foot scaffolding platform to house not one but two DJ booths. Music sorted and the next thing they needed was obviously drink on tap. No problem, some thoughtful chap had brought along a full bar which was set up on the side of the road with a choice of draught beers.

The mountain vibrated from the music and general rowdiness in Dutch corner from morning until, well, morning. If the local police passed by, the DJ politely turned down his music and gave them a shout-out, *'Letsch hear it for our friendly neighbourhood copsch!'*

The friendly *'copsch'* continued onwards, probably not having been instructed as to how to deal with such a thing at French police training college. Once out of sight, the music would be wound back up.

And so it continues until the night before the Tour arrives when the Tour traffic (logistics, officials, team buses etc) start to make their way up the mountain having just packed everything up at the finish town earlier that day. What seems like thousands (and probably is) of cars, lorries, coaches and motorbikes crawl up the mountain, somehow managing to get enormous, articulated lorries around the narrowest and sharpest of hairpin turns, often within millimetres of parked motorhomes and tents but never so much as clipping a wing mirror. Having said that, I suspect the truth is that they do clip the odd wing mirror here and there, but I didn't experience such a thing. The back end of my motorhome (which was where I was sleeping) was hanging out into the road a tiny amount and I could hear the lorries passing within inches of my head, but that was as close as they came. It's a good job really as I suspect if they had given the motorhome a little nudge, we would both have careered off down the mountain in a manner similar to a Top Gear 'I hate caravans' stunt.

At the bottom of the Col du Grand Colombier the boys looked fine, pretty fresh to be fair. It was a different story at the top. Oh how I laughed when Stephen described the ride as brutal.

'Get used to it,' I gleefully replied.

At last, the crap holiday Gods were tilting things in my favour. Suddenly it didn't seem so bad to me that I was having a rubbish time; after all, if everyone else was too, then there was more of a chance of someone suggesting we go home.

Feelings of getting an early pass back to England were soon snatched from my grasp however when some helpful chap (or chapess) pointed out that, at some point on the descent of this *Col*, our riders would have passed the halfway point of the whole Tour. For some reason this just made everyone feel like the challenge was more achievable than it had been yesterday. 'Oh so we are carrying on then are we?' Apparently we were.

Driving up a mountain lined with Tour spectators (many of whom are drunk) and littered with cyclists riding up at varying speeds can be a bit hairy. Spectators are prone to jumping out in front of you to wave their flags, cheer or to put their thumbs up (I have no idea why). Cyclists will often behave unpredictably. The reason for this is simple, they are usually knackered. Many won't have ever attempted anything like this before so a bit of weaving across the road and impromptu stopping without warning is to be expected. Picking your way past the cyclists is a slow and often nigh on impossible thing to do and as soon as you pass one, there are twenty more in front of you. Plus you have the same volume of traffic coming down the mountain towards you. It's hard enough in a car but in an old, overloaded, 7.5 metre long motorhome, it is, shall we say, challenging.

However, give me the uphill bit any day because driving down the other side is a hundred times worse. Suddenly the cyclists, who just moments ago could barely push their pedals round, have a new lease of life. Just as they were beginning to think that pedalling was over-rated, they find that it is now completely obsolete. 'Whoosh, look at us! We were turning ourselves inside out a minute ago but now we can steam down the mountain at 50 km/h without a care in the world.' Down they came, weaving in and out of vehicles; I lost count of the number of times a bike would whizz past the motor-home and then duck in front to avoid decorating the windscreen of an approaching car. No regard for the quality of the motorhome's old brakes and clearly no concerns about being rear-ended by four tonnes of fibre-glass, steel and energy gels. The brakes struggled all the way down and for most of the descent I was relying on the engine to control our speed, remaining in second gear. How I didn't squash a cyclist or two en route I have no idea. Maybe I did and just didn't notice.

The crowds on the mountain aren't any less enthusiastic for the actual race. Although the last couple of kilometres have barriers up to keep the fans away from the riders, they are free to mix all the way up to this point. It's a recipe for disaster and it amazes me every year that more accidents don't occur. The spectators (which we have already established include many who are more than slightly tipsy) fill the road, parting like the Red Sea at the last second as the leading riders approach. I've been witness to a girl in her twenties, who, after having downed her own bodyweight in wine during the morning, decided that, as the road had now been closed to allow the Tour to pass by, the best place for a little sleep was bang in the centre of the aforementioned road. Fortunately her friends managed to persuade her that perhaps this wasn't the best decision of her life and encouraged her to move to the side of the road moments before the *peloton* steamed past.

Needless to say, the One Day Ahead team sped off within the first few metres of the descent and we didn't catch up with them until 15 km later when they were starting to pant up the side of the next climb, the cat 3 Col de Richemond, a mere baby of a mountain. This game of cat and mouse was to continue for much of our time in the mountains; the fact is that getting down a mountain is considerably faster on a bike than it is in a motorhome. Tour riders can reach speeds of 90 km/h or more on a descent and will regularly out-brake and pass not only Tour cars but also motorcycles. Descending at that speed is a real skill and not something for the faint-hearted. During my own descent of Alpe d'Huez, I had my hands clamped round my brake levers for much of the journey. It was only when I reached the bottom that Mick bothered to inform me that keeping the brakes on runs the risk of heating up the wheel rims to such an extent that the inner tube could burst. Oh thanks for that, ever helpful advice as always.

The final cat 3 Col de Richemond was indeed just a baby mountain and looking at the stage profile, I was sure it would be possible to carry the speed from the descent of the Col du Grand Colombier and freewheel up the side of the Richemond. The boys said this definitely wasn't possible but I suspect they were just trying to make their efforts for the day sound more impressive than actually they were.

With the boys duly refreshed with food and fluids, Sara and I set off for the finish. Once over the last climb, the team had a pleasant downhill coast of about 20 km, just turning very slightly uphill at the end. After the HC climb earlier in the day, I doubt they even noticed it.

An hour or so later and four very hot, sweaty and exhausted chaps climbed into Motorhome One. After distributing protein shakes, I turned the motorhome towards our destination for the night, Albertville. We already had a spot lined up as my handy book of French *aires* had told us that there was an *aire* in one of the car parks overlooking the town.

Motorhome Two was already parked up in the *aire* when we got there and we found them tucked in the corner of a large and mostly empty car park just outside of the main town. The car park was positioned part way up a road which led from the town up a hill. This gave us a superb view over the town and also illustrated that, although it was probably only a kilometre or two, the town was much too far away for any of us to be bothered to walk down for a drink or food. Motorhome Two fired up the cooker and we filled ourselves up on chilli and rice.

As soon as the sun went down, the temperature dropped almost instantly so we all retired to our respective motorhomes. About an hour later, we heard a tap, tap, tap on our door. It was Emily. Everyone had gone to bed in Motorhome Two but she wasn't ready for bed and knew we would still be up so she'd snuck over for a glass or two of wine. She told us that Nicole and Jess were still extremely keen to do some more cycling, especially while we were in the mountains. I explained how hard it had been keeping up with the boys today with just one main mountain pass and Emily could see how the job would be made even more difficult with two stragglers to look after. Sara impressed upon her the importance of not being pushed into acting as support for both the boys and the girls because it wasn't fair and would leave her in the motorhome all day, on her own, effectively doing everything.

While we were sitting chatting, Sara also asked Emily if there was anything that she specifically wanted to do whilst on this trip. She told us that she was keen to see one of the main mountain passes, ideally without having to drive over it. Sara and I agreed that when we got to the Col du Tourmalet, Emily could come with us in Motorhome One for the day. This would mean that Jess would have to drive Motorhome Two. It was likely that Nicole would want to cycle up the Tourmalet and that she would want Jess to go with her so we could already see that this was a potential heated discussion waiting to happen. However, it seemed a small price to pay to ensure that Emily got a day off to do what she wanted.

Of course, while our boys had been slogging their way through another 194.5 km, the pro Tour riders were enjoying their first rest day. The rest day was a distant memory to me though and the next one couldn't come soon enough.

STAGE 11
Wednesday 11th July 2012
ALBERTVILLE – LA TOUSSUIRE (LES SYBELLES)
Mountain – 148 km

'Vous êtes des assassins!' (You are murderers!)
Octave Lapize - Winner of 1910 Tour, said to Tour organisers after experiencing true mountain climbs

Soon enough morning came and once more I awoke to find myself in a nondescript car park somewhere in deepest France. Today's stage would later be described by Mick as being 'gruesome.' I could have told him that before he even left the motorhome.

At just 148 km, today's stage certainly wasn't going to be one of the longest but with a couple of HC climbs as well as a cat 1 and a cat 2 thrown in for good measure, it wasn't going to be a walk in the park either. Nicole had decided to ride some of the stage too, despite Sara and me voicing the potential problems of the motorhome keeping up with the boys on the descents. Needless to say, our advice was largely ignored and needless to say, Emily and Jess spent much of the day playing catch-up with the boys. I think Nicole made it part way up the first mountain before hitching a lift in our very own broom wagon. A largely pointless effort given the knock-on effect of potentially delaying the boys in getting their food and drink breaks. Oh well, these youngsters just wouldn't be told.

In Motorhome One it was another day off for Sara and me but rather than sit around idly enjoying the beautiful sunny weather to which we had fast become accustomed, we decided we would much rather spend our day washing out dirty cycling shorts and completing other, similarly unpleasant, tasks. With the boys and Motorhome Two gone, we slipped into a finely tuned process. Sara would pile the washing up on the draining board and wash and scrub it before passing it to me. I would then stand outside the motorhome manually wringing as much water out of the, frankly still grubby, kit before hanging it on our improvised washing line (the cycle rack) to dry.

With the washing done, Sara set to work giving the motorhome yet another spring clean. I took the opportunity to sort out some of my 'motorhome jobs.' The car park had a motorhome service point in the corner, which meant I could empty the toilet cassettes and fill up with water. I plodded back and forth with our portable water container and topped us up. It would have been quicker to drive the motorhome over to the tap but I had just hung all the washing out and moving the motorhome would have meant unhanging it all. I couldn't be bothered with the extra hassle.

It occurred to us that, given the easy access to water at this spot and the fact that we weren't in any great rush, we might even be able to treat ourselves to a luxury shower each. A hot shower every morning is something most of us take for granted but living for any period of time in a motorhome, especially with several other people, forces you to be sparing with water. To have an unlimited supply on tap and to be able to leave the shower running while I washed was wonderful. Not quite as wonderful as being at home admittedly – my own shower has a water pressure high enough to strip paint and is big enough that I can turn around without knocking all of the shampoo and shower gel off the tiny shelf and all over the bathroom floor. It also doesn't have a shower curtain which clings to me as soon as it gets wet thus making the whole process of washing both difficult and not that enjoyable. But I had long since forgotten my shower at home and the dribble of hot water (the fact that the water was hot was some consolation I suppose) trickling out of the miniature shower head was heavenly. It would have been nice to have come out of the shower and into some freshly laundered clothes rather than the shorts and t-shirt I had already been wearing for two days but it appeared that this was asking too much. I rummaged through my holdall only to discover that the washing fairies hadn't been today. You can't have everything.

I stuck the kettle on and got a fold up chair out of the storage cupboard on the side of the motorhome. Mick had managed to squeeze six chairs into a cupboard which was clearly designed to hold about three. This, coupled with the fact that one of the cupboard door locks was broken, meant that you really had to want to sit down to be bothered with the hassle of removing and replacing a chair. Getting one out was easy. Getting it back involved a twenty minute punch-up with the contents of the cupboard and the door itself. I had time for a fight today though so I relieved the cupboard of a couple of chairs and sat down to read while Sara had her luxury shower.

Today's Tour route formed a loop so the boys would end up almost back where they had started. In addition, tomorrow's start point was only about 60 km away from where we now sat. This meant that, other than a bit of shopping, we had nothing else to do for the rest of the day. Had we been following Jess' plan, today would be the day to go and do some sightseeing. Truth is, we were both exhausted and whilst I am sure Albertville has much to offer a tourist with time to kill, motivation to do anything was lacking in Motorhome One. Sara joined me with a cup of tea and a bag of Adnan Cakes. There is something about a brew that makes everything seem alright. I've always been a big drinker of tea and Sara and Mick are the same, no sooner than the mug is empty and someone jumps up to boil the kettle again. I've always considered that this love of tea dates back to the days when I worked in an office. Nipping to the kitchen to make a cuppa was an opportunity to grab five minutes break from work, which gives you a pleasant feeling. I'm sure a psychologist would tell me that, twenty years on, I still associate a cup of tea with the same pleasant feeling, hence my desire to drink so much of it. There's probably some truth in this theory but today, having another cup of tea just meant that I could delay getting in the flipping motorhome and driving to nowhere for nothing.

After having our usual morning moan and confirming that yes, we were most definitely completely selfless and almost Saint-like in the way we were putting up with this confounded trip, we started to discuss the change in group dynamic which was to occur the next day. When we had first sat in the pub to discuss the One Day Ahead challenge, Stephen had grand ideas of letting all manner of friends and relatives meet us along the way, either to ride or just for a bit of a jolly. These plans were swiftly knocked on the head by the rest of us but we hadn't been able to dissuade Stephen from having both his brother and sister fly out to join us for some of the mountain stages. His younger brother, Christian, was originally planning to meet us halfway through the Tour, with the intention of riding the second half of the route in its entirety. Although Christian wasn't as strong a rider as the rest of the group, the original feeling was that, by the time he joined us, the rest of the team would be getting tired and not riding at such a high pace.

Therefore, even though he was a weaker rider, he would be able to keep up with a team which already had over 1,700 km in their legs. A few days before Christian was due to fly out, Mick expressed concern that, actually, far from getting tired, the team were getting stronger and were riding as hard, if not harder, than they had done in the early stages. It wasn't the outcome any of us were expecting but it was a fact that their bodies had quickly settled into the routine of riding 200 km every day. Bringing a weaker rider into the group would only have one effect and that would be to slow the group down and this wasn't something that anyone wanted. Cue difficult telephone call by Stephen to his brother to tell him he couldn't come.

His sister was another matter though. Hannah wasn't planning to ride whole stages, just bits and pieces of the route in the same way as Nicole had been doing. She was due to arrive the next day. It was going to be interesting to see how things changed as Nicole would now have another girl in her camp when fighting the 'I want to ride today' battles. I'd met Hannah once before and she struck me as someone who would be happy to get stuck into an argument if she felt it justified. Our position hadn't changed and Sara and I had no plans to start supporting two lots of riders regardless of how strongly the argument was pushed.

Two or five cups of tea later and with the washing basically dry, we decided to make a move to the supermarket. An extra body meant extra food and we really needed to do a weekly big shop. As neither of us enjoyed supermarket shopping, we had done our best to do lots of quick shops – in and out – rather than face an hour or more filling up a trolley. But we couldn't put it off any longer. It was time to trolley up.

At least the conversation changed while we were in Carrefour. Instead of complaining about supporting the boys, we could now grumble about how much we hated shopping. Bread, pasta, milk, Adnan Cakes, wine, chicken, this was our staple diet for most of the three weeks in France. Neither of us were benefiting much in the waistline department but at this stage of the game, I'd given up caring. It had become obvious very early on that going for an hour's ride each day was going to be totally impractical and I gave up on the idea within about twenty four hours of arriving on French soil.

With the shopping done, the motorhome was now back to the state that I liked it the best – full of water and food and with an empty toilet. The fuel tank was also full, so all was well with the world, at least in the case of the motorhome. Since the problem with Stephen's American Express card earlier in the trip, he had been lending us another card to pay for fuel but what we hadn't realised was that, although his company was paying for the diesel for the motorhomes, they had put a limit on what they would contribute. It seemed that he didn't think this rather important piece of information needed to be shared with the group until we got close to the agreed limit, which we now were. The result of this was that Sara was now using her own card to fill up the motorhome and pay motorway tolls thereby incurring more costs on behalf of the group (she had been paying for food too), which would at some point need to be repaid with everyone making a contribution. This was a conversation which no one seemed to be comfortable having as we already knew that at least two of the group had come along thinking that the whole trip was going to be a freebie. It was a conversation which needed to be had though and before we reached Paris because otherwise it would be all too easy for everyone to go their separate ways and never be seen or heard of again. I made a mental diary note to bring the topic up on the next rest day in four days time, if indeed no one had brought it up before then.

An hour after loading up with shopping and we were driving into Saint Jean de Maurienne, a lovely town situated in the foothills of some stunning mountains. After a quick circuit of the town, we spotted a sign pointing to *'Camping Car Parking – Le Tour.'* This looked promising and indeed it was. Yet another supersized field had been set aside for visitors to the Tour and their motorhomes and of course, it was free. The sun was still blazing so with the motorhome parked up, I set up the folding chairs and we settled down to wait for the others.

I decided it was probably time for my second shave of the trip. The growth on my face had long since passed the designer stubble phase and was now well into the 'feels grubby and horrible' stage, at least for me. I can usually just about tolerate three or four days of growth but anything over that and I just feel dirty. The budget showers and lack of fresh clothes had left me feeling generally grubby anyway and I had therefore managed to put up with a few extra days of face hair but it was time for it to go. As I sat on the motorhome steps hacking away at something which my electric shaver clearly wasn't designed to tackle, it occurred to me that it would be funny, nay hilarious to shave everything off bar a moustache. Sara, Mick and I had long debated the decorative qualities of a moustache or a lip slug as Sara liked to call them. Mick had worn quite a beast of a slug in the eighties and I think, given the choice, he would grow it back in a heartbeat. I'd never gone in for the moustached look but this was too good an opportunity to miss. Even though I was working without a mirror, I did a pretty good job, sufficient to have Sara in stitches when I went back into the motorhome.

'You've GOT to leave it for Mick to see, it's brilliant!' she commented.

Today was the day that Matt's parents were due to arrive and it wasn't long before we got a phone call to say that they were in the town and where could they find us? Directions were given and they were soon parked up behind us, erecting a tent next to the motorhome. As it turned out, as well as Matt's mum and dad, there were another couple who had come along for the ride. My initial thoughts were that we weren't going to be able to cope with looking after another set of bodies but they were quick to point out that they had come with the intention of being fully self-sufficient. A point borne out when I saw the portable cooking stove being removed from the boot of the car and set up in front of the tent. Sara insisted that they eat with the rest of us tonight though, especially given that they may not even be able to stay in the same spots as us going forward. After all, it was fine to pitch a tent in this field but they would have struggled pitching it in the car park that we had stayed in the night before.

Seven and a half hours after leaving Albertville, four exhausted riders climbed into Motorhome Two at the stage finish. It had been a tough day and the four stiff climbs had taken it out of the boys. When I later spoke to Adnan about the ride he told me that for the first time on the trip, the group had separated quite a bit on the climbs, each rider pushing their way to the top at their own pace. They then re-grouped at the top before descending to tackle the next mountain. Temperature had also been an issue – riding up the mountains was swelteringly hot in the sun but it soon changed when they went over the summit and started the descent as the wind chill made it quite cold. You will often see the pro Tour riders being given newspapers at the top of mountains which they stuff down the front of their jerseys as a defence against the wind chill. When my mum saw this happening for the first time on television, she asked me if the newspapers were 'to give them something to read on the way down'. After I stopped laughing she claimed to have been joking but I'm not so sure.

The support team had experienced similar issues with keeping up on the downhills as we had the day before. Hopefully this situation would be greatly improved with the arrival of Matt's family as they could now help with support and work in tandem with the motorhome team. Matt was obviously pleased to see his parents, not least because they had brought his other cycling shoes out. I suspect his foot had been hurting more than he had let on but at least this wouldn't be a problem going forward. It turned out that Matt's dad was also quite the cyclist and had brought his bike so that he could tackle a climb or two. I could see that, at some point in the next few days, we were going to end up with One Day Ahead team members strung out all over the mountains of southern France.

Mick noticed my new facial furniture straight away and was as enthusiastic as Sara for me to continue with the growth of my new sluggy friend for the rest of the trip.

'I'm sure Helen will love it,' he said.

At this point, no one else had seen my creation and then Emily stuck her head in the door to ask something. I answered her question and noticed a quick glance down to my lip then back to my face. She'd seen it but she didn't make any comment. A few minutes later, Adnan came into the motorhome and did the same thing. And that's when the penny dropped that they didn't realise this was a bit of fun and they actually thought that I was going through a bit of an image change. They thought that I thought that my new moustache looked cool. In other words, they thought I was an idiot. Needless to say, after clarifying the situation, the shaver came back out and the lip slug was swiftly despatched. Thank goodness I had enough charge left in the battery.

'I thought it looked alright' said Mick. That should have been enough to tell me that it didn't.

In terms of overnight spots, I think this field in Saint Jean de Maurienne was one of my favourites of the whole trip. It was incredibly scenic, with huge mountains all around. The weather was perfect and it almost felt like we were on holiday. Almost. I was soon back to earth with a bump when Sara handed me the stage profile for the following day. It showed that tomorrow's stage was the longest of the whole Tour at 226 km. There were two cat 1 climbs in the first 80 km alone. It was a good job that we had enjoyed a decent rest today because tomorrow looked like it could be hellish for the boys.

There were 175 riders at the start line for the Tour this morning where, no doubt, they were keen to crack on with the first uncategorised climb of this year's race. Peter Sagan led the first successful escape from the *peloton* at the 2 km point. He was joined by two other riders and at 19 km they had a lead of 20 seconds over the main group. By the 26 km mark, there were just two riders out in front but by the 32 km mark, they had been joined by another twenty-three riders and 18 km later this lead group had an advantage of 4 minutes 30 seconds and were averaging a speed of 49.8 km/h. At 80 km, the group had stretched their lead to 7 minutes and with 70 km to go, Lotto-Belisol had put five riders on the front of the *peloton* to start bringing the breakaway back.

Voeckler and Arashiro led the escape on the early part of the Grand Colombier and the *peloton* reached the foot of this climb 6 minutes behind. For the first 9 km of the 17.4 km ascent, the yellow jersey, Brad Wiggins, accompanied by four Team Sky colleagues, led the race upwards. They failed to catch Voeckler, who took the King of the Mountains points at the top.

Nibali attacked coming down the other side and put Wiggins under more pressure. By the valley floor, Nibali was 55 seconds ahead of Wiggins but was eventually caught on the ascent of the Col de Richemond with about 2 km left to climb. With 15 km of the stage left to go, Wiggins was 3.30 minutes behind the lead group.

Ever-popular Frenchman, Thomas Voeckler, Team Europcar, won the stage and picked up enough points to take the King of the Mountains jersey from Kessiakoff. Wiggins finished in 13th place. Good enough for him to hold on to the yellow jersey for another day.

Tour positions at end of STAGE 10

Stage winner: Thomas Voeckler/Team Europcar

Yellow: Bradley Wiggins/Sky Procycling
Green: Peter Sagan/Liquigas-Cannondale
Polka Dot: Thomas Voeckler/Team Europcar
White: Tejay Van Garderen/BMC Racing Team

STAGE 12

Thursday 12th July 2012
SAINT-JEAN-DE-MAURIENNE - ANNONAY
DAVÉZIEUX
Hilly – 226 km

'Shut up legs; just do what I tell you!'
Jens Voigt - Tour de France rider

When Mark Cavendish was asked to describe today's stage, he remarked that the first half of the stage was 'as close to hell as you can get.' Good job that these words wouldn't be spoken until Cav had completed the stage tomorrow or perhaps our riders would have had reservations about hopping on their bikes. As it was, they weren't aware of Cav's opinion although a quick nose at the stage profile would have been enough to let them know that their lovely little jaunt in the French countryside was well and truly over. I had also noted that Nicole had been remarkably quiet on the 'I want to ride my bicycle, I want to ride my bike' front. It is obviously true what they say about the Tour being sorted out in the mountains.

It was important to get off at a decent hour today, the longest stage of the race with some killer climbs; this was going to be a long day for everyone concerned. Unfortunately things didn't quite go to plan and after plenty of faffing around, the team ended up starting their ride several hours later than planned. I think perhaps the novelty of riding their bikes might have been wearing off now that much of the riding was in an upwards direction. I was coming round to the idea that perhaps I was in the right place in the motorhome and the boys' cycling holiday was beginning to look almost as crap as my motorhoming holiday. One thing which would help to lessen the pressure on the support teams was that we now had some assistance in the form of Matt's parents. It would be far easier for them to tail the boys in a similar manner to the actual Tour de France team cars, keeping them topped up with water and snacks and leaving Sara and me to concentrate on getting to our agreed stop points. When we had originally talked about the logistics of this ride, we had considered taking a moped along with us. This would have given me the option to whizz back and forth to the riders with drink bottles and snacks and might have saved having to haul the motorhome over some of the bigger climbs. In the end we had decided this was a luxury we could do without, but having our own team car was certainly a good alternative. While we battled through 226 km with the boys, Motorhome Two were heading off to pick up Hannah from somewhere, an airport? A train station? I had no idea but she was somewhere close and would be with us until the end of the trip.

The day started with a gentle 20 km downhill ride to the foot of the Col du Grand Cucheron. Another massive mountain. Another hot day. Another army of cyclists and spectators to pick our way through. Whilst I personally could have done without all the spectators and cyclists, they were a source of great motivation to our riding team. The spectators didn't seem to give two hoots who they were cheering for, if you were on a bike, you got cheered. If you were in a team, recognisable by your matching team kit, you got cheered even louder and if you were really lucky, you might even get a free bottle of beer. It did happen, a couple of times in fact. Having experienced this support during my own ride up Alpe d'Huez, I understood how it could help drag you up the stiffest climbs. You are just about ready to fold and chuck your bike down the side of the mountain when a random spectator starts to run alongside you, willing you to keep going. Chances are they aren't even speaking English but you get the gist and you keep pedalling. A few metres up the road, you drop your newly found support team and are ready to pack it in again but don't worry, the next supporter jumps out at you ready to push you up a little bit more. And so it goes on and eventually you find yourself at the top of the mountain. This makes riding up mountains sound a lot easier than it actually is. I probably should have mentioned something about the burning legs, gasping for every breath, lungs on the verge of explosion and general nausea which accompanies you all the way up.

Matt's parents were to trail the boys up the first climb and we were due to meet them at the foot of the second climb, about 60 km into the stage. Having their own support car worked really well. Being much smaller than the motorhome, it was easier for the car to nip through the other traffic on the mountain and pull into small parking spaces to wait for the riders to catch up. The car team were kept busy topping up water bottles and handing out snacks all the way up the mountain. It was about as close to a fully functioning professional cycling team as we were going to get.

At the 60 km mark, the boys pulled in for a brief stop and some food. The temperature was in the mid thirties and I was sweltering just from driving the motorhome. Hauling a bike to the top of not one but three categorised climbs didn't sound like much fun. The riders moved the chairs, which I had set up in the sun, round to the back of the motorhome to the only bit of shade they could find. I pointed out that they were lucky to get a break; it wouldn't happen on the pro Tour. The professionals did their eating on the bike. Each stage has a feeding zone, which is an area where team staff are permitted to hand out food and drink to their riders. This is supplied in a special bag called a *musette*, which is nothing more than a basic cotton bag with a long strap which enables the rider to sling it over their shoulder. The rider takes the bag and without stopping, proceeds to empty the bag, either by eating the contents (sandwiches, fruit, energy bars etc) or by distributing the food throughout his jersey pockets. The musette can then be disposed of, in a similar way to water bottles, for a handily positioned fan to grab and take home as a souvenir. I had suggested that maybe it would be easier for us to chuck a couple of apples in a carrier bag and hand them to our team through the motorhome window as they passed but for some reason, they weren't keen on riding the Tour with this level of authenticity.

Lunch devoured, everyone set off to continue their individual adventure once more. By the time we met up with the boys at the next feed stop, they were all looking decidedly red in the face. They had just conquered the second cat 1 climb of the day, the Col du Granier, although I am not sure that conquered is really the right word. Mick said they had grovelled their way up it and I think his description is probably more accurate, especially given that it was now 4:00 pm and they still had almost 140 km left to cycle. Honestly, what had they been doing all day? In need of some good news, I dug out the stage profile and pointed out that the rest of the day was nearly all downhill, with just a small blip at the end. They probably wouldn't even need to pedal for most of it. This revelation didn't seem to help pick their spirits up and they all seemed to have hit a bit of a psychological low. This was the first time on the trip that they really felt that the One Day Ahead challenge might get the better of them. Well if you think I have driven halfway around France for you lot to give up, you can think again! Sara and I did the only thing we could in the circumstances. We packed up the motorhome and while the boys were considering whether this was the point they pack it all in and load their bikes onto the bike rack, we drove off.

With any endurance event, getting to the end is as much a mental challenge as it is physical. Cycling is no different. First there is the boredom aspect. Doing the same thing over and over again, for days at a time, will eventually drive anyone to distraction. It helps if you have someone along for the ride to chat to and different scenery each day to enjoy (I can't imagine how painfully dull it must be cycling round a track for hours at a time) but sitting on a bike for eight hours a day will soon become tiresome regardless of how strong your legs are. When the physical pain starts to set in, the voices in your head pipe up telling you to stop, you've done enough, it's not worth it, who cares, why are you doing this to yourself, what's the point? At first it is easy to suppress these voices but they start getting louder and louder. Your mates might be able to drag you along for a bit but soon all you can hear is the voice in your head telling you to stop. The real challenge is to smash through that voice and ignore his cries for release from the suffering. Most people are unable or unwilling to do this. Most people are more sensible than to try. Our team all had experience of pushing themselves through the pain barrier and I don't for one minute think that any one of them would have actually given up just because they were feeling a bit fed up. However, just to be on the safe side, I figured the best thing to do was take the option away from them.

With no motorhome to climb into, they had no other choice than to pedal to the finish. Plus of course, driving off and leaving them in such a desperate state was very, very funny.

So with little option but to pick themselves up, dust themselves off and pedal onwards, that's exactly what they did. They covered the next 110 km at an average speed of 35 km/h, helped in no small way by the fact that it was nearly all downhill. Somewhere along the route today they had come across our solo cycling friend, Frode. He was battling with his own voices and was also enjoying a day of extreme suffering. He rode with the One Day Ahead team for a few kilometres but in the end, couldn't keep up with their pace and dropped back. Not for the first time our team wondered whether Frode would manage to complete his challenge alone or if indeed he would even make it to the end of today's stage.

The final cat 3 climb, the Côte d'Ardoix, proved to be, as predicted, a mere blip and they flew up it, arriving at the stage finish somewhere close to 8:00 pm. No one was talking about going home by this time and they had beaten back the mental demons of defeat to get the job done. Our weary cyclists were asleep on the motorhome floor within minutes of leaving the finish town. I would have quite happily dozed off myself but we still had to get to the overnight stop which was 140 km away. When I heard Sara snoring, I realised that I was the only person onboard still awake. It occurred to me that no one had thanked me for my tough love earlier in the day but their satisfied snores were thanks enough. They weren't of course, I would have preferred money.

It was dark and late by the time we reached Saint-Paul-Trois-Chateaux. Motorhome Two had been there for hours and they had managed to find parking places in a car park in the centre of the town. The car park manager had been over to say that we had to be out of the car park by 8:00 am the following morning as it was to be used for official Tour traffic. If the boys were hoping for a lie in, they were going to be sorely disappointed. Matt's parents had left us earlier in the afternoon and after liaising with Motorhome Two, had found a campsite a few kilometres out of town to overnight in. They would catch up with us somewhere along the route the next morning.

After a long and hot day, I had completely forgotten about our new arrival, Hannah, who had now been picked up and was bouncing around our makeshift camp with all the enthusiasm of an excited puppy. I recalled how we had all shared a similar enthusiasm just a week and a half before. Now we were all irritable, short-tempered and grumpy or was that just me? I exchanged some pleasantries with Hannah but all I really wanted to do was go to bed. So that's what I did. It was the first time I had gone to bed before everyone else but the long days were catching up with me and I just needed to sleep. I was vaguely aware of Emily sneaking into the motorhome for her nightly glass of wine but I couldn't tell you how long my roomies stayed up for. I was out like a light.

It seems that the idea of four categorised climbs in one day was enough to put even the pros off today; with several more retirements from the Tour and 174 riders making it to the start line. The retirements included the former yellow jersey, Fabian Cancellara. An early break-away led by Robert Gesink (Rabobank) saw thirty riders off the front of the *peloton*. After a bit of back and forth action, there were twenty eight riders in the lead group at the top of the Col de la Madeleine, with a lead of just under 3 minutes on the main group.

At 79 km, Cadel Evans and a team mate launched an attack on the yellow jersey group and managed to get 20 seconds ahead but were caught within 5 km of starting their attack. At the top of the second HC climb, the *peloton* had reduced the gap between them and the leaders to 2 minutes and 10 seconds.

The final climb saw a handful of attacks and with 6.5 km to go to the summit, Evans was dropped from the yellow jersey group. This would eventually cost him 1 minute and 26 seconds to the overall leader in the GC.

With 10 km to go to the end of the stage, Pierre Rolland of Team Europcar found himself out on his own and he pushed on hard to the end of the stage, which he won. Pinot claimed second place and Froome took third. Wiggins rolled in sixth and continues to hold the yellow jersey position, with his team mate, Froome, 2 minutes and 5 seconds behind him in second place.

After lending the polka dot jersey to Thomas Voeckler for the day, Fredrik Kessiakoff took it back and will wear it again tomorrow.

Tour positions at end of STAGE 11

Stage winner: Pierre Rolland/Team Europcar

Yellow: Bradley Wiggins/Sky Procycling
Green: Peter Sagan/Liquigas-Cannondale
Polka Dot: Fredrik Kessiakoff/Astana Pro Team
White: Tejay Van Garderen/BMC Racing Team

STAGE 13

Friday 13th July 2012
SAINT-PAUL-TROIS-CHÂTEAUX – LE CAP D'AGDE
Flat – 217 km

'It doesn't get any easier, you just go faster.'
Greg LeMond - Tour de France rider

I opened my eyes to the standard glorious sunny day and
Adnan beaming down at me. He was remarkably cheery
for someone who had barely recovered from a day of
hell and who was about to endure yet another one. Mind
you, he did have a bag of Adnan Cakes in his hands
which he was slowly working his way through. That much
sugar is enough to put a smile on anyone's face.

'Frode made it,' he said.

Frode and his driver had turned up in the same car
park late the night before, Frode finishing some hours
after our team and well after the sun had gone down. I
really felt for him, he must have had an awful day and
having to continue cycling after dark wouldn't have been
very enjoyable. I wondered whether he had actually
finished the ride or just done what I would have done
and thrown his bike into the back of their motorhome
with strict instructions to his mate not to tell anyone,
'There's a fifty Euro bonus in it if you just keep shtum.'
Any driver of mine could have doubled his money for
the three weeks with side deals like this.

The main reason, however, for Adnan's smiling face
was that he had just had his morning peek at the Tour
guide and seen today's stage profile which was gloriously
lacking in lumps and bumps. The length (third longest of

the Tour) didn't bother him in the slightest and he laughed heartily at the attempts of the weeny cat 3 to put him off. Today we would leave the Alps far behind us and head south towards the coast, ending up, all being well, at zero metres above sea level in Agde, just west of Montpellier. In theory, the boys should have all been celebrating the fact that they were leaving the mountains at last and I am sure that they would have been except for one thing. With the Alps behind us, the Pyrenees were now directly in front of us and after a brief respite today, the boys would soon be back to riding stage profiles which looked more like the back of a stegosaurus than a cycling route.

I stuck my head out of the motorhome door and the car park was a hive of activity, much of it surrounding Motorhome Two. One cyclist, two cyclists, three cyclists, four cyclists, five cyclists… Mmm, too many cyclists given that Adnan and Mick were still sitting at our breakfast table. Hannah clearly wasn't here to waste any time and she, Nicole and Jess were kitted up and preparing to cycle the stage. I suppose it made more sense than riding one of the mountain stages but once again, zero consideration appeared to have been given to whether Emily was happy doing all the support. I caught Emily's eye and beckoned her over.

'Did they ask if you were okay with them riding?' I asked.

As I suspected, they hadn't but Emily was too polite to make a fuss and didn't want anyone else sticking up for her either as it would only cause arguments. As she rightly pointed out, we only had another seven stages after this one and then we would be done. Seven stages seemed an awful lot at that moment in time but I respected Emily's decision and agreed not to say anything.

There was no sign of any dilly-dallying from the riders today; amazing what a difference a lack of mountains can make and the somewhat expanded group set off at 8:00 am. The two motorhomes left in convoy together, conscious of the time restriction set by the car park manager the previous evening. As we drove out, the blinds in Frode's motorhome were firmly shut and there was no sign of life. I also noted the car park manager standing outside his hut glaring at the two motorhomes and half dozen cars still in parking bays. I suspect Frode was about ten minutes away from an early morning wake up call.

Given that this was a holiday(!) and that so far I hadn't seen the sea (not even on the journey to France since we had taken the train rather than the ferry), I was almost looking forward to spending a day at the coast, especially given the blazing temperatures we were experiencing. I say almost because obviously this wasn't an ordinary holiday; it was in fact, a rubbish holiday and therefore on the only day that the Tour went anywhere near the beaches of the south of France, Sara and I weren't supporting and were tasked with staying inland to drive to tomorrow's start town. To make matters worse, tomorrow's start town was Limoux, which is positioned, according to Jane, exactly 305 km from our current location. The temperature was forecast to reach close to 40° and the old motorhome was severely lacking in the air conditioning department. Mick had explained how the air con worked earlier in the week. There was a choice of two options: you could have full power or half power. Full power involved opening both front windows in the cab, for half power, you just opened one. If we were completing the Tour de Iceland, this solution would have been perfect. We weren't and it wasn't. The only advantage to not supporting this particular stage was that Sara and I could get our driving done by mid-afternoon, whereas the others would have a transfer of around 140 km after they had finished riding. Emily would have already driven 217 km by that time so I hoped that Jess or even one of the boys might offer to share the load a bit although I knew that this was just wishful thinking.

As the temperature crept up in the motorhome it became more and more uncomfortable. It was too noisy to have the windows fully open on the fast roads and anyway being blasted with hot air isn't exactly refreshing. When we stopped for fuel my shorts and t-shirt were clinging to my back and legs, damp with sweat. How long had I been wearing this t-shirt for now? I was beyond caring and comforted myself in the knowledge that everyone else was in the same boat. I spotted an air pump on the opposite side of the forecourt and thought it made sense to check the levels in the tyres. Although the front two tyres were brand new, we had covered a fair distance since they were replaced and I had no idea when the rear tyres were last checked. I'd like to think that Mick had checked them before we left but there was no telling. Mick is actually a superb mechanic and is excellent at looking after other peoples' cars. Unfortunately his and Sara's vehicles sometimes end up being a touch neglected. I moved the motorhome over to the air line and set about removing the dust caps. Even this was exhausting work in the heat. How were the boys managing to cycle in it and more to the point, how were the girls getting on? I stuck the air line onto the first valve and panicked slightly as it started letting air out of the tyre. The compressor was obviously having a bad day too because try as I might, I couldn't get it to do the one thing it was designed for and it appeared happy only to let air out rather than putting it in. The tyres were slightly low but there wasn't much I could do about it here so I replaced the dust caps and got back into the cab. We tried two or three more garages on the way to Limoux and had the same problem at each one, each time letting a bit more air out of the tyre. Mick told me later that some of the European compressors are only designed to pump up to about 40 psi, which is fine for cars but not larger vehicles which need pressures closer to 60 or 70 psi. European motorhomers must have a secret place to pump their tyres up because I never found a pump capable of doing it.

Having given up on the air idea as a bad job, we got back into the sauna and moved to the rear of the petrol station so we could have a bite to eat. We sat behind the motorhome, using it as a shade, and noticed that there were three large washing machines in the car park against the back wall of the cashiers kiosk. In England I would have assumed that they had been dumped but here they looked too clean and neat. Closer inspection revealed that this was actually the French interpretation of a launderette. The machines were all coin-operated and without the restriction of opening hours. 'I'm off to get some petrol darling, oh and I'll do a wash while I'm down there too.' I'm not sure who would normally choose to do their washing at the petrol station but it was certainly a tempting idea for us. Unfortunately lack of time, lack of the right coins and lack of any motivation to try and obtain said coins from the petrol attendant meant that we didn't bother. Nice idea though.

Back on the road and the heat and monotony of driving was enough to send me to sleep. It was in both of our interests that I resisted this urge but Sara nodded off a few times. I didn't notice her rouse from one such cat-nap and almost jumped out of my skin when she exclaimed, 'I'd recognise that bastard anywhere!'

She spat the words out with such venom that I was wracking my brain trying to work out who it was she hated so much.

'Who? Where?' I asked.

Sara was pointing out of her side window, 'There, right there, Mont Ventoux.'

From the random swearing and cursing which followed, I was able to ascertain that if Mont Ventoux had a Facebook page, Sara would not be one of its friends.

The reason for this extreme hatred, of what most people would consider to be a wonder of nature, stemmed from an event some years previously. The event in question involved Mick, Sara, two bikes and of course, Mont Ventoux and it probably doesn't take a genius to work out the gist of what happened.

Mont Ventoux is an epic Tour de France climb. With an elevation of 1912 metres there are three routes to the top on a bicycle. When it comes to the Tour, the chosen route is, as you might expect, the hardest one. Riding south from Bédoin, the route rises 1617 metres over 21.8 km. The first 6 km is easy with a gradient of just 3.9% but then things start to get a bit more interesting. If you say it quickly, it doesn't sound so bad but unfortunately riding it quickly is another matter – 16 km with an average gradient of 8.9%. It is also likely that, during the last few kilometres, you will be battered with strong winds. *Venteux* means windy in French and winds of up to 320 km/h have been recorded at the summit. For much of the year you will find winds of over 90 km/h towards the top of the Ventoux and the road is regularly closed because of these winds. The top of Mont Ventoux is almost lunar in appearance and it all looks rather desolate and depressing to be honest. It is the sort of climb which will push any cyclist to their limit.

Sadly, one of the things Mont Ventoux is best known for is indeed a rider who was pushed to his limit. British Tour rider, Tom Simpson died on the Ventoux whilst competing in the Tour de France in 1967. Simpson famously fell from his bicycle after starting to weave up the road and asked spectators to put him back on his bike. He made it to within a kilometre of the summit before collapsing and dying from heat exhaustion caused by several factors including dehydration, amphetamines and alcohol. There is a memorial to Tom Simpson near the top of the mountain and to this day, cyclists will leave tokens of remembrance there such as water bottles and other cycling-related items.

The Ventoux is a vicious climb but for some reason Sara was persuaded by Mick to have a crack at it. She tells the story far better than I can but the basics are that they both cycled from their motorhome at the top of the mountain, down to Bédoin. They then both started the ride back up. Mick got bored riding 'so slowly' (sound familiar?) and picked up his pace, leaving Sara struggling along in the rising temperature which ultimately got up to around 40 degrees. Sara didn't see Mick again until she arrived back at the motorhome. It took her all day to cycle up the Ventoux. Mick tells me that she did look a bit 'red in the face' when she eventually made it. I bet she did! Mick then found himself on the receiving end of, in his words, a bit of an outburst and a gross overreaction, before saying to Sara, 'What took you so long? I could've ridden up faster on my Chopper.'

I could see why she had such strong feelings about the Ventoux and I suspect that Mick wasn't far behind on that same list.

This was the point at which the idea for the 'Chopper Challenge' was first mooted. Although Mick had ridden up Alpe d'Huez the previous year on his Mk I Raleigh Chopper, it was the Ventoux where the idea was first formulated. Sara suggested that maybe Mick should put his money where his mouth was and actually try to haul himself up a mountain or two on the birthday present he received when he was 10 years old. Never being one to shy away from a challenge, Mick happily accepted.

'How hard can it be?' he asked, 'It's only a bit of pedalling after all.'

Anyone who was around in the seventies will know that the Raleigh Chopper was the bike to have. Looking back this is strange because it was completely impractical but, and this is the reason it was such a success, it looked really cool. A big wheel at the back, a small one at the front, a long banana seat (complete with warning label telling you that it wasn't safe for two people – yeah right) and long, upright handlebars. These handlebars were particularly dangerous as they were bolted to the top of the steering stem and because they were so long, any amount of force on the bars would cause them to move. Mick kindly demonstrated this for us in his garden during a test ride. He bounced down a couple of steps and as his weight moved forward so did the handlebars, collapsing over the front wheel. Mick disappeared over the top but jumped up a second later exclaiming, 'It's a good job I know how to fall!'

The most lethal part of a Chopper (for a 10 year old boy at least) was the gear knob. It was possibly the coolest part of the bike, it looked like a car gear stick and was positioned on the top tube. This was a perfect location to catch any unsuspecting youngster right between the legs if he had to stop suddenly or if he just slipped off the saddle (or if his handlebars collapsed).

Fortunately for Raleigh however, the Chopper was offered for sale long before anyone was bothered about health and safety so none of these issues were of any great concern.

Raleigh had made a cool bike but they hadn't made a bike which was easy (or even safe) to ride and the Mk I version was the worst of the lot. As well as the design issues above, it suffered from speed wobbles and was also prone to the odd inadvertent wheelie. The press branded it a dangerous toy. Overall the Chopper was difficult to ride, heavy and certainly not designed for long distance travel. Even if you could ride it, you risked having your undercarriage removed by the groin-cracking gear lever at any moment. The last thing it was designed for was completing mountain stages of the Tour de France.

We allowed Mick some flexibility to bring his Chopper up to date. He would be allowed to weld the handlebars to the steering stem purely for safety and he would be allowed to fit slightly longer pedal cranks and clipless pedals. Everything else on the bike had to be standard. I offered a small contribution of clipping a playing card to the frame with a clothes peg so that it flicked in the spokes as the wheel rotated making the bike sound like it had an engine. Well at least that's what it used to sound like when I was ten. In my forties it sounded like a playing card being flicked by the spokes of a bike wheel.

There is some video knocking around somewhere of Mick riding up Alpe d'Huez on his Chopper and it really is a sight to behold. Here we had this 50 year old, grey-haired man, on a bike which was nearly as old, racing up a mountain and overtaking people half his age on carbon road bikes. Two years later, Mick tackled the Ventoux, the mountain which had taken Sara all day to ascend. Mick rode up on the Chopper (or his mountain bike, as he was now calling it) in a smidge over two hours, again passing many carbon bikes on the way. He also managed to get himself on TV as he was just about to start his ride when Chris Boardman and Ned Boulting (ITV4) were starting the same ascent. Boardman is heard to shout, 'Man on a Chopper!' as Mick passes by behind him.

They should have filmed Mick ascending, it would have been more interesting than watching people ride up on modern bikes, although if Mick had used up his words for the day the conversation may have been lacking.

Mick's efforts on his Chopper on Mont Ventoux and Alpe d'Huez served to illustrate the point that it was possible to scale these monsters with limited gearing. The early Tour riders didn't have the luxury of gears and Henri Desgrange didn't allow derailleur gearing to be used until 1937, arguing that surely it was better to triumph by the strength of muscles than the artifice of a derailleur? Desgrange was of the opinion that variable gears were only for those aged over 45 years – Mick would have been fine then!

Fortunately for everyone concerned, the Ventoux wasn't included in this year's Tour so the closest we got to it was seeing it in the distance as we passed by. Even from 20 or 30 km away it looked pretty formidable and I made a mental note not to get sucked into riding up this beast of a mountain at any point in the future.

With Mont Ventoux decreasing in size in the motor-home wing mirrors, Sara and I pushed on to Limoux and found a rather handy car park with a few motorhome spaces right in the centre of town. It was early evening and quite hot and muggy so we sat outside and got stuck into a bottle of wine while we waited for Motorhome Two to join us, which they did a couple of hours later. The boys had enjoyed a good ride, although with the transfer at the end, it had been a long day. It had definitely been a much-needed break from the climbs of the previous few days but the lads had suffered a bit with strong headwinds and blistering heat.

While Sara started to make the dinner, Adnan suggested we wander down to a nearby bar for a drink. I'd probably had quite enough already but to my alcohol-fuddled brain, it seemed like a good idea. We found a typical French bar, crowded with locals and ordered a couple of beers. Adnan told me once again how much he was enjoying the trip and said how grateful he was to everyone who was supporting him. Having the assistance of the support teams meant he and the other riders could concentrate purely on cycling and not worry about where the next meal was coming from or where they would sleep for the night. I was glad that Adnan was having a good time, he is a great guy and I was enjoying his company. However, this didn't change the fact that I wasn't enjoying my own Tour de France experience and I couldn't wait to get home. After a couple of beers, we strolled back to the motorhome to find dinner was ready.

At some point that evening, after another drink or two, my brain decided that now would be the best time to let the group know how much fun I wasn't having. I think it came as a bit of a surprise to them (well not Sara but everyone else). It came as a bit of a surprise to me. I can remember sitting in a folding chair listing everything I hated about the whole event, driving, cooking, washing, finding water, emptying the toilet, looking for overnight stops, going round the supermarkets, filling up with diesel. It was quite a rant.

Stephen stepped in, 'C'mon Rich, it's not all bad, there must be some bits you are enjoying?'

There weren't, Sara was right, it was shit.

I then decided to phone Helen and let her have both barrels too. Good old alcohol! Poor Helen had had a minor version of today's moan every evening since we left so I imagine she was getting pretty sick of it. The real giveaway to this was when, fed up with listening to me whinging, she hung up on me.

I sloped back to the group, 'Helen hung up on me,' I informed them.

No one else spoke. I think they were probably scared of what it might provoke. Someone suggested I went to bed, I'd feel better in the morning. They were probably right so I did. Alcohol is very good at exaggerating whatever feelings you are experiencing. When we had arrived in Limoux, I hadn't felt that bad, a bit tired and irritable maybe but certainly not on the verge of a meltdown. Note to self, try drinking less.

More retirements meant that 166 riders signed on for the longest stage of the 2012 Tour de France. The *peloton* started strongly and there were no successful breakaways until 15 km when nineteen riders escaped. By the 45 km point, the lead group contained eleven riders who were 45 seconds ahead of a second group. The main *peloton* was 1 minute 35 seconds back. By the foot of the second climb, the leaders were 2 minutes and 35 seconds ahead of the *peloton* and some attacks and a bit of tooing and froing were seen. After 120 km, there were five men in the lead with an advantage of 4 minutes over the main group and by 50 km they had increased this lead to almost 13 minutes.

The lead riders worked well together until the 5 km mark when they started to think about the individual opportunity of a stage win. The stage ended with David Millar being forced to lead out Jean-Christophe Peraud. Peraud started his sprint with 250 metres to go but Millar kept pace with him and crossed the line first to win his fourth Tour stage.

Bradley Wiggins finished in 12th place and maintains his hold on the yellow jersey. There were no other jersey changes today.

Tour positions at end of STAGE 12

Stage winner: David Millar/Garmin-Sharp

Yellow: Bradley Wiggins/Sky Procycling
Green: Peter Sagan/Liquigas-Cannondale
Polka Dot: Fredrik Kessiakoff/Astana Pro Team
White: Tejay Van Garderen/BMC Racing Team

STAGE 14
Saturday 14th July 2012
LIMOUX – FOIX
Mountain – 191 km

'Skin and bone heal for nothing. Carbon fibre costs money.'
Mick – One Day Ahead team

Amazing what a good night's sleep can do for your state of mind. I awoke feeling much better than I deserved to and far more positive. A quick text to Helen to apologise for whatever I had said the night before which had caused her to hang up and I was firing on all cylinders. I might not have had the best time over the last couple of weeks but the team were now over two thirds of the way to achieving something pretty amazing both in terms of the cycling achievement and the money raised for the charities we were supporting. I needed to get my head around the fact that this was going to be one of those situations where you don't actually enjoy the event until you get home and start talking about it. A bit like the Tour de France I imagine – three weeks of pain and suffering but if you get a finisher's medal at the end of it, you have a story you can tell for the rest of your life.

Things could also have been a lot worse. Looking back, the whole trip had gone very smoothly and the riders hadn't suffered any major problems whatsoever. Matt and Stephen's accident in the first week was now forgotten, Matt had new shoes so his feet were fine and between them the boys had only fallen victim to about three punctures so far in over 2,000 km. Remarkable really, I was expecting crashes, punctures and other mechanicals on a daily basis. There had been far more problems to resolve with the motorhomes, what with getting Motorhome Two stuck in the mud on the first night and our dodgy tyre situation. Quite the opposite of what I would have predicted. Travelling by bicycle is obviously the way to go. Our luck had to take a turn for the worse at some point I guess and today, when I was feeling almost upbeat, was as good a day as any.

The weather had turned distinctly wet during the night and the forecast for the day wasn't great with more rain and strong winds forecast. As if the poor weather outlook wasn't enough to contend with, the riders would also be back in the mountains as they were about to start their assault on the Pyrenees. 191 km to cover today, starting with a category 2 climb to warm up, followed by a couple of cat 1s to finish things off. On a lighter note, the last 40 km of today's stage was downhill.

No one was in a particular rush to get going and I don't blame them. It was pouring with rain and the type of day you would normally decide definitely wasn't for cycling. Unless of course you were a Tour rider, in which case, you wouldn't have had a choice. After delaying their start for as long as they could, the boys came to the conclusion that the weather wasn't showing any signs of improvement and they may as well just get on with it. Sitting in the motorhome wouldn't get them to Foix and it was only a bit of rain after all – men or mice? They looked a sorry sight as they donned wet weather gear and free-wheeled out of the car park. Another day on which I was grateful to be driving the motorhome and not cycling.

Matt's parents were still around and providing additional support to the team so Sara and I had agreed to meet up with the boys before they started the first category 1 climb, about 80 km into the ride. By the time they arrived at our meeting point, it was clear that the day wasn't progressing well and the rain was having a detrimental effect on morale. I think it was only the second time that the boys had to sit inside the motor-home to eat their lunch rather than outside. We had done well with the weather in the main and only suffered a couple of really miserable days the whole trip, today and the day in Belgium with the rain and strong head-winds. I suspect if there had been three or four days in a row like this, we might have been on the train home somewhat sooner than anticipated. We agreed a meeting place at the foot of the second mountain, which was approximately 60 km away, and threw the boys back out into the rain. I shouted some words of support along the lines of, 'If it was easy, we'd all be doing it!' as they pedalled off. I think they appreciated it.

To get to our next meeting point, Sara and I had no choice but to go into the mountains ourselves. Where possible we would avoid going over the bigger climbs and skirt round the bottom but this wasn't an option today. As we climbed higher and higher, we found the conditions were getting steadily worse. Visibility was very poor due to fog and mist and it was also quite breezy. The rain was on and off but all in all it made for a very unpleasant experience. The roads in this part of the Pyrenees were also not ideal for a large motorhome. They were narrow with plenty of tight bends, many hairpins and substantial drops to the sides. The French seemed to think that dotting the odd concrete block along the side of the road was enough to stop you driving off the edge. These blocks were only about a metre high and I suspect that if I had driven into one, we would have nudged the block over the side and swiftly followed it down the huge drop it was trying to protect us from.

When we got to the vicinity of our meeting point, it was clear that finding somewhere to park up was going to be a challenge in itself. By this time, we were miles from anywhere, right out in the sticks, on a small mountain road which barely had passing room for two vehicles, never mind parking places. Every now and then we would pass a tiny house or shack built onto the side of the mountain. We wondered who would choose to live in such a remote location, a location which was probably cut off from the outside world by snow for many months of the year. Even during the summer the occupants would be many kilometres from the nearest village. It seemed a remote and extreme place for anyone to decide to live.

We were still trying to find somewhere to pull over when Sara's phone started ringing. My first thought was, 'Wow, we are in the middle of nowhere but there is still phone reception!' It was Mick calling to tell us that Adnan and Stephen had crashed and they needed rescuing as Adnan had broken a wheel. This wasn't good news, not least because we knew that Adnan would be fuming if the crash was Stephen's fault. He had already told us that he hadn't been overly impressed with Stephen's cycling and I had seen it first hand when I rode the time trial stage. The team had now suffered two crashes since they started their challenge and the common denominator was Stephen. The boys were only a few kilometres away from where we were so we started to head in their direction. Shortly afterwards, Mick phoned back to say that they had managed to borrow a wheel and would meet us at the bottom of the first cat 1 climb. This was only a kilometre away and as luck would have it, there was a tiny little hamlet at the foot of the mountain with a small area of wasteland at the side of the road, just big enough to park a motorhome.

Mick had told us that Adnan and Stephen hadn't injured themselves, which was obviously very good news. However it was a concern that Adnan's wheel was damaged. We had some spares onboard but nothing of the standard of Adnan's bike, which was brand new, purchased specially for this trip and mostly carbon fibre. I wasn't sure if the wheels were carbon but if they were, they would have been expensive and I suspected that Adnan wouldn't have his smiley face on when he got back to the motorhome.

Adnan was the first to arrive back at the motorhome having stormed down the mountain in what I assume is as close to rage as Adnan gets (i.e. not very 'ragey' at all). He was well ahead of the others which gave him a few minutes to tell us what had happened. He and Stephen had been riding next to each other, behind Mick and Matt. Matt, who was in front of Stephen, had stood up out of his saddle resulting in a momentary slowing of speed. Stephen's front wheel very nearly clipped Matt's rear wheel and Stephen panicked and unclipped his foot from his pedal. As Stephen tried to put his foot down he omitted to take into account the fact that Adnan was riding next to him and before making it to the floor, his foot hit Adnan's bike. Result? They both ended up on the ground. At that point, no damage had been done but unfortunately another rider, who was nothing to do with our group, took it upon himself to cycle over Adnan's wheel. He then cycled off. Adnan was fairly forgiving of this chap, explaining, 'It wasn't really his fault, he had the choice of riding over either a wheel or me - both of us were lying in the road and in his way.'

I asked Adnan if he was lying in the road because he was tired and fancied a little nap. I think I saw the slightest twitch of a smile but I can't be sure.

The whole incident had, understandably, annoyed

Adnan considerably. What was irritating him the most was that Stephen wasn't accepting any responsibility for the crash and hadn't offered an apology, which Adnan felt he was owed. Adnan also confirmed that his wheel was carbon and it was completely ruined. Cost of a replacement wheel? £600. I had whole bikes worth less than this. Adnan had been lucky in one respect as a team of Belgian riders, who were also riding the Tour route, passed by shortly after the accident. Our boys had seen this team previously and had chatted to them during other stages. These riders had full mechanical support cars with them, including a selection of spare wheels. Stephen had therefore asked if they would lend Adnan a wheel so that he could at least get back to our motorhome. The team put it to a vote within their group and all the riders bar one agreed to lend Adnan a wheel. I'm not sure what the problem was with the one miserable sod who wanted to leave Adnan at the top of a mountain in the pouring rain but fortunately he was out-voted. Adnan said he looked really grumpy and put out when they swapped one of their shiny new wheels for Adnan's bent one. I suspect he would have been even more upset when, later in the day, the rest of his team agreed that Adnan could hang on to the replacement wheel until the end of the Tour as long as he promised to return it to them in Paris.

Mick, Matt and Stephen soon joined us at the motorhome and I filled up their water bottles for the umpteenth time while they tucked into sandwiches and cakes. The weather at the top of the last climb had been appalling and although it wasn't that cold in the foothills of the mountain, it had been absolutely freezing on the descent. It was also fairly hairy as the roads were very greasy from the rain. I thought of those large drops at the side of the road and could see how easy it would be for someone to misjudge a corner or skid and suddenly find they were careering over the edge. It doesn't bear thinking about.

One more category 1 to get over and then a nice free-wheel all the way home (if the stage profile was to be believed, which I suspect it wasn't). The team were confident that they could get to the end of the stage without further support from Sara and me so we updated Jane with our destination of Foix and turned the motor-home around. The fastest route was actually for us to go over the same climb as our cyclists were riding, the Mur de Péguère. The alternative was a diversion which would take us many kilometres out of our way. As we reached the turn off for the Mur de Péguère, the traffic ahead of us started to slow down and back up. Ahead we could see a police car and several officers talking to the drivers. Next we noticed the large '*Rue Barrée*' sign in front of the turning we wanted to take. We had only driven past the road half an hour ago and it was open then but the police had now decided that the mountain was too busy with motorhome traffic and had closed the road. Mick later informed me that the road got very narrow towards the top and any available parking spaces had already been claimed. There were also large numbers of cyclists attempting the climb and the narrow roads meant there was nowhere for vehicles to overtake so it was easier just to shut the road down. They were still letting cyclists through though so our guys were fine and it was only Sara and me who had to take the detour.

The Mur de Péguère is one of those climbs which, when you glance quickly at the stage profile, doesn't look too bad, 9.3 km with an average gradient of 7.9%. Then you look a bit more closely and see that the gradient is between 16% and 18% for the last 3 km of the climb. When I realised this later on in the evening, I was glad that we had been diverted as it would have been most embarrassing struggling up the mountain in first gear while all the lycra boys were overtaking us.

If the One Day Ahead riders thought they had suffered a bad day in the mountains, the professional riders didn't have a much better time when they tackled this stage the next day. When the riders made it to the Mur de Péguère they discovered that someone had scattered tacks across the road. This led to about thirty punctures in the *peloton* but in true Tour tradition, no one gained any time as the riders followed the unwritten rule which states that the Tour is won by legs alone and not by gaining an unfair advantage over a competitor. This gentleman's agreement can seem odd when compared to other sports but it is something which is very much a part of the modern Tour de France. It would be most unusual for the holder of the yellow jersey to be attacked by a challenger if he had an accident or a mechanical problem with his bicycle and although the *peloton* wouldn't actually stop, it would be completely normal for them to slow down to such a pace that it would make it easy for the race leader to catch them again once the problem was resolved.

During Stage 15 of the 2010 Tour, yellow jersey holder, Andy Schleck was battling up the final climb of the day against one of the main contenders for the jersey, Alberto Contador. 3 km before the pair reached the summit, Schleck's chain slipped and jammed in his back wheel and Contador took the opportunity to attack and sped off up the mountain. The result of this was that Schleck lost 30 seconds to Contador on this stage as well as the yellow jersey. The backlash was prompt. Schleck hit out at Contador for not showing 'fair play' and Contador was on the receiving end of boos from the crowd when he donned the *maillot jaune* at the presentation ceremony at the end of the stage, as well as criticism from other riders both past and present. Later that evening, Contador released a video recording via YouTube to apologise for taking time off Schleck in this manner, stating that he was unaware that there had been a problem with Schleck's chain when he started his attack. Contador went on to win the General Classification of the 2010 Tour by just 39 seconds over Schleck, although he was later disqualified and stripped of this title after providing a urine sample which tested positive for a banned substance. Contador blamed food contamination but it was to no avail and Schleck now holds the title of 2010 Tour de France winner.

Mind you, a few tacks on the road and a bit of unfair play would have been the least of the riders' worries had they been competing in the early Tours. Tales of itching powder in the cyclists' shorts, spiked drinks and sabotaged bicycles, as well as nails and glass thrown in the road were commonplace. In the 1904 Tour on the slopes of the Col de la République, fans of local rider, Antoine Faure, set up a road block and set about the other riders with cudgels whilst allowing Faure to speed off up the road. During the same Tour, fans blocked the road with trees on one stage in an attempt to slow down rival riders and Maurice Garin and Lucien Pothier were chased by fans in a car for 6 km as they tried to run them off the road!

Underhand tactics such as these weren't restricted to the 1904 Tour. In 1910, Gustave Garrigou found that his bike had been tampered with when the hub fell off and all the ball bearings fell out. A year later, Garrigou won the Tour but suffered death threats along the way due to the fact that a fellow competitor, Paul Duboc, was poisoned and Duboc's fans claimed Garrigou was responsible. In 1937 Roger Lapébie discovered that some devious character had sawn through his handlebars. Riding the Tour de France is indeed an occupation fraught with danger.

Fortunately our boys suffered no such sabotage and went on to complete the day's cycling with no further mishaps, steaming up to the finish line like a train. Matt was in front on The Gate with Mick sitting just behind him. Mick told me later that the speed Matt had managed to attain on his massive bike was incredible and it was like 'sitting behind a motorbike.' We loaded the bikes and boys onto and into the motorhome and we were just about to set off when Mick noticed a public toilet and decided he would pay a quick visit. He had removed his cycling shoes and replaced them with sandals but didn't bother to take his socks off. To complete his look, he was still wearing his lycra cycling shorts plus a rather fetching 'Raleigh' cycling top. Retro tops were all the rage but I had to laugh when Sara watched him plodding across the car park and said, with a mix of disgust and shame in her voice, 'Look at him thinking he's cool and trendy in his retro cycling top. It's not retro, it's just really old. He's had it since the 1970s!' It was for good reason that Mick's CB handle was 'Fashion Victim.'

With Mick back on board and no doubt wondering why everyone was suddenly laughing at the top he had been wearing all day, we headed towards Samatan, which would be our start town for the next day's stage. It was late when we arrived and it was getting dark. We met up with the girls in the other motorhome and they explained that there didn't seem to be many options in terms of parking for the night but that they had found somewhere which seemed suitable on a small industrial estate. They directed us to the spot and we tucked the motorhomes behind a large factory unit.

While we were eating a rather late dinner, Jess pondered, 'I wonder what they do in the factory?'

I replied that I suspected that they made foie gras.

'Really? What makes you think that?'

'Er, the massive sign above your head which says, Foie Gras Factory?'

It seemed a reasonable assumption.

Another difficult day ticked off and as I climbed into my bunk I realised that we were now only a day away from the second and final official rest day and two days after that, we would start to head north on our way to Paris.

The pro Tour started their stage this morning at St-Paul-Trois-Chateaux and by 15 km an eight man breakaway had formed. The lead group extended their advantage and by the 35 km mark they had gained 9 minutes 20 seconds over the *peloton*. The average speed of the race for the first hour was 41.8 km/h.

Eventually the Orica Greenedge team decided to reel the escapees back in and by the intermediate sprint stage at 126.5 km the gap was down to 3 minutes 40 seconds.

With 36 km to go, the team of BMC moved to the front of the *peloton* and caused a split in the group but all of the main GC contenders managed to hold on to the front group. By the 10 km to go point there were just two riders out in front, with a lead of only 25 seconds on the yellow jersey group. These two were caught with 2.5 km left to race.

Despite an attempt by the Team Sky train to bring a rider across the line first, they weren't able to match the pace of André Greipel and Peter Sagan, who fought each other for the win right up to the line. Greipel claimed the stage with a last minute lunge to the line.

No changes to the jersey wearers today but the pros will be back in the mountains tomorrow so watch this space…

Tour positions at end of STAGE 13

Stage winner: André Greipel/Lotto-Belisol

Yellow: Bradley Wiggins/Sky Procycling
Green: Peter Sagan/Liquigas-Cannondale
Polka Dot: Fredrik Kessiakoff/Astana Pro Team
White: Tejay Van Garderen/BMC Racing Team

STAGE 15
Sunday 15th July 2012
SAMATAN – PAU
Flat – 158.5 km

'The world lies right beyond the handlebars of any bicycle.'
Daniel Behrman – Author

Our quiet spot behind the factory was quite noisy when the first rays of sun peaked through the motorhome window. I pushed up the blind to see that we appeared to be parked at the edge of a car park for the weekly market. No one seemed to be bothered in the slightest by our presence though and we weren't in anyone's way so if they weren't worried, I didn't see why we should be.

Sara and Mick were already awake and I sat up, banging my head on the underside of Adnan's bunk bed (again), which woke him too. While we were sitting having breakfast, we spotted a couple of men, who I guessed were in their sixties, come out of the rear door of the foie gras factory. They were on a cigarette break and had been standing chatting for a few minutes when it became obvious that something had caught their eye. I couldn't see what they were looking at from my seat in the motorhome, but they were getting very animated and excited about whatever they had spotted. I stood up to look out of the side window and then it all became clear. Jess was outside in some rather short shorts and was bending over doing something to one of the bikes. This explained the gesturing from these old boys and I didn't need to be fluent in French to understand what they were saying. All four of us sat and watched as they carried out various mimes to Jess' rear; they were completely unaware that we could see them. After a minute or two, I thought we should add a new dimension to the show so I hooted the motorhome horn and waved at the two chaps. Jess was also alerted to their presence but rather than take this as their cue to hurry back into the factory, they continued with their demonstration whilst giving Jess and the rest of us a thumbs up. In the end it was Jess who didn't know where to look and she who hurried back into the motorhome. Once their entertainment had vanished and with cigarettes finished and stubs deposited on the floor, the chaps disappeared back into the factory, no doubt to take out their frustrations on some poor goose.

The stage today looked to be relatively unchallenging. According to our Tour bible, it was flat and only 158.5 km. No problem, should have it done by lunch then. Further investigation revealed that there were a couple of category 4 climbs and one category 3 but hardly anything to be worried about. Motorhome Two was tasked with providing support today along with assistance from Matt's parents. Sara and I had the normal rest day jobs of filling up with water, diesel and food, sorting out the toilet cassettes and finding somewhere to stay for the night. As the following day was an official rest day (i.e. an actual day of rest rather than a day of rest which involves doing nearly as much work as a non-rest day), we had all decided it would make sense to try and book into a campsite for a couple of nights. Today's stage finished in Pau and this was also the start town for the stage after the rest day. It was possible that there might be somewhere in Pau for motorhomes to park up but if not, we would try and find a local campsite.

Motorhome Two got another bashing this morning as it was leaving our camp. The foie gras factory had a low roofline which partially stuck out across the road. I am guessing that this had been hit on numerous occasions in the past as there was a metal warning sign hanging from the roof on a pair of chains. Emily, for whatever reason, didn't see the warning sign but fortunately the motorhome was low enough to fit under the eaves of the roof. Unfortunately it wasn't low enough to fit under the warning sign itself and it made one hell of a noise when she clumped it. I thought for a moment that she wasn't going to stop, perhaps figuring that it might be best to just push on through but the flurry of French traders from the market who jumped out in front of her gabbling away and pointing at the top of the motorhome seemed to do the trick. Emily reversed up and drove round the sign without even bothering to inspect the damage. I imagine she was too embarrassed and just wanted to get away from the scene of the crime. A later inspection revealed no major damage to the roof of the motorhome, just a couple of light scratches. A few more inches and it would have been a different story as it would have been the factory roof which was struck and not a movable sign.

With the riders and support motorhome on their way, Sara decided to try and get some of the washing dry before we set off. The sun was out and it made sense to take advantage of it. I went off to explore and found that at the end of the road there was a small campsite. The toilet block and motorhome service point were right next to the entrance and it was too handy to pass by. While Sara sorted out the washing, I made a few trips with the portable water container and also emptied the toilet cassettes. Given our new found water supply and the fact that we had time to spare, it seemed only right that we treat ourselves to a luxury shower each. While I was on my third or fourth cup of tea and while Sara was in the shower, I had a minor panic whilst trying to set the sat nav for the day's journey. Jane was temperamental at best and today was not going to be the exception. For some reason Jane would not locate any satellites and was apparently completely unaware of where she was or what she was doing. Being an expert in modern technology, I carried out all the normal fixes for this type of problem, i.e. turning Jane off and on again and then repeating the same thing five or six times just to make sure but without any luck. It seemed that as fast as we dealt with one job, another was swiftly dropped into our laps. I told Sara the great news that we would now be spending the day trying to buy a sat nav from somewhere. We did have maps with us but they weren't detailed enough to follow the Tour route on and a sat nav was a basic essential. More expense and more hassle.

Before we left Samatan, I thought it would be funny to put Adnan's broken wheel into one of the factory bins and send him a photo of it, explaining that I had managed to get rid of it. I was right, it was very funny but unfortunately Adnan didn't think so.

I started up the motorhome and drove down the side of the factory towards the main road. As we passed the low roofline, several traders from the market jumped out in a panic shouting and pointing. I was nowhere near either the roof or the sign but they weren't taking any chances. The two smoking factory workers popped out for another cigarette as we passed the end of the factory and they waved goodbye. What a lot of good we were doing, raising money for charity and even finding time to brighten up the day of a couple of excitable old Frenchmen.

A few kilometres down the road while we were trying to work out the best place to find an electronics store, Jane suddenly burst into life. I pulled over and picked her up. Everything seemed to be back to normal and working fine. Looks as though Jane was just having a moment or wanted a lie in but whatever, she was now back to her normal self and seemed more than capable of continuing to lead us around France.

Pau was a couple of hours drive away and as we got closer to the town, we started spotting signs for 'L'Étape du Tour' (Stage of the Tour). Every year there is an organised event which gives amateur cyclists the opportunity to ride one of the stages of that year's Tour de France route. The Étape attracts over 10,000 riders and will usually cover one of the mountain stages in either the Pyrenees or the Alps. The event is run as a race although most entrants would be aiming just to finish. Finishing an Étape is a great achievement and for many amateur riders it will be the high point of their cycling 'career.' Not quite as impressive as attempting the whole Tour of course but impressive nonetheless.

As we drove into Pau, it began to look as though this year's Étape was starting in the town. This could be good for us because there was a possibility that the organisers may have arranged parking for the entrants and any motorhomes which they might bring along. It wasn't long before Sara spotted a sign directing motorhomes to a parking area. That'll do just fine thank you very much. The sign also told us that the Étape had been held the previous day. This wasn't necessarily a problem as the parking area might still be open in case people wanted to stay on and wait for the actual Tour to arrive. We followed the signs into a small industrial estate and immediately saw some motorhomes and caravans up ahead but something didn't look right. I think it was the dogs, children and two scrap cars which told us that this might not be the type of tourists we wanted to overnight with. A man wearing standard issue grey trousers and braces over a white string vest stood up and pointed further up the road. Clearly we weren't welcome here then. A short distance up the road there was a large open space which contained several piles of full bin bags. There were a couple of standpipes in the centre of the space and a motorhome sign nailed to the fence. This was obviously what had been the *Étape* motorhome parking area but it wasn't looking particularly welcoming now and we decided we could find somewhere better.

There were actually two *Étape* events run in 2012. The first covered the route of Stage 11 in the Alps and the second, Stage 16 starting from Pau. This was the stage that our team would tackle in two days time and it was going to be particularly tough. Only 60% of entrants finished the race within the official cut-off time. These riders only had to ride one stage and almost half didn't manage it. This does help to put the efforts of the One Day Ahead team into perspective.

In the centre of Pau we found a large car park which was big enough for several hundred cars. We had discussed the possibility of going to a restaurant to eat this evening as we weren't going to have an early start the next day and this car park was ideally located for such an excursion. There were already half a dozen motorhomes parked up so we decided to join them. It didn't take too long before we noticed the ITV4 lorry on the other side of the car park and this was our first clue that perhaps we weren't going to be able to stay there. It was possible (and given the ITV4 lorry, likely) that this parking area was going to be used for the Tour traffic. If that were the case, we could expect to be moved on at some point that evening. Climbing out of the motorhome I spotted a yellow sign on a lamp post and when I looked properly, I saw that nearly every lamp post had a similar yellow sign. The signs were to inform the public that the car park would be closed from midnight that night as it was indeed going to be used for the Tour traffic. Had we consulted the Tour Guide, we would have realised that the stage finish was on the road which ran alongside the car park. There was definitely no way we were going to be able to stay here but in terms of somewhere to wait for the boys and Motorhome Two, it was ideal.

Sara had spoken to Nicole and the boys were getting on fine, no more problems or crashes today. They expected to be with us within an hour. This gave us some time to arrange somewhere to park for the next two nights. It was unlikely that we would find anywhere to park in the town of Pau itself so I pulled down one of the campsite books from a shelf above the dining table and started to look at local sites. There was one about 5 km from the town which looked as good as any so Sara called them to see if they could accommodate us. The owner answered and confirmed that he would be glad to put us up for a couple of nights and advised us that the cost would be twenty Euros per motorhome. The site also accepted tents which meant that Matt's parents could stay at the same place.

Early in the first week of our trip, the boys had met a reporter who worked for a French television channel. He was reporting on the Tour and they got talking and explained what they were up to. Our story obviously grabbed the reporter's interest and he said he would like to do a small piece about the boys and their Tour attempt. Telephone numbers had been exchanged and the two parties had tried to meet up several times but the logistics of us being one day ahead of where the reporter needed to be had meant that, so far, nothing had worked out. Our team were due to meet with the reporter on the day of Adnan and Stephen's crash but he had been held up when the final mountain of the day was closed and so in the end, he ran out of time.

We were still hoping that something could be done before we reached Paris but in the meantime, Sara had an idea. She decided to go and knock on the door of the ITV4 lorry to see if she could speak to anyone from this British television company. ITV4 provides live coverage of the Tour de France and it would be fantastic for our charities and sponsors if they were prepared to give us a brief mention. Sara went over to the lorry while I sat in the motorhome watching. I was half expecting her to get shouted at by some grumpy English lorry driver who was having as good a time as I was and whom Sara had just woken from his afternoon nap. As it was, no one was home but not being one to be beaten at the first hurdle, Sara left a note on the windscreen of the lorry. This in itself was quite amusing. Sara is five foot nothing and watching her jumping up to try and reach the windscreen wipers of this huge truck was most entertaining.

Shortly afterwards, the rest of the team arrived. As today's stage was comparatively short and without too many lumps and bumps, the riders had finished relatively early. Adnan started to tell me that it had been a tough ride and something about a 50 km/h headwind but I must have glazed over because he didn't push the topic. It wasn't that I didn't care, I was simply getting used to them finishing each stage without too many problems. 'Yes, yes, I'm sure some of it was a bit uncomfortable and made you puff a bit but you're here now, it's done, let's forget about it and move on to the next stage.'

Someone noticed that there was a tap located next to one of the motorhomes and for some reason it was decided that it would be a good idea to get the physio out of the way here so that the boys could all have a shower. We could then fill up with water from this tap. It seemed like a perfectly reasonable plan and it is only when looking back that I wonder why it didn't occur to anyone that we were about to drive to a campsite which would have plenty of water and their own showers. It was probably something to do with the fact that we had all grown used to hunting for water every day and when we saw a free and accessible tap, no one wanted to pass the opportunity by.

Emily set up her physio table and dealt with the boys' legs in turn. I had been suffering since the beginning of the trip with a considerable amount of pain in my left shoulder. The seating position of the motorhome didn't seem to suit me and regardless of how much I adjusted it, I couldn't get comfortable. As we had some spare time, I asked Emily if she would mind giving my shoulder a good pummel. She obliged and confirmed that it felt pretty knackered but doubted that anything she did would make it any better while I was still driving 200 km a day. It wasn't only the riders who were suffering the pain of the Tour each day.

It was early evening when we drove into the campsite *Les Sapins* and what an excellent choice we had made. The site was fairly small and not particularly crowded and we were instructed to park in the corner which gave us loads of room for the vehicles and tables, chairs, bikes and other rubbish that inevitably found its way out of the motorhomes. We paid for two nights and were given the usual welcome briefing which accompanies any visit to a French campsite. This briefing will normally involve the owner telling you where the toilet block is, where the chemical toilet disposal point is and most importantly, what time the bread man comes in the morning. I have stayed on numerous sites in France and boy do they love their bread! Whenever you check into a French campsite, you will be given details of how to order bread, what time it will arrive and where to get it from if you miss the delivery. Most site owners will expect you to give them an order there and then, this obviously being what the other Europeans do. I've never ordered bread and always receive a most peculiar look when I turn down the offer; 'You don't want to order bread? Really? How strange you English are!'

Regardless of whether you order bread or not, you will almost certainly be woken by the bread dude when he arrives at ridiculous o'clock every morning. Sometimes they come on a bike with a basket and an incredibly annoying bell, ding, ding, ding, ding!!! The worst bread man I ever came across was a chap with a small van. I've no idea what the van was, I'd never seen one before; I think he may have put it together in his shed from bits of other vans that he had lying around. What I do know however is that he had fitted it with air horns which were absolutely piercing, especially at 6.30 am. I was amazed that everyone tolerated it but as far as I could tell, it was only me who was miffed, everyone else seemed over-whelmed with gratitude that he had bothered to take the time to deliver their bread in the first place. You will also find that, even in the tiniest hamlet, there will always be a bakery and it will usually be open. I have been to villages and towns in France with half a dozen shops, all of which were closed, except for the baker. The baker is always open. What is this fascination with bread? In any event, we didn't bother to order any bread so that's another campsite owner who thinks the English are weird.

I thought I had spotted a restaurant a short distance up

the road just before we turned into *Les Sapins* so Mick, Adnan and I went to investigate. There was indeed a restaurant or at least the remains of one. We couldn't quite work out if the windows were boarded up and the building was derelict or whether it was just closed and had very tatty window shutters. Regardless, there seemed little chance of anyone cooking our dinner for us tonight. We made a note of the other facilities available to us during our stay; a supermarket, a discount shoe shop and a warehouse store which seemed to sell household stuff. It wasn't entirely clear though and being Sunday and France, all three shops were shut. What a lot we had to look forward to the next day though.

Back at the motorhomes we passed on the disappointing news that we wouldn't be dining out tonight and that, as the supermarket was shut, it was a case of eating whatever we already had in stock. *Quelle surprise*, pasta it is. During dinner, Sara's phone rang and another surprise, it was the driver of the ITV4 lorry. He explained that he was only a driver and therefore not in a position to make any arrangements but he would gladly pass on Sara's details and some information about our challenge to the right people. We all thought it was very kind of him to have taken the time to ring back and I am sure he passed the details on to whoever makes the decisions on these things. That person obviously threw Sara's number in the bin though as this was the last we heard from ITV4.

The prospect of a proper day off had everyone feeling completely relaxed that evening and we all sat out late into the night chatting and drinking. It was another one of the few occasions when it actually felt like we might be on holiday. We weren't of course but it did feel like it for an hour or two. The subject of finances still hadn't been addressed and things were getting more out of hand every day. Sara had paid for several hundred Euros worth of food and diesel and Emily was owed quite a bit too. In contrast, Adnan hadn't paid anything towards the trip and kept asking me what he owed because he hated the idea of not paying his way. I had no idea and I wasn't sure anyone else did but the matter needed resolving. I tentatively raised the subject while everyone seemed to be in good spirits and suggested that we sit down as a group and go through everything the next evening. Several of the group took the stance of, 'I'm not interested in getting involved in the discussion, just tell me what I owe' and that suited me. Quite frankly, as far as I was concerned, the fewer people involved in the discussion the better. Nicole had been keeping a record of what they had paid out in the Motorhome Two group so I agreed that I would sit down with her the following evening so that we could get the finances straight before we left for the last week of the trip.

It was well after midnight when we called it a night but it was a nice change to be having a late night because we were enjoying ourselves rather than because it had just been a really long day.

163 riders lined up at the start of Stage 14 and the day started with a brisk pace and a number of unsuccessful breakaway attempts. It took 35 km before anyone could pull away from the *peloton* and at this point, Peter Sagan and two other riders managed to escape. The *peloton*

temporarily split into two groups at the 38 km mark and at one point there was a gap of 1 minute 45 seconds between the two but they came back together at 54 km.

By this time, Sagan's group were in the lead with a counter-attack group of eight behind them. The second group caught the lead group at 56 km, by which time the *peloton* were 1 minute 10 seconds behind.

As the *peloton* hit the bottom of the first cat 1 climb (the one which had seen Stephen and Adnan crash the previous day), they were 15 minutes behind the leaders. The lead group were split apart whilst ascending the Mur de Péguère and with 20 km to go, there were now five riders in the lead group, one of whom was Luis León Sánchez. Sánchez made a break from the group at 11 km and stayed away until the finish, thus winning the stage.

When the yellow jersey group reached the top of the Mur de Péguère a number of riders suffered punctures due to the tacks which had been thrown into the road. Bradley Wiggins managed to escape but when he was made aware of the situation, he held up the rest of his group to ensure that no one gained any time as a result of the attempted sabotage. Wiggins continues his hold over the yellow jersey and the other three jerseys also remain in the same hands going into tomorrow's stage.

Tour positions at end of STAGE 14

Stage winner: Luis León Sánchez/Rabobank Cycling Team

Yellow: Bradley Wiggins/Sky Procycling
Green: Peter Sagan/Liquigas-Cannondale
Polka Dot: Fredrik Kessiakoff/Astana Pro Team
White: Tejay Van Garderen/BMC Racing Team

REST DAY
PAU
Monday 16th July 2012

'I think the most ridiculous sight in the world is a man on a bicycle, working away with his feet as hard as he possibly can, and believing that his horse is carrying him instead of, as anyone can see, it's he carrying the horse.'
George Bernard Shaw – Playwright

What a fantastic feeling it was to be able to wake up and not have to do anything. France had treated us to another glorious day of sun and today we were going to be able to enjoy it. After a leisurely breakfast sitting outside the motorhomes, the boys decided they were going to go for a short training ride just to keep their legs moving. I opted to tag along and removed my bike from the roof of the motorhome for the second and last time in the trip.

It is easy to see why so many cyclists flock to France each year and why it makes the perfect country for the Tour de France. We rode out of the campsite and within a kilometre we were out in open countryside, cycling on quiet roads lined with trees, fields and the occasional hamlet. Riding in such pleasant surroundings and without the worry or stress of impatient car drivers makes cycling pure pleasure and I was once again envious of the fact that the boys had spent the last couple of weeks doing this. Then I remembered some of the huge mountains they had scaled and the envy abated somewhat. I rode alongside Adnan and we pedalled along at no great speed, chatting about nothing in particular. It was easy riding and much of the route turned out to be downhill and the cool breeze generated as we freewheeled down the hills was a welcome respite from the temperature, which had been creeping up all morning. After about 10 km we turned our bikes round and started to head back.

One of the first things I learnt when I started cycling was that it is usually better to cycle uphill before you get the reward of the downhill. If you find yourself flying down a road without having put the effort in to get to the top of that hill in the first place, chances are you will have to put the effort in later on in your ride. It is always better to get to the top of a climb and know that you can now freewheel for ten minutes, than to coast down a hill knowing you've got to drag yourself up the side of another hill immediately afterwards. I'm sure the number of hills on the way back had increased and it was certainly harder work returning to the campsite than it had been leaving it. Adnan and I were a few hundred metres ahead of the other three and then Adnan started to drop behind me too, he said he was going to wait for the others but I think he was just struggling to keep up with my blisteringly fast pace! By the time I had made it to the top, there was no sign of any of them. The campsite was only round the corner so rather than sit at the side of the road waiting I took the opportunity of being first back to camp, in doing so taking the glory of the stage win.

The rest of the group turned up about fifteen minutes later and the reason for their delay was immediately clear. They had been to the bakers and Mick was riding along with a bundle of French sticks under his arm. All he needed was a stripy top and a beret and the locals would have thought he was the new bread man.

One luxury shower later and we all sat down to a lunch of French bread, cheeses and cold meats. Sara spotted a red squirrel in the hedgerow, something which is rarely seen in England nowadays. It was an idyllic setting. While we were eating, some other British cyclists came over to say 'Hello.' They had ridden the *Étape* a couple of days before. This was the stage that our team were riding the next day. We asked how it was. 'Absolutely awful,' was the reply. We already knew that it was going to be tough; there were four categorised climbs to tackle including the mighty Col du Tourmalet. It sounded like these other Brits had really struggled and some of their group had failed to complete the entire stage. When we explained that our team had ridden the whole Tour route to this point, they looked suitably ashamed and I imagine they went home with the intention of taking up an easier hobby to save future embarrassment.

When the Tourmalet was mentioned, Hannah immediately jumped into the conversation saying that she was going to ride up it tomorrow. Sara and I looked at each other. We were supporting the next day and we had also agreed to take Emily with us so that she could see the mountain without having the hassle of having to drive over it. Tomorrow was going to be a hard enough stage without us having to support an extra rider or two. We had seen this situation coming a few days before but a suitable time to discuss it hadn't arisen. It seemed that time was now.

'Just so you are all aware, we have agreed that Emily can come with us tomorrow to give her a break. Therefore Jess is going to need to drive the second motorhome and I'm afraid if Nicole and Hannah want to cycle, then she will need to support them. Sara and I won't be able to support the girls as well as the boys.'

And so ended the calm and enjoyable day. Hannah would not or could not understand why it was a problem for us to sit around at the top of mountains waiting for the girls to catch up. There was no acknowledgment of how quickly the boys would be descending or how busy the mountains would be, which in turn would make it hard for us to keep up with the main group of riders. Nicole was also of the same view, despite the fact that she had seen at first hand how easy it was for the cycling team to get away from the support motorhome on some stages. Neither of them appeared to care about the fact that if they rode, Jess would be left to drive the motorhome on her own. She hadn't been keen to drive in the first place but expecting her to do it alone, I thought, was pretty selfish. There was even a comment along the lines of 'Why does Emily get to do what she wants to do?' Absolutely unbelievable given how much Emily had done for the group already.

It was clear that Hannah and Nicole were not going to back down and I suspect that this was as much Stephen's fault as anyone else. Stephen had obviously sold the trip to them on the basis that they would be able to do as much riding as they wanted. It was a nice idea but there was enough work in supporting four decent riders, without trying to look after some distinctly average riders who were lagging behind. Sara and I repeated the same thing over and over again, the priority of this trip was to get the boys to the finish, everything else came second. It wasn't sinking in and in the end I had to walk away telling the girls that Emily was with us for the day, we would support the boys and it was up to the three girls what they did. Sara told me later that Hannah and Nicole refused to back down and Jess eventually reluctantly agreed to drive the motorhome on her own, I suspect just to bring the matter to a close. I did feel sorry for her, it wasn't fair and I felt a bit guilty that she was in this position but I also knew that if we had taken on the work of looking after Hannah and Nicole, it would have given us a much tougher day and may have meant the boys missing food stops, which was not an option.

Mick and I headed off to the supermarket to pick up some supplies. Sara had refused to do yet another supermarket shop on her day off and she had given us a list of essentials. An icy blast of air conditioning hit us as we walked through the automatic doors. The outside temperature must have been close to 40° and it could really do with cooling down for the mountain stage tomorrow. I chatted to Mick about it, the heat didn't really bother him but he agreed that a few degrees cooler would be better all round. Unfortunately, the weather was one thing we didn't have any control over. As we filled our baskets up with supplies, Mick discovered that the baskets (which had two wheels and a long handle, rather like a wheeled suitcase) would slide in quite a dramatic fashion around the corners if you gave them a bit of a swing in the right direction. The more weight in the basket, the better the skid. I'm not sure what the other shoppers made of the pair of us flinging our baskets around each corner but we decided it was time to go when Mick's basket caught a slight ridge in the floor and he very nearly threw four bottles of wine straight across the tiles.

'We would definitely have had to do a runner if they had broken,' said Mick, the responsible adult who was supposed to be on this trip to look after the irresponsible youngsters.

Back at camp and everyone was doing their own thing. The girls were sunbathing; Stephen and Matt were cleaning their bikes. Sara was washing clothes. Emily had her physio table set up and was working on one of the cyclists who had been chatting to us earlier. Adnan was in the motorhome having also been to the shops.

We had somehow walked straight past him, although I suspect that he had seen us messing around with the baskets and had hidden so as not to be associated with us. He had kindly bought Sara and me a magnum of wine to say thank you for our help. I think he thought it would last us until Paris. It didn't even make it to the next day. A nice gesture and very much appreciated.

Rest days are a strange thing. When I first watched the Tour, I assumed that the riders longingly looked forward to the rest days and then spent the day lazing around in bed. This is far from what actually happens. For starters, many riders would rather just push on through and not bother with the rest day, especially the second one when the finish is almost visible on the horizon. Stopping for a day merely gives their bodies a chance to slow down and relax. It gives them the chance to catch up with family and friends and if they are on the edge of giving up, it might be enough to push them over the edge. If you are caught up riding stages every day, you don't really get time to think as you are on the constant and unrelenting Tour merry-go-round. Stop for a day and you have thinking time and might start to ask yourself why you are putting your body through so much suffering and wouldn't you be better off at home, sleeping in your own bed each night? I didn't need a rest day to ask myself these questions. I'd been asking myself since Belgium. Tour riders don't get a proper rest anyway, they still ride, as our team had done but they will usually do quite a hard ride of two or three hours. The only riders who get out of this training ride will be the ones who are injured and who might actually be allowed to rest up for the day. On top of the training ride, there will also be press conferences and other media obligations to fulfil, especially for the higher profile riders such as the current holders of the various jerseys. When it comes to professional cycling, rest days are a paradox. In the early years of the Tour, riders would be rewarded with up to three rest days between each stage. The stages were much longer though – in the first Tour in 1903, the longest stage was 471 km in length and the average length across all six stages was over 400 km. I imagine you would need a couple of days to recover after cycling 400 km in one hit, but by the same token, the last thing you would want to do is get up and do it all again after a break. I can see why a rider may be more inclined to keep pressing on and this feeling was noticeable in camp towards the end of the day. There is only so much sitting around you can do and with home just a few days away, people were itching to start moving again.

First though, there was the money situation to be dealt with. Things still felt a bit tense between the two motorhomes following the discussion earlier about Jess having to drive. Still, no point in shying away from it, the financial issue needed addressing and we had agreed to deal with it today. Everyone sat down with their scraps of paper detailing money spent and money owed and Nicole and I went through item by item to try and ascertain who owed money and who was owed money. It took ages to wade through everything but eventually I had calculated that most of us needed to chip in one hundred and fifty Euros. This would be enough to pay back people like Sara, who had spent more than everyone else and also provide each motorhome with a kitty for food for the remaining week. For some reason though, Nicole had come up with a different figure and thought everyone needed to pay slightly less. We compared notes and I saw that Nicole was including Emily in her calculations. Nicole was expecting Emily to share the costs, but I didn't think this was the arrangement we had made with her employer. I checked with Adnan, who confirmed that the deal was that Emily would provide her services for free and she would be taken care of in terms of food and other essentials. Remember, Emily wasn't someone we knew before the trip, she had agreed to come along for the adventure and to represent the physio company that she worked for. At a stretch you might think that she should contribute towards a bit of food but certainly not the diesel, toll fees and camping charges. At this point, everyone from Motorhome Two started to back Nicole in saying that Emily should pay, including Stephen who had been with Adnan when the original agreement was made! Emily said that she had absolutely no problem in paying and was, understandably, totally embarrassed by the whole thing. But there was no way that anyone in Motorhome One was going to let Emily stump up a penny. We knew that the bottom line to this argument wasn't actually anything to do with whether Emily should or shouldn't pay, it was to do with the fact that some people in Motorhome Two had run out of money days ago and they were being subsidised by the others. Not Emily's problem and again, mainly down to Stephen who had implied that this would be a free trip for all concerned.

Eventually it was agreed that Emily wouldn't have to contribute to the costs of the trip, as indeed was only right. Nicole was put in charge of collecting the money from their motorhome and Adnan and I paid what we owed directly to Sara so that she was partially reimbursed. Stephen was also responsible for making sure that Sara received in the region of four hundred Euros for fuel once we had made it home and he had been able to reclaim it from his employer. One of my concerns in respect of the finances was that if they weren't sorted out before we got home then the matter would probably never be resolved. I got the impression that some of the group wouldn't have had too much of a problem walking away from their monetary responsibilities. It transpired that my fears were well founded as Sara never received the money she was owed for fuel.

If the atmosphere between the two motorhomes had been tense before the rest day, you could positively cut it with a knife by the time we all packed up and went to bed. Mick, Sara, Adnan and I sat in Motorhome One having opened the magnum of wine and there was a tap at the door. It was Emily; she had come to get away from the massive row now going on next door. Apparently Nicole was angry that Stephen had left her to deal with the money side of things and felt that he should have taken more responsibility. Stephen's excuse was that he was busy concentrating on cycling. I don't think Stephen ever really got a handle on how much work the support teams were doing and he was oblivious to the problems he had caused by telling everyone that they wouldn't have to pay for things and that they could ride as much as they wanted to.

Emily had been embarrassed by the whole thing but we reassured her that there was no need for her to have been. It had worked out well that we were taking Emily with us tomorrow as it would allow some time for things to cool down a bit. Only five more stages to go…

The 15th stage of the Tour opened with 162 riders still in the race and the attacks started straight away. After 65 km there was a group of five off the front with an advantage of 1 minute and 30 seconds over the *peloton*. A sixth rider bridged the gap between the *peloton* and the breakaway group at 82 km. By the time the leaders had reached the point with 45 km to go, they had increased their lead to 7 minutes and 45 seconds and they continued to add to this lead, moving ahead by 11 minutes and 40 seconds with 11 km to go.

By this time the *peloton* weren't going to catch the escapees and as the leaders neared the finish line, they started to jostle for the stage win. After a couple of failed attacks, the win was eventually taken by Pierrick Fedrigo, FDJ-Bigmat. The *peloton* continued to lose time all the way to the finish but none of the jersey competitions were affected and Wiggins will wear yellow once again tomorrow.

Tour positions at end of STAGE 15

Stage winner: Pierrick Fedrigo/FDJ-Bigmat

Yellow: Bradley Wiggins/Sky Procycling
Green: Peter Sagan/Liquigas-Cannondale
Polka Dot: Fredrik Kessiakoff/Astana Pro Team
White: Tejay Van Garderen/BMC Racing Team

STAGE 16

Tuesday 17th July 2012
PAU – BAGNÈRES-DE-LUCHON
Mountain – 197 km

'I'm fascinated by the sprinters. They suffer so much during the race just to get to the finish, they hang on for dear life in the climbs, but then in the final kilometres they are transformed and do amazing things. It's not their force per se that impresses me, but rather the renaissance they experience. Seeing them suffer throughout the race only to be reborn in the final is something for fascination.'
Miguel Indurain - Five times Tour de France winner

Here we go again. I had fallen asleep without closing the window blind the previous night and when I awoke, I was sweating from the heat of the sun being reflected through the plastic window. It was only 7.30 am but it already looked as if it was going to be another scorcher of a day.

Four famous, or perhaps that should be infamous, climbs for the team to haul themselves over today. Today's stage ran for a total distance of 197 km and almost 30% of that distance would be spent cycling up two HC and two category 1 mountains. If I used the time it took me to get up Alpe d'Huez as an average, it would have taken me over twelve hours to scale the categorised peaks and I would still have 140 km to cycle at the end of it. Let's hope the boys can pedal a smidge quicker than I can. So, with the Col d'Aubisque, Col du Tourmalet, Col d'Aspin and the Col de Peyresourde all beckoning, today was not the day for a late start.

It seemed I wasn't the only one who had been roused

by the sun. Sara and Adnan were up and Mick was also stirring. Adnan emerged from the bathroom with shaving foam all over his head, apparently his hair was getting long and it was time for a cut, which he duly completed with a razor. Perhaps he was hoping he would be more streamlined for the descents.

There was also activity in Motorhome Two and Nicole and Hannah were kitted up and obviously raring to go. I had been under the impression that they wanted to try to ride all of the big climbs but common sense had prevailed and the girls had decided to give the Col d'Aubisque a miss and start with the Tourmalet. I'd told Jess the previous evening that the mountain would be absolutely heaving with spectators and cyclists so if she didn't want to drive the motorhome through this chaos, maybe the better option would be to park at the bottom and let the girls ride back to her when they had finished. They could then pick a longer route around the bottom of the mountain. Eager to avoid making her adventure in the motorhome any more hairy than she needed to, she agreed that this made sense and thanked me for the tip. I'm not sure how Hannah and Nicole felt about the fact that they would now have to deal with the prospect of an intimidating descent back to Jess but you know what they say, go big or go home.

Today ended up being one of our earliest starts, the guys wanted to get going in the hope that they could conquer at least one mountain before the full force of the midday sun was upon them. It was a short drive to the start point in Pau and Sara, Emily and I dropped them close to the large car park in the centre (which was now jam-packed with Tour vehicles). Emily was under strict instructions that she was to do absolutely nothing for the day. It must have felt like Christmas. We still had Matt's parental back-up support team and they were going to follow the riders in the car for the whole day. This would ensure that they had easy and constant access to drinks and food and meant they wouldn't be worried about conserving fluids or running out. Matt's dad had brought his bike along and was also going to ride up the Tourmalet so our team would be well represented on the mountain today. Part of me was jealous as I would have liked to have had a crack at it myself. I knew I was considerably fitter than when I attempted Alpe d'Huez and it would have been nice to prove that I could get up something so colossal in a half decent time but it just wasn't practical. Something to save for another year.

Our team were confident that they could make it to the foot of the Tourmalet without any support from Sara and me, which meant we could avoid the Aubisque altogether. This suited me fine, the fewer mountains bursting with crazy fans I had to negotiate, the better. I was more than happy to leave the boys to it.

The Col d'Aubisque has been a regular feature in the Tour de France since it first appeared in 1910. It was, in fact, one of the first mountain passes to be included in the race. In 1951, the holder of the yellow jersey, Wim van Est, was defending his position on the *Col* when he lost control of his bike and fell off the side of the mountain. He fell 70 metres and was incredibly lucky to stop on a small ledge, with no serious injuries. Van Est's team manager took a rope from the team car and threw it down to him but it wasn't long enough to reach so the team had to extend the length using spare bicycle tyres. It took the entire team stock of forty tyres to reach Van Est and when he was pulled up, the tyres were stretched and ruined. Fifty years on, a memorial was placed on the spot where Van Est fell, it reads, *'Here on 17 July 1951 the cyclist*

Wim van Est fell 70 metres. He survived but lost the yellow jersey.'

The cycling Gods were smiling as the team reached the first climb and all four riders made it up without anyone falling off the side. This was fortunate not least because we didn't have forty tyres between us with which to haul any careless fallers back up. By the time we met the lads at the foot of the Tourmalet, it was close to midday and the temperature was in excess of 40°. This was going to be one hot and uncomfortable climb. Lunch was brisk; the boys didn't want to waste any time. The high temperatures meant that eating was a struggle and it was a case of forcing food down. Failure to eat would have meant falling foul of the dreaded bonk at some point and with three mountain passes to tackle, this wasn't something which was on anyone's agenda. As the Tourmalet was the largest of the four mountains they would be crossing today, we agreed we would drive up and park after the summit, just in case anyone needed anything else before continuing.

If you have never been up close and personal to one of the really huge mountains of the Alps or Pyrenees before, the first time is an eye-widening experience. Emily had seen some mountains during the previous couple of weeks but nothing on the scale of the Tourmalet. Her open mouth and comment of, 'Wow, that is big!' said it all. There was a car park at the foot of the climb and as we drove past, we spotted Motorhome Two there. Jess was sitting in the sun reading, Hannah and Nicole had started their ride. I think Jess had the right idea.

As predicted, the mountain was buzzing with activity. Every available parking spot at the side of the road was occupied by a motorhome. In between the motorhomes, people had squashed cars and even tents. On the slopes leading away from the road there were more tents. On the road itself, there was a train of cyclists which we could see disappearing far up the mountain. It seemed that every type of person and every type of bicycle was represented here today. Old, young, all nationalities, mountain bikes, road bikes, expensive carbon models to old fashioned steel antiques, the Tourmalet had it all. If we craned our necks to look almost vertically up, it was possible to see the continual stream of cyclists all the way to the summit, the route flanked by hundreds of motor-homes and thousands and thousands of spectators. The atmosphere as we drove along was the very definition of electric, every rider was cheered all the way up, every vehicle was acknowledged and waved at. Sara and I had expected no less and we weren't disappointed. The Tour riders wouldn't even be here for another twenty four hours; tomorrow would be incredible on the mountain.

I think Emily was overwhelmed, 'I'm so glad I didn't have to drive through this lot,' she said.

There are two monuments at the top of the Tourmalet, one is a bust of Jacques Goddet, the director of the Tour from 1936 to 1987 and the second is a large statue of Octave Lapize on a bicycle gasping for air as he struggles to complete the climb. Lapize was the first rider to reach the summit of the Tourmalet in 1910, the first year the mountain formed part of the Tour route. Almost immediately after we passed the monuments and the summit, the crowds started to thin out and within fifty metres they had all but disappeared. If you want to watch the Tour de France on a mountain stage, the place to be is on an ascent. Positioning yourself on the descent will guarantee you a fraction of a second of entertainment as the riders speed past you at up to 90 km/h. No doubt the descent would be much busier with fans tomorrow as those who left it to the last minute to turn up would have no option but to position themselves in the cheap seats but today, the far side of the Tourmalet couldn't have been quieter. A few kilometres beyond the summit we found a large parking area and I turned the motorhome side on to the road and Sara hung our Union Jack from the window so that the boys would spot us easily.

Cycling up the Col du Tourmalet turned out to be a lot harder than the boys had expected and the main reason for this was the heat. Mick was the first one to reach us at the motorhome and he used up a few of his words for the day to tell us that it had been 'a bit on the hurty side.' The boys were usually quite good at keeping together on the climbs but there was a good fifteen minutes between them all getting to our stop point. It occurred to me that we hadn't spotted Nicole or Hannah on the drive up; I wondered how they were getting on. Shortly after the boys arrived, Matt's parents' car turned up. Matt's dad had made it to the top of the Tourmalet and was, understandably, very pleased with himself. No time for basking in the glory though and it was straight back to work. Having the extra support car had been a godsend and I think the boys may well have struggled without it. It had been necessary for them to top up with water several times during the ride up the mountain purely because of the temperature. This would have been nigh on impossible to have facilitated with the motorhome as there wasn't anywhere suitable to stop on the way up. Trying to swap water bottles on the move from a car is one thing but doing it from a 7.5 metre motorhome, whilst weaving in and out of hundreds of cyclists and spectators would have been something else altogether.

With the two *hors categorie* climbs out of the way, there was just the matter of 150 km and two category 1 climbs to deal with before nightfall. Sounds easy if you say it quickly but time was pushing on and it was looking like it might be a late one. Our next meeting point would be at the start of the final climb of the day, the Col de Peyresourde. It's basically a straight road from the Tourmalet to the Peyresourde, the only real downside being that the Col d'Aspin is in the middle of it. For this reason, these three mountains are usually grouped together when they feature in Tour stages. Suitably fed and watered, the guys saddled up and continued their descent – enjoy it while you can!

Just as we were about to head off, Motorhome Two pulled up beside us. Nicole and Hannah had managed to drag themselves to the top of the Tourmalet and confirmed that it was a brutal ride, not helped one bit by the temperature. I don't think they had enjoyed the descent back to Jess much and there wasn't any sign of either of them wanting to do any more cycling today. Jess didn't appear to have enjoyed her day of driving either, especially as she had just driven through all the crowds and cyclists on the Tourmalet rather than taking the scenic route around the bottom. Once again Emily came to the rescue and having witnessed the spectacle of a Tour mountain in its full glory, she offered to resume her role as driver. Emily also suggested that Motorhome Two go ahead to the finish to collect the boys so that Sara and I could meet them at the top of the Aspin before going to tomorrow's start town to try and find somewhere to stop for the night.

The crowds on the Aspin were just as impressive as they had been on the mighty Tourmalet. At least this would help carry the boys to the end of the stage. The temperature in the motorhome was stifling and this was, without doubt, turning into the worst day of the trip in terms of heat. We were both sweltering and dripping in sweat; goodness knows what it must have been like for the cyclists. I was praying that we would find somewhere decent to stay tonight, somewhere with a tap close by, just so I could have a luxury shower. I was also beginning to regret not having used that washing machine at the petrol station last week. I was all out of clean clothes now and I wasn't the only one. If this heat kept up, it was going to get very stinky in our motorhome over the next few days.

We met the boys at the top of the Aspin but they didn't want to stop so it was just a case of topping up water bottles and they were on their way. It was about 5:00 pm by the time we reached the base of the Col de Peyresourde and the boys were all but done in. Not for the first time however, there was one more mountain to go. The final climb might have been the shortest of the day at 9.5 km but in some parts the gradient reached 10%. I decided not to remind them of that fact and told them to concentrate on the 9.5 km; I mean, when you convert it to English, it's not even 6 miles. I'm sure they were cursing me for being so efficient in topping up their water as they only got to stop for about five minutes but there was no point in hanging around, the bikes weren't going to pedal themselves.

The boys got ahead of us quite quickly as we were caught behind other cyclists and traffic so they were long gone by the time we reached the police road block located about 1 km down the road from where we had stopped.

As we sat in the queuing traffic, we could see that the police were letting cars through but not motorhomes, which were being turned around and sent back the way we had just come. This could only mean one thing. The mountain was already full up and there were no more parking spaces. Knowing that some people will try and park anywhere, the police had obviously decided that it was easier just to stop the motorhomes from having access to the mountain. It wasn't really a surprise that the Peyresourde was so busy as the Tour was going to be passing over it twice in the next two days. Tomorrow they would ride in the direction that our boys were going today and the following day they would come back the other way. This meant that anyone with a prime viewing position would get to see the race twice. It also meant that the One Day Ahead team would, in theory, be riding over the mountain tomorrow when the official Tour would be coming the other way.

As we had no intention of staying on the mountain, we didn't anticipate a problem getting through the road block. The police were letting cars through so the road couldn't have been physically blocked or closed, it must purely be that there wasn't any room for more campers. We pulled up to the female police officer who looked as though she had had better days.

'Montagne fermé,' she snapped and pointed back the way we had come.

The mountain clearly wasn't closed as she had just let two cars drive up it in front of us. I asked if she spoke English, she didn't. In broken French, Sara and I tried to explain that we wanted to pass over the mountain to the next town, not actually stop on it. We pulled out a map and pointed to the town we were going to but she wasn't having any of it. In the end, I nodded agreement and turned the motorhome round. As I was turning, I noticed another road which sort of led in the same direction as the mountain road. I wondered if maybe this led round the bottom of the mountain, which was a better option than going back the way we had come. Shortly after taking this route, the road started to turn and lead away from the mountain and in the opposite direction to the way we wanted to go. I pulled over and dug out the maps – no point in relying on Jane for this one, we needed to do it the old way.

I couldn't quite believe it when I looked at our options. To go around the mountain, we had to retrace our steps and then make a detour of over 100 km. This was ridiculous especially as I was sure there was no reason why we couldn't drive over the Peyresourde other than the fact that the police officer wrongly thought that we wanted to camp on it. Unfortunately it didn't look like we had much choice. We really needed Mick and his French skills but he was probably halfway up the mountain by now and I couldn't see him being very keen on cycling back down again just to sort this problem out. Reluctantly I turned the motorhome round and started to head back to the blocked junction so we could start our two hour detour.

Approaching the junction, we were just in time to see the police officer wave through a motorhome, which toddled off up the mountain on exactly the same route which we were told we couldn't take. The motorhome had French plates and the driver obviously had a better command of the local language than I did. This confirmed one thing in my mind though, that the mountain road was open for the right people. Although there was a police car parked across the entrance to the mountain road, it was blocking the route from the way we had originally come, not from the road we were now exiting. There was actually enough room for me to squeeze the motorhome behind the police car and up the mountain. I looked at the gap and I looked at Sara. The police woman was in heated debate with another motorist and had her back turned to us.

'Oh just go,' said Sara, 'What can she do? She's hardly likely to chase us or she will have to move the police car and then everyone will drive up.'

It was a good point. Worse case scenario she might radio ahead and we might get stopped at the other end but given that she was being selective in which vehicles she was allowing to pass, I really couldn't see this happening. Even if it did, at least we would be on the right side of the mountain.

So I pulled out of the junction, nipped behind the police car and shot off up the mountain as fast as our overloaded motorhome would carry us (which, admittedly, wasn't very fast at all). As far as I could tell from looking in the wing mirrors, the police officer didn't give us a second look. It isn't in my nature to disregard the instructions of a police officer but on this occasion I am happy that it was the right thing to do. A 100 km detour for no reason was not something I relished and as it turned out, we were quite right, it would have been completely unnecessary. The mountain was extremely busy with parked motorhomes but there was absolutely no problem with driving along the road and we reached the other side within about fifteen minutes. We passed several police cars too and none of them paid us any attention so I think we could be safe in the knowledge that we weren't on the French 'most wanted' lists.

Half an hour later and we had reached the most motorhome unfriendly town of this year's Tour de France. Bagnères-de-Luchon was not only hosting the finish of the stage tomorrow but also the stage start the following day. It was therefore a high profile Tour town and could expect a lot of visitors. Because of this profile and in line with other significant stage towns, we had expected a field or maybe a car park to be set aside for visiting motorhomes. In fact, it seemed that the town was going out of its way to make it difficult for visitors to park. We found several decent sized car parks which were completely empty and which would have accommodated numerous motorhomes. Unfortunately they had all height barriers across the entrances making it impossible to get in. This wouldn't have been so bad if the barriers were permanent as there wouldn't have been much the authorities could have done to change things. However all of the barriers were of the adjustable type which were hinged and could be swung out of the way if required. It seemed very short-sighted of the town officials to prevent motorhomes from parking in the town thus losing the local shops and businesses potential extra trade. This was especially the case when you consider that it was the very same business owners who would have paid for the town to be a host town in the first place via their taxes.

It was getting late now and it was also starting to get dark. We hadn't heard from Motorhome Two for a while but it was unlikely that they would have made it to the finish yet. When they did eventually arrive, we knew they would all be hungry and would expect to be directed straight to a parking spot where dinner was waiting. I started to head out of the town and the motorhome suddenly bounced into the air with an extremely loud crash. Sara and I had been referring to the French speed humps as 'plate smashers' ever since we had arrived. The French seem to go out of their way to ensure that their speed humps aren't signed or marked in any way. The tarmac is carefully matched to that of the surrounding road so as to ensure that the humps are almost completely invisible. You can just about make them out in the daytime although often it is only at the very last minute. You then have a choice of either hitting the hump at your current speed or slamming the brakes on, causing all the cupboard doors and drawers to fly open thus depositing their contents across the floor. At night, you have no chance. I guess we hit the hump at about 30 km/h and I was certainly well within the speed limit. I'm not really sure why the hump was there, probably just to catch English drivers unawares and to give the locals some amusement. Regardless, we (or rather Sara) lost four plates, a large glass oven dish, a serving dish and some assorted crockery as a result of this incident. I did suggest that maybe this was why camping shops sold plastic tableware for motorhomes but Sara politely pointed out that it would be a cold day in hell when she had plastic plates in her motorhome. Thinking about it, we were probably carrying 5% of the total vehicle weight in the twelve piece dinner service that was crammed into the kitchen cupboards!

Eventually, with absolutely no other option and for the first and only time, we had to accept that there was nowhere to park other than a quiet residential street. This was far from ideal and if there were any other choice we would have taken it but there wasn't. We found a lay-by which had some houses on one side and a small park on the other. This would have to do. Sara started to prepare some dinner and we waited to hear from the rest of the team. Even though it was now dark, it was still very hot and humid. We had been uncomfortable all day and there wasn't enough water on board for the two of us to have showers and still have enough for Adnan and Mick. Once we had stopped, I noticed that Sara seemed a bit snappy; maybe she was more bothered about her plates than she had let on. It was more likely that she was just hot like me and had also worked out that she wouldn't be getting a shower tonight. Eventually we heard from Motorhome Two and tried to direct them to our home for the night. It became a source of considerable frustration when their sat nav wouldn't locate the street we were on and they finally gave up and asked us to come and find them. This meant we had to clear the table of the dinner plates and cutlery and Sara had to stand at the hob holding the pans in place so that the dinner didn't end up decorating the carpet. I then drove back to the town to try and find the other motorhome. Forty five minutes later and even hotter and more bothered, we made camp for the second time. Sara had really had enough by now and was happy to take a snap at anyone who she thought warranted it. Most of us worked out very quickly that the best thing to do was keep a safe distance. It took a little while for the penny to drop with Mick and he got the brunt of it. I honestly don't think he noticed though, he was a very tired teddy.

It wasn't necessary to debrief the stage with the guys - I knew what they would say. It was long, hard and hot and they didn't enjoy it one bit. Was it the worst stage yet? Not by a long straw, that honour still went to the early stage in Belgium with the strong headwinds and rain. I still find this hard to believe but they all agreed so who was I to argue?

Just before I fell asleep, I remembered that, following their rest day today, the actual Tour riders would be coming over the Peyresourde in the opposite direction to our boys tomorrow afternoon. That should make for an interesting spectacle!

STAGE 17
Wednesday 18th July 2012
BAGNÈRES-DE-LUCHON – PEYRAGUDES
Mountain – 143.5 km

'It is the unknown around the corner that turns my wheels.'
Heinz Stücke - German long-distance touring cyclist

The temperature didn't let up all night which made for muggy conditions in the motorhome. Opening the window next to my bunk had merely served to allow more hot air to waft over me and I woke feeling as tired as when I had got into bed six hours earlier. My general mood was good though and my elevated spirits were due to one thing, today we would see the back of the mountains and would start our journey north to Paris and HOME!

Sara also seemed more cheery and Mick put a smile on our faces when he showed us the Garmin, which had recorded his maximum speed for yesterday's stage – 86.7 km/h. He had recorded this speed coming off the Col d'Aubisque which, he went on to explain, he 'flew down.' Obviously. Rather him than me. It reminded me of when he was descending Alpe d'Huez on his Chopper and a Frenchman on a road bike came up behind him and wanted to get past, so to alert Mick to his presence, he whistled at him. Mick wasn't overly impressed with this given that he was riding at a reasonable pace, so at the next hairpin he didn't bother braking and shot past the French rider whistling as he went. I'm sure that this was not a story which would be retold in the bar later, *'Ah, oui, a crazy rosbif, he overtakes me on le Chopper!'*

The main topic of discussion over breakfast was, however, the small matter of how the team were going to get over the Col de Peyresourde later in the day when the entire Tour de France would be coming over in the opposite direction. The Peyresourde had been the last climb of yesterday's stage and was also the final mountain to be crossed in today's stage. Before they reached it, our guys would have to tackle four other categorised climbs (including the HC-rated Port de Balès) so the chances of them getting the 128 km to the foot of the Peyresourde ridden quickly and before the road was closed, were slim. Actually the general consensus was that this would be completely impossible. The Peyresourde would be closed well before the Tour riders reached it in order to allow the Caravan through. Although our team had been starting each stage much earlier than the Tour riders' (most Tour stages were starting after midday), they were riding noticeably slower than the professionals. The pros were obviously in a race, whereas our boys just wanted to finish. So if the Tour *peloton* took, say four hours to complete a stage, it might take our riders six or seven hours to ride the same route when you included the time taken for food stops etc. The Caravan would probably be crossing the Peyresourde around 3:00 pm and the road across the mountain would be closed at least an hour before then. Try as we might, we couldn't see any way in which our team were going to be able to complete their reverse ride over the mountain pass this afternoon. Only one thing for it then, they would have to do it this morning instead. There had been a few minor deviations of the Tour route here and there for our boys. For example, having to bypass a one-way street rather than go down it the wrong way (the street would be closed during the actual Tour) and the Peyresourde could now add itself to this small list of amendments. The finish of today's stage was actually situated on the summit of the Peyragudes. This summit is to be found at the top of a small road which forks off from the main road across the Peyresourde. Therefore, the team decided to start their day by riding up the Peyresourde to the Peyragudes. They would then turn around and cycle back the way they had come, to start and ride the rest of the stage in the correct order.

With the route for the day sorted, there wasn't much more to do but get the bikes ready and get pedalling. I spotted a few twitchy curtains while we were sorting the bikes out which was hardly surprising. I think I would have been the same if I had woken to find two motorhomes and the makings of a cycling team opposite my house. I'm sure the locals were relieved when they realised that we weren't a permanent fixture and had left by 9:30 am.

I was looking forward to a slightly less hectic day and it was great to know that, as far as the mountains were concerned, Sara and I were done. I'd checked the map and we could get to our next destination without having to go anywhere near a mountain pass. By teatime we would be 150 km closer to Paris and the Pyrenees would be a distant memory. My priority for the day, however, was to have a shower, ideally a luxury one! We had next to no water in the tank and so after our customary four or five cups of tea, we headed off in search of a tap.

As a motorhomer, there is nothing more pleasing than to see the French sign for a motorhome service point. The sign is a picture of a motorhome with an arrow underneath pointing to a tank of water. It is supposed to signify the motorhome dropping its waste water. If you are low on water or need to empty your toilet cassette, this is the sign you are looking for and as luck would have it, about 10 km into our journey, we saw one. The most common place to find a motorhome service point is at an *aire* or on a campsite but sometimes they just exist in the middle of nowhere. Such was the service point we found today and not only that, but it was a good one too. As with so many things, service points come in good and bad varieties. The bad will be dirty and uncared for and the last place you would want to fill your water tanks from. In complete contrast, a good service point is a gem of a find and will be clean, well laid out (with drinking water well away from the chemical disposal point) and easily accessible. We had stumbled upon a good service point. It was in the middle of nowhere, there were only three buildings anywhere to be seen; I think to call it a hamlet would be stretching the definition of the word. But for whatever reason, this community had seen fit to provide passing motorhomers with the convenience of an excellent service point. I was able to reverse the motorhome up to the point and offload our grey water (water from the shower, washing up etc) and simultaneously fill the tanks with clean water. The toilet cassettes were dealt with too and in a matter of minutes all was well with the world once more. Two luxury showers later and another quick top-up of water and we were on our way. It was great to feel clean again.

It was early afternoon as we arrived at Blagnac, the host town for tomorrow's start and the place was bustling with activity. This was a town which was taking its position as a stage start seriously and all through the town were references to the Tour – little coloured jerseys in shop windows, models of bicycles along the side of the road and flags and bunting stretched across the street. We had become slightly numb to Tour paraphernalia as it tends to be everywhere along the route of the Tour de France. Farmers will design huge bicycles out of bales of hay or decorate their fields with images relating to the Tour which can only be seen from the helicopters providing the television coverage. Enormous model bicycles of a similar size to Matt's Gate will be displayed on roundabouts or even on the rooftops of houses and I have even seen buildings painted in the colours of the competition jerseys – yellow, green and polka dot. Blagnac was no exception and we had high hopes of being able to park somewhere other than a local housing estate tonight.

Blagnac didn't disappoint and we soon picked up some parking signs for '*le camping car*' and discovered that the town had made a huge field available for their motor-homing visitors. Cost to park for the night? Absolutely nothing. Thank you Blagnac!

There were a few motorhomes already parked up but as the Tour wasn't due to arrive until the following day, the majority of the field was completely empty. We weren't expecting Motorhome Two to return for a few hours yet so Sara and I spent a not unpleasant afternoon sitting in the sun, drinking tea and reading. It was still warm but comfortably warm, not the awful, humid heat that we had experienced the day before. At least our cyclists should have had a better day.

The girls and our riding team arrived at the field to catch the last of the sun and tables and chairs were set up for dinner. The boys showered and Sara took the pile of dirty cycling kit so that she could start washing it before we ate in the hope that it would dry before the sun disappeared completely.

Shortly after she had started washing the kit, Sara called me into the motorhome.

'Nicole and Hannah have put their stuff in with the boys' for washing;' she said, 'since when is it my job to wash their kit?'

It wasn't clear whether the girls had ridden their bikes today or whether this was their dirty kit from the day before but either way, it wasn't down to Sara to do their washing for them. I could see why Sara was annoyed, what an absolute cheek to throw their washing into the pile and expect Sara to sort it out. I wanted to say something but Sara asked me to keep quiet.

'We'll be home soon, just ignore it, I've washed the kit now but I'm not doing it again,' she said.

Reluctantly I agreed to bite my tongue but no sooner than I had, Nicole stuck her head out of the door of Motorhome Two announcing that some garlic bread was ready. I was in the process of wringing the water out of her cycling shorts and ignored the request to 'come and get it.' Two minutes later she called Sara and me again.

This time I responded, 'We'll be there in a minute, we are just finishing washing *your* cycling kit!'

'It's not my kit,' shouted back Nicole.

'Really?' I said as I held up the small pair of white women's cycling shorts, 'Well I'm pretty sure these aren't Mick's.'

Nicole disappeared back into the motorhome. No apology, no explanation, no understanding of what she had done wrong. After dinner, Sara told Nicole and Hannah that she thought it was a bit unfair of them to just throw their washing in the pile and expect it to be done. Nicole's response was basically 'I don't see what the problem is, we have been taking it in turns to do the washing every evening.' She completely missed the point that yes, we had been sharing the washing of the boys' cycling attire but nothing else, Sara and I hadn't given her our cycling kit to wash when we had ridden. What planet was she on? It seemed our original nickname for the kids was spot on and we were most definitely the parents. This was really the last straw for me and Sunday couldn't come soon enough.

Earlier in the day, Stephen had spoken to the French television reporter who had expressed an interest in doing a piece about the boys' challenge. Once again it had been impossible to agree on a meeting place and time due to the twenty four hour time difference in their two schedules. As we moved into the closing stages of the trip, it seemed unlikely that One Day Ahead would be 'coming to a TV screen near you' any time soon.

As for the ride, all four cyclists agreed it was much easier than the previous day, primarily because of the lower temperature. The crowds were amazing and Mick celebrated reaching the top of the final mountain by launching an empty water bottle into the air, telling the 'shedloads' of back-breaking climbs exactly where they could go. I felt that we had reached the stage whereby the riders could be confident that they were actually going to complete this challenge. The incredibly tough stages were now behind them and other than a long, flat stage tomorrow, there was just a short time trial to bash out before the final, celebratory run into Paris. There might have been a bit of tension in the air as we settled down for the night but everyone was confident that the One Day Ahead challenge was a done deal.

Now what was that old saying about counting chickens?

Yesterday's rest day gave a few more riders the opportunity to say enough was enough and the starting line of Stage 16 of the 2012 Tour saw 155 riders still in the race.

At the 22 km mark, in a move instigated by Alexandre Vinokourov, Astana Pro Team, a group of thirty-eight riders made a dash for freedom and broke away from the rest of the group. By the base of the Aubisque they were ahead by 3 minutes and 40 seconds, this lead was increased by a further 5 seconds before the summit. Thomas Voeckler, Team Europcar, reached the summit first to claim maximum mountain points.

By the time the *peloton* reached the start of the Tourmalet climb, they were 5 minutes and 35 seconds behind the leaders. Further attacks came as the riders raced upwards and the lead group started to split into smaller groups. Voeckler was again first over the top of the second huge climb of the day.

Voeckler continued to collect points as he led over the Col d'Aspin and by the time he reached the Col de Peyresourde, accompanied by Brice Feillu of the Saur-Sojasun team, he was 1 minute ahead of the next group of riders. The main *peloton* were now 9 minutes and 20 seconds behind. With 22 km to go, Voeckler dropped Feillu and took the final summit points of the day. No one was up to catching Voeckler and he also helped himself to the stage win and the polka dot jersey.

Wiggins in yellow finished in 12th place, over 7 minutes behind Voeckler but he didn't lose any time on the main contenders for the jersey and will be wearing yellow again for the final day in the mountains tomorrow.

Tour positions at end of STAGE 16

Stage winner: Thomas Voeckler/Team Europcar

Yellow: Bradley Wiggins/Sky Procycling
Green: Peter Sagan/Liquigas-Cannondale
Polka Dot: Thomas Voeckler/Team Europcar
White: Tejay Van Garderen/BMC Racing Team

STAGE 18

Thursday 19th July 2012
BLAGNAC – BRIVE-LA-GAILLARDE
Flat – 222.5 km

'The whole world has become much more interested in security. There is so much misery in this world that everybody looks for peace and quiet. The Tour de France refuses security. It involves and needs the concept of facing pain and defeat. Sacrifice is partly responsible for the Tour's popularity. Sacrifice is part of cycling's legend, certainly part of the Tour's legend.'
Jacques Goddet - Director of the Tour de France 1936 - 1986

There were no two ways about it; today was going to be long, probably the longest yet. I had been both looking forward to it and dreading it in equal measures. I was looking forward to it because by the time I crawled into bed tonight, we should be within spitting distance of Paris. I was dreading it because to get that close to the French capital, we would have to travel over 600 km whilst still carrying out our normal support role. The route for the day was a straight line north from our current position, 222.5 km of cycling and then another 400 km to Bonneval where tomorrow's stage would start. I knew that the riders probably wouldn't finish the stage until late afternoon and I would then have to drive double the distance I had already covered up to that point. I focused on getting home, sleeping in my own bed, changing into some clean clothes, never getting wrapped up in one of Mick's stupid ideas again.

Adnan was looking decidedly ropey when he emerged

from the bathroom; I asked if he was okay.

'Not really, I feel awful,' he replied.

I could tell he was ill when he didn't laugh at my follow up line informing him that it was a good job he didn't have to spend the day cycling halfway across France. We had faired superbly in terms of sickness and injury and other than my dizzy do and Matt's sore foot and scraped shoulder, we hadn't suffered at all. One of the easiest ways to pick up a bug whilst cycling is from a dirty water bottle but we had been incredibly careful about keeping our bottles clean and so far the riders had all been fine. Maybe our luck had run out as Adnan really appeared to be struggling and obviously wanted to climb back into bed, but equally didn't want to give up now that we were so close. Mick suggested that the riders should leave a bit later to give Adnan another hour or two in bed to try and sleep it off. Everyone agreed and Adnan got his head down and tried to sleep.

Matt's parents were leaving us today and we all got to see them before they left as they had pitched their tent in the same field as us last night. They seemed to have enjoyed themselves and it had certainly been a tremendous help having them available for the mountain stages. I honestly think we would have struggled to support the team properly had they not been there. They had a clear out of their hire car before they left and returned various water bottles, clothing, bits of bike and other rubbish which they had accumulated. Other donations included another map of the Tour route (I think I knew it off by heart now) and some Euros for the charity collection which had been donated by a stranger at the top of the Tourmalet. Apparently this had happened while Hannah and Nicole were resting at the top after completing the climb and their response to the donation was, 'Oh good, that'll pay for dinner tonight.' Fortunately Matt's mum heard and took charge of the cash so that she could ensure it ended up in the right place. I was stunned when I heard this story and it did nothing to make me feel any better towards the girls following the laundry episode of the previous evening.

An hour or so later and Adnan was still not feeling any better but he had decided he was going to ride regardless. If he had to stop to be sick then so be it. I didn't like to say it at the time but riding whilst sick is all part of the Tour experience and the pros do this on a regular basis. We had heard a rumour that some riders in the Tour had been so uncomfortable in the heat two days prior that they had been throwing up over their bikes, themselves and their colleagues as they tackled the climbs. No one said they could have an extra hour in bed to sleep it off.

I could completely understand why Adnan was so determined to get on his bike. It would have been awful if he had given up at this point. He wanted to be able to go home saying, 'I've ridden the entire Tour de France route,' not, 'I rode most of it but then felt sick.' Naturally all of the boys wanted Adnan to finish the ride too, this was a group effort and they wanted to finish as they had started, together. They all agreed to ride at whatever pace Adnan was comfortable with, just to get through the stage, regardless of how long it took.

'Yeah, sure, take your time, it's not like I've got 600 km to drive today is it?!' I shouted after them.

Of course, I didn't actually shout this but it is possible that I may have thought it.

Given the late start and the distance we needed to travel, I went to speak to Emily about where we should meet later. It was obvious that we were going to have a late finish today and it was possible that it might end up being too late to drive all the way to Bonneval. It therefore didn't make any sense for Motorhome Two to do what they would normally do and drive to the next start town. I suggested that we meet them at the finish town of Brive la Gaillarde and then we could decide where to head for. I suspected that we would probably end up driving part way to Bonneval and would then finish the journey tomorrow morning. There was some flexibility to do this as the next stage was a time trial and only 53.5 km in length. After three weeks' training, the boys should be able to knock this out in about ninety minutes. Arrangements made, Sara and I left the others to it and pointed the motorhome north.

We had agreed to meet up with the boys more regularly given Adnan's state of health. At the first agreed stop, about 45 km into the stage, we had to wait much longer than we would have normally expected. This wasn't a good sign. There were no climbs of any significance in the first 45 km but the boys were clearly not riding at their normal pace. Mick arrived first and he looked concerned. Adnan was really struggling and didn't feel any better. Hardly surprising, I don't ever remember the doctor saying to me that the best way to cure a stomach bug is to go on a 200 km cycle ride.

Shortly afterwards, Adnan, Matt and Stephen rode up. Matt and Stephen helped themselves to some food; Adnan went and sat in the motorhome. I went to see how he was.

'I feel awful, honestly, if this was day one or two, I would pack it in and go home. I'll be damned if I'm giving up now though.'

I had to admire Adnan, he was certainly determined. But determination alone won't get you through a 222.5 km stage of the Tour de France, he needed to eat too. He didn't fancy pizza, sandwiches, crisps, anything in fact. Eventually he was persuaded to eat half a Snickers bar. Shortly afterwards he disappeared behind the motor-home, probably to bring it back up again.

Stephen, Matt and Mick were equally determined; determined that they weren't going to leave a man behind and that they would drag Adnan to the finish if they had to. I expect Stephen's Marine training came in handy here – they never leave a man behind either! In terms of support, the boys were completely molly-coddled today and had five or six food stops compared to the normal two or three. I suppose it could have been worse, Adnan could have been ill on the longest stage of the Tour rather than the second longest.

Every stop was the same; Adnan looked on the verge of collapse and couldn't face eating anything. At least he was drinking and the energy drink contained carbo-hydrates which seemed to be what was keeping him going. It was easy for Sara and me to say things like, 'just keep going,' or 'nearly there now' but Adnan was really suffering. The relief he felt when he crawled into Brive la Gaillarde must have been unbelievable. Adnan looked as wrecked as I had seen any of the riders look. It was no surprise when he got straight into bed. The stage might have been an easy one but the hardest day of the trip was no longer the wet, windy Belgian one, at least not in Adnan's eyes.

It was early evening by the time we found Emily and the girls and Bonneval was over 400 km and a five hour drive away. I didn't fancy another five hours behind the wheel and I doubted that Adnan would want to be bounced around in the bed for that long. We got out the maps and looked for a suitable midway point. Cross-referencing the map with our book of *aires*, we found a town called Theillay which was 280 km away. Jane estimated a two and a half hour drive, definitely preferable to the alternative.

Four hours later (thanks Jane!) we pulled up at the motorhome *aire* in the village of Theillay. The *aire* was little more than a patch of ground outside the fire station and opposite a cemetery but at 11:00 pm none of us really cared. The boys had been snacking on biscuits, cakes and bread during the drive and it seemed too much to ask the girls in Motorhome Two if they were going to cook dinner now. I had some cold pizza and the last of a French stick before joining Sara, Mick and Emily for a well-earned glass of wine and reflected on the fact that the boys were now well past the 3,000 km mark.

I made my way to my bunk at the back of the motorhome and checked on Adnan. He was sleeping and still hadn't eaten anything other than half a Snickers bar. I had my fingers crossed that a good sleep would be enough to sort him out for the next day.

153 competitors lined up for the final mountain stage of this year's Tour de France. It was over 25 km into the race before any riders managed to break away from the *peloton*. Several attempts at escaping were quickly pulled back. Perhaps nearly three weeks in the saddle were starting to take their toll? On the descent of the first climb, a group of seven riders managed to pull ahead by a few seconds. Behind them came a second counter-attack group and then the main group.

By the top of the second mountain, the lead group were 40 seconds ahead of the group of ten counter-attackers and 1 minute and 40 seconds in front of the *peloton*. At the 68 km mark, the second chase group caught up with the leaders. At 71 km the lead group had an advantage of 3 minutes and 5 seconds over the bunch.

The Liquigas-Cannondale team took up position at the front of the *peloton* at the start of the second climb and drove all the way to the base of the fourth mountain, the Port de Balès. On arrival at the Port de Balès, the lead group had lost some of their advantage and were now 2 minutes and 15 seconds ahead.

Several attacks were seen as the lead group raced to the summit of the Port de Balès and the group was in a fragmented form as it went over the top, whilst the main *peloton* continued to make ground. In the closing kilometres of the stage, the leaders were gradually reeled in and only Alejandro Valverde, Movistar, was able to stay out in front, ultimately winning the stage by 19 seconds.

Chris Froome rolled in second and Bradley Wiggins was third. Wiggins said in an interview after the race that as he hit the summit of the last climb, he started to allow himself to think that he was going to win the Tour de France. It certainly looks that way now and barring a disaster, Wiggins looks set to make history this week as the first Brit ever to win the *maillot jaune*.

Tour positions at end of STAGE 17

Stage winner: Alejandro Valverde/Movistar

Yellow: Bradley Wiggins/Sky Procycling
Green: Peter Sagan/Liquigas-Cannondale
Polka Dot: Thomas Voeckler/Team Europcar
White: Tejay Van Garderen/BMC Racing Team

STAGE 19
Friday 20th July 2012
BONNEVAL – CHARTRES
Individual time trial – 53.5 km

'If you aren't throwing up, you aren't working hard enough.'
Anon (although most probably Mick – One Day Ahead team)

It was a treat to wake up to a grinning Adnan standing in the middle of the motorhome munching Adnan Cakes.

'Do you realise I rode an entire stage of the Tour de France on half a Snickers? That's hardcore, even the pros don't do that! Bunch of girls needing their little bags of sandwiches and fruit.'

Adnan was feeling better then. My finger crossing had done the trick and Adnan felt fine, albeit hungry. Hardly surprising given that he had burnt off about 7,000 calories the previous day but ingested only 125. It is a wonder he didn't feel a whole lot worse. Still, nothing a couple of bags of Adnan Cakes couldn't sort out.

'What's he doing now?!' shrieked Sara.

Adnan and I were alerted to the fact that Mick was outside and was heading off towards the fire station with an unknown Frenchman. Fifteen minutes later Mick returned following, what he described as, 'a very nice shower'. It transpired that Mick had been saving his words up and had managed to tell the fireman what we were up to and also the fact that he was himself a retired firefighter. The French *Pompier* was, by chance, a cycling fan although I have no idea how they came to be discussing the shower facilities. He was just about to leave for the day to go to his real job (80% of French firefighters are volunteers), but he offered to leave the station open so that we could all use the showers if we so wished, asking only that we pushed the door shut when we left. I initially assumed that there were other people in the building but it was completely empty. What a wonderful random act of kindness.

It was still over 130 km to Bonneval and the start line of today's stage. Today should be a pushover of a ride for the boys, completely flat and just 53.5 km. It would be a time trial for the professionals but for the One Day Ahead team it was an opportunity to take it easy. I mean, really, 53.5 km? I doubt it would even warm their legs up. The boys wouldn't need support but they would need transport to Bonneval, although as I pointed out to them, if they rode the 130 km from our current location and then tagged the time trial on the end, they would still have ridden less than they had on most days of this trip. It was the turn of the girls in Motorhome Two to support the boys, so they drew the short straw of driving them to the start. They set off at 9:30 am and Sara put the kettle on.

I had been thinking about riding today's stage and Sara offered to drive the motorhome if I wanted to, but honestly, I just couldn't be bothered. The weather was cooler and there were even a few spots of rain, which made cycling even less appealing and I was completely lacking in enthusiasm. I wasn't interested in cycling, I was interested in getting home and we were oh so close now. We spent a couple of hours building ourselves up to the drive to Chartres and when we had run out of tea bags, we decided it was time to get going.

The weather was definitely more 'British' as we moved further north and by the time we reached Chartres, I found myself digging around at the bottom of my holdall for a fleece. After two and a half weeks stuffed in a bag with the rest of my dirty clothes, it was ready for the bin but a quick shake and it was instantly transformed into a wearable garment (none of us were winning any prizes for fashion by this stage of the trip). Motorhome Two and the boys were waiting for us near the end of the stage finish. As expected, the boys had bashed out the time trial with ease and it had only taken an hour and a half to complete the short, flat course.

The One Day Ahead team were now just one stage away from completing their objective and we started to think about celebrating our achievement. Whilst it could be argued that our celebrations were twenty four hours premature, we didn't really have any choice. Mick had booked us on to the early evening Eurotunnel Shuttle back to the UK tomorrow, which meant that as soon as the boys had finished riding, we needed to drive straight to Calais. The reason for this was that Mick had decided that, after riding the Tour de France route, the best thing to do on Sunday would be to compete in the British Mountain Bike Cross-Country National Championships. Of course, that's exactly what any normal person would do. If nothing else, at least he had put himself through one hell of a training regime in the lead up.

Therefore, we had decided to hold our main celebratory meal tonight and we had also opted to stay in Chartres for the night. Alongside one of the main roads through the town, we found a wide pavement area which was used for parking. There were a number of cars parked up but also a handful of motorhomes so we added ours to the line. It looked as though we had struck lucky once again with parking, as we were now located just a few minutes walk from the centre of town.

Everyone was on good form and I couldn't be happier. There was a tiny, tiny part of me that was actually sorry that it would soon all be over. Just to be clear, this was a really tiny part, molecular level stuff.

Chartres had a wide range of restaurants and eatery options and we mooched through the streets comparing the alternatives. Adnan and I were keen on finding somewhere a bit special, somewhere we could really mark the occasion and we spotted a pleasant looking French bistro with a set menu advertised in the window at a cost of fifty Euros a head. This seemed reasonable for three courses including wine and we pointed it out to the others. Immediately Hannah baulked at the price and started waving her arms at a menu in a second restaurant. Actually, the use of the term 'restaurant' is probably being generous, maybe café would be a better description.

'Look, what about this one, twelve Euros for three courses and wine?'

Adnan and I looked at each other both wondering how ill you could get from eating three courses and wine which cost a total of about eight quid. Obviously we were going to have to find some middle ground and the pizzeria a few doors down seemed to fit the bill, offering a starter and pizza for sixteen Euros a head. Bargain!

We must have looked a ramshackle bunch when we walked into the restaurant. Someone, I assume the manager, almost broke into a sprint to get to us so that he could hustle us out of the view of his other patrons. Mick asked if they had space for ten and we were directed to a large table right at the back of the dining room. We were all used to each other wearing creased, grubby clothes and looking generally unkempt but I'm sure we provided a talking point for the other diners that evening.

Garlic mushrooms to start, followed by a ham and cheese pizza, lovely! Admittedly I had eaten pizza almost every day since we arrived in France as it was a staple of the boys' daily diet but this one was so much better. As the wine flowed, the tensions of the three previous weeks seemed to drain away and suddenly all of the issues which had dominated our thoughts during the trip seemed insignificant. Who cares if the girls want to ride today? Are we really that bothered about washing an extra pair of cycling shorts? Is it really a big deal if we spend twelve Euros on food or eighteen?

No sooner than I had started to relax and the bill arrived and I was brought back to earth with a bang. If there is one thing that I can't stand, it's when you go out for a meal with a group who start bickering about how much they are going to contribute when the bill turns up, 'I didn't drink so I'm not paying for that,' 'I didn't have a starter,' and so on. Needless to say, we now had this charade to go through. Even with drinks, the bill only worked out at twenty Euros each; it wasn't a fortune by anyone's standards, although apparently it was. I was able to step out of the discussion as Mick told me he was paying for mine as a thank you for the work I had put in getting him round France.

'What about me?' piped up Sara.

'You're my wife,' he replied, 'you didn't have a choice!'

The punch in the chest was enough for Mick to realise that he was also paying for Sara's meal.

Eventually there was a pile of money on the table which was sufficient to cover our debt. I highlighted the fact that we didn't appear to have left a tip. Faces quickly turned south. Oh, I'll get the tip then shall I? Twenty Euros should cover it. So much for a free meal!

It wasn't particularly late when we left the restaurant and we headed back to the motorhome for our last night.

Emily joined Mick, Sara and me for a nightcap and asked if she could cadge a lift home with us tomorrow. The rest of the group were staying in France for an extra night but Emily had, understandably, had enough and was as ready for home as Sara and I were. I think Mick and Adnan would have been quite happy to stay on.

'Fancy doing another lap?' I asked Adnan,

'I'd love to,' came the reply.

Stage 18 and 153 riders took to their bikes today. It would take a lot for anyone to drop out now with Paris just around the corner. The race started quickly and it was 21 km before an escape group, led by Dmitriy Fofonov, Astana Pro Team, got clear of the *peloton* but after 26 km there were six riders just 40 seconds ahead. Omega Pharma-Quickstep were pulling the main group along and by 40 km, the leaders had been caught.

A new breakaway group of sixteen riders formed after 71 km and at the 84 km mark, they were 3 minutes and 15 seconds ahead of the rest of the group. BMC and AGR2 worked together to pull back some of this time and the gap was down to 2 minutes 10 seconds by the 120 km point.

At 120 km a large dog ran on to the road and caused a crash involving a number of riders. Fortunately there were no serious injuries and all riders were able to continue. I believe the dog was also fine, running back into the crowd after getting the shock of his life.

The lead group had diminished in size slightly by the 28 km to go point and there were now fourteen escapees with an advantage of just 45 seconds. Several riders attempted to break out of the lead group but without success and the *peloton* finally caught the leaders inside the final kilometre.

With no significant climbs, this was always going to be a stage for the sprinters and Bradley Wiggins started a perfect lead out for Mark Cavendish who began his sprint 300 metres from the line. No other rider could match his pace and Cav claimed the 22nd Tour de France stage win of his career.

No changes today in the jersey competitions and Wiggins is one step closer to bringing home that coveted yellow jersey. Wiggins excels at time trials so he will almost certainly be looking for a stage win tomorrow.

Tour positions at end of STAGE 18

Stage winner: Mark Cavendish/Sky Procycling

Yellow: Bradley Wiggins/Sky Procycling
Green: Peter Sagan/Liquigas-Cannondale
Polka Dot: Thomas Voeckler/Team Europcar
White: Tejay Van Garderen/BMC Racing Team

STAGE 20

Saturday 21st July 2012
RAMBOUILLET – CHAMPS-ÉLYSÉES, PARIS
Flat – 120 km

'I am 68, but still ride every week with some friends, maybe 60 km at a time, but we enjoy a glass of wine and some Parma ham afterwards.'
Eddy Merckx - Five times winner of the Tour de France

The final stage of the Tour de France is, to a large extent, a ceremonial affair rather than a day of racing. The winners of the various jerseys are usually wearing them by this time and riders will enjoy the most leisurely ride they have had for three weeks. It is a tradition that riders do not attack to try and gain time in the General Classification competition and the final stage is seen as a gentle roll into Paris. It is not uncommon to see riders in the *peloton* enjoying a glass of champagne or a cigar as they head towards the capital. From the point of view of the yellow jersey holder, Stage 20 is a victory parade and a chance to move through the *peloton*, chatting with other riders who will take the opportunity to congratulate him on his achievement. The final stage is a day for the sprinters and it is only in the closing kilometres of the race that things get serious and a battle will take place for the last stage win of the Tour.

The Tour has always finished in Paris and has come to a conclusion on the Champs-Élysées every year since 1975. Once the riders reach the Champs-Élysées, they complete eight laps of a circuit which takes them up one side of Champs-Élysées, round the Arc de Triomphe, back down the other side of the Champs-Élysées, round les Tuileries and across Place de la Concorde. The official length of this last stage would be 120 km with around 50 km of this distance made up by the laps of the Champs-Élysées circuit.

Sitting at the breakfast table, Mick was tapping away at the Garmin, which had kept a running total of the distance the boys had cycled since our first day in Belgium. Including the rest day rides, the extra few kilometres here and there to get to exact start locations and the odd additional kilometre or two for detours or where they had simply gone the wrong way, the boys had already ridden a couple of hundred kilometres over the official Tour distance of 3,497 km. There were still 70 km to ride to get to Paris and Mick was therefore mulling over whether it would be cheating to miss out the eight laps of the Champs-Élysées circuit. I could see the logic; after all, the boys were already well in excess of the total distance that the Tour riders would have ridden so they had certainly covered the kilometres. The Champs-Élysées isn't particularly challenging, there is a slight incline and it is laid with cobblestones but it wasn't something which any of the boys were going to struggle with. In fact, the main challenge of the circuit would be the fact that the road would be open and no doubt teeming with traffic. Anyone who has ever tried to drive around the Arc de Triomphe in a car will know how stressful it can be so I could see why the idea of trying to do it eight times on a bicycle was mildly off-putting. The decision was made that riding up the Champs-Élysées to the Arc de Triomphe would be more than sufficient and very much safer and with that we left Chartres for the final start town of Rambouillet.

It was no surprise when we got to Rambouillet to find

that Hannah and Nicole had decided to ride the 70 km to Paris. I couldn't really blame them, it was the last chance they would get and if it wasn't for the fact that I didn't think it was fair to leave Sara to negotiate the Parisian traffic, I would probably have ridden it myself. The girls set off marginally before the boys and everyone riding agreed that they were happy to do the stage without any support along the way. This was good as it was going to take some time for us to work our way through the busy Paris roads and then we had to try and find somewhere to park two motorhomes, ideally close to the final finishing point of the Tour, the Arc de Triomphe.

Surprisingly, the traffic into Paris was light, not what I had expected at all on a Saturday afternoon, the day before the Tour de France arrived. For the first time in my life, I approached the Place Charles de Gaulle, the road which circles the Arc de Triomphe, in a motor vehicle. To make things interesting, I had chosen a 7.5 metre long motor vehicle which, in this country at least, had the steering wheel on the wrong side. Twelve separate avenues terminate at the Place Charles de Gaulle to create an oversized roundabout. The road is wide, certainly sufficient for ten lanes of traffic if not more and it is the type of road you would normally expect to be split up with painted lane markings or controlled by traffic lights. Indeed, just down the road from my house there is a reasonably large roundabout which has just four roads leading into it and as well as lots of painted lanes, there are also five sets of traffic lights. The Place Charles de Gaulle has neither lanes nor lights, it is a total free for all. Because of the angle of our road leading on to the Place Charles de Gaulle and as I was situated on the right-hand side of the motorhome, I couldn't see any of the traffic coming towards us from the left.

'Let me know when it's safe to go,' I said to Sara.

271

'Mmm, I'm not sure it will ever be safe as such,' she replied, 'I should just go if I were you.'

At least we weren't in the new motorhome.

I pulled out and wondered if any of the cacophony of horns I could hear were aimed specifically at me. Possibly, possibly not, but regardless nothing had driven into the back of us and now we were most definitely in the flow of traffic circling the Arc de Triomphe. The problem we now had was that we needed to get out. We completed one lap to check which exit we actually needed and then a second just for good measure. I'd drifted too far towards the centre of the massive single lane to get out on the first pass of the Champs-Élysées and needed another lap to push our way back to the edge. We escaped unscathed but it was utter madness, for the boys to cycle through that lot eight times would have been suicidal.

Almost as soon as we had turned on to the Champs-Élysées, we noticed a painted lane on the right-hand side of the carriageway in which no traffic was driving. It wasn't clear whether it was a drop-off zone or maybe a taxi waiting area or nothing more than an area in which you weren't allowed to park or drive.

'That'll do,' said Sara.

'Really?' I replied, 'I'm pretty sure you won't be allowed to just park two motorhomes on the Champs-Élysées.'

Sara shrugged. She didn't say anything but I know she was thinking, 'Good luck in finding somewhere better.' I didn't fancy doing circuits of Paris looking for spaces which didn't exist so I indicated and pulled over. Emily was behind, having been in convoy since Rambouillet and she tucked in behind us. I was convinced that it would be no longer than five minutes before we were asked to leave. If I had done the same thing in London, I doubted that it would have been that long. We weren't sure how far away the boys were but they must have been close so Sara, Emily and Jess set off to their final finishing point at the Arc de Triomphe. Someone had arranged for some trophies to be made for the boys. The trophies consisted of four metal sculptures of cyclists racing, mounted on a wooden plinth. Each had a brass plate on the front with the rider's name and details of the One Day Ahead challenge. Mick's plate read, *'Mike.'* That should please him given that I had never heard anyone call him Mike.

'What does Adnan's say? Adam?' I asked.

Sara rolled her eyes when she saw. I laughed. It was typical and for me it summed up the whole adventure perfectly.

Fifteen minutes after our arrival and there was no sign of the boys and no sign of any police interest in my, surely illegal, parking. A movement in the wing mirror caught my eye and I spotted a scruffy looking individual walking up the side of the motorhome. He came up to my door and tapped on the window. I had no idea what he wanted but I was pretty certain that whatever it was, it wasn't going to be to my benefit in any way whatsoever. I waved him away but he was persistent and waved his hand around, mimicking the action required to open the window. I shook my head; that wouldn't be happening. Realising that he was going to have to conduct his scam of choice through the glass, he bent down to the floor and appeared to pick up a gold ring. He then held it up to the glass and gestured as if to give it to me. At this point, whilst convinced that this was an elaborate ploy to relieve me of some cash, I wasn't sure how the scam would play out. Regardless, I wasn't going to open the window to find out and eventually my little friend grew bored and toddled off to try his luck elsewhere.

When I got home, I Googled 'Paris gold ring scam' to find out what it was all about. I must admit, I was expecting something a bit more ingenious, you'd have to be a complete half-wit to fall for this one. Basically the ruse goes thus: the scammer tells the victim that they have dropped a ring and tries to return it to them. The victim will then either take the ring and pretend that they did indeed drop it or refuse, saying it doesn't belong to them. If the victim takes the ring, the scammer suggests a reward or finder's fee might be appropriate. If the victim refuses the ring, the scammer says that he is willing to split the 'valuable find' between them but explains that he doesn't have time to take the ring to a jeweller for appraisal or sale. Either way, the hope is that the victim is so driven by greed and the thought that he is about to get his hands on a solid gold ring, that he hands over ten or twenty Euros. Happy with his cash, the scammer hands over the ring and both parties go their separate way. Of course, the ring turns out to be made of tin or some equally worthless metal, what a surprise. As I say, you would have to be a total numbskull to fall for this.

Amazingly the gold ring scam artist was the only person to knock on my window for the entire two hours that I sat on the Champs-Élysées. Every time a police car drove past, I expected them to pull in or turn around and move me on but it never happened. My thanks therefore go to the Paris police, your indifference made my last day in France rather more stress free than I had anticipated it would be.

My phone rang. It was my sister calling from home. Various people had been doing their bit to get the word out about the One Day Ahead challenge while we were away. Sara's sister had been in charge of updating the blog and social media and my sister had also been doing what she could to spread the news of our Tour. My sister was calling to tell me that she had just come off the phone to Sky News; apparently they were in Paris and were interviewing people about the Tour de France. Sky now had my phone number and I could expect a call. This was exciting stuff, we had been trying to win some television exposure since day one and if Sky were in town and looking for news to fill some time, we would be happy to oblige. The Sky researcher called me minutes later and as we spoke, I watched the boys come riding up the Champs-Élysées, Union Jack flags flying like capes from their shoulders. Only a hundred metres to go.

'We'd love to do an interview with the team,' enthused the researcher, 'unfortunately we've just left the city centre but we will be back tomorrow, can we talk to you then?'

I explained that half of the team were travelling back to the UK today but gave her Stephen's contact details so that she could get in touch with him the next day. I'm not sure whether an interview with half the team wasn't as appealing or whether the researcher lost Stephen's mobile number, but he didn't hear from her the next day. I don't know why I was surprised, despite talking to three different television stations since arriving we just weren't destined to get our fifteen minutes of fame.

I missed the presentation of the trophies, the popping of the champagne and the celebratory photographs under the Arc de Triomphe but the whole group was reunited a short while after I had watched Mick, Adnan, Stephen and Matt pedal their way up the home straight. Nicole and Hannah had left the boys before the final few kilometres, allowing them to complete this momentous journey as they had started, four boys together.

Sara opened another bottle of champagne and Mick must have got a bit of dust in his eye because I'm sure it was leaking slightly. Maybe he was sad because his trophy had the wrong name on. Still no one seemed bothered about the fact that we were parked on the main road through Paris and we started to wonder how far we could push things. During the previous three weeks, Emily had carried out physio in a number of strange places, from car parks to fields to residential streets. It was completely normal to see Emily setting up her massage table wherever we had chosen to make camp.

'Do you think I could get away with doing some physio here?' asked Emily, 'It would make a fantastic photo with the Arc de Triomphe in the background.'

Turns out she could and it did. Stephen was happy to oblige and climbed on the table which was situated behind Motorhome Two and on the edge of the Champs-Élysées. The motorists passing by seemed to enjoy this spectacle, tooting their horns and waving as they passed. It was a crazy end to a crazy three weeks.

We had pushed our luck far enough on the Champs-Élysées and time was pressing on, we had a train to catch. Goodbyes were said, congratulations were passed on and mention was made of meeting up back in England for a meal. I doubted it would happen. We had started out as one group but very quickly a divide had begun to form. This division had steadily widened as the Tour went on, Motorhome One on one side and Motorhome Two on the other. Emily was the only exception, a Motorhome One team member, stuck in Motorhome Two. She now joined us for the trip home and I sat in the driving seat for the final time. I had agreed to get us out of Paris and then Sara said she would drive the last hour back to Calais.

Driving out of the capital, I suddenly remembered our solo riding friend Frode. I hadn't seen or heard of him for a few days and wondered how he was getting on.

'He joined us for part of the ride today,' said Adnan cheerfully, 'he's fine - he should be at the end by now.'

I was pleased Frode had made it to the end. He seemed like a nice guy and was always smiling when we saw him. His was a tremendous achievement considering he had ridden the whole route on his own.

Half an hour later, I switched seats with Sara. I had driven almost 5,000 km around France and now, at last, I would soon be home.

The second to last stage of the 2012 Tour de France was an individual time trial, each man riding alone and against the clock. If anyone had wanted to challenge Bradley Wiggins for the yellow jersey, they would need to gain over 2 minutes on this short stage and that was never going to happen.

Wiggins was the last rider to tackle the course and did so at a blisteringly fast pace. He was the only rider to complete the stage with an average speed in excess of 50 km/h and in doing so confirmed his win of the 2012 Tour de France. Wiggins would ride to Paris wearing the yellow jersey which he has held since Stage 8 and make history as the first British man to win the Tour de France.

Tour positions at end of STAGE 19

Stage winner: Bradley Wiggins/Sky Procycling

Yellow: Bradley Wiggins/Sky Procycling
Green: Peter Sagan/Liquigas-Cannondale
Polka Dot: Thomas Voeckler/Team Europcar
White: Tejay Van Garderen/BMC Racing Team

2012 MTB XC NATIONAL CHAMPIONSHIPS
Sunday 22nd July 2012
READING

'Life is like riding a bicycle. To keep your balance, you must keep moving.'
Albert Einstein - Theoretical physicist

It was very nearly midnight by the time Mick and Sara dropped me off at home. Mick had taken over the driving once we were back in England and our first stop was at their house. He needed to pick up his mountain bike. We said goodbye to Adnan and Emily at this point too as they continued their journey home in Emily's car which she had left on Mick and Sara's driveway.

The 2012 Mountain Bike Cross-Country National Championships were being held the following day in Reading. Mick and Sara were driving straight there and would sleep in the motorhome. Our journey to Reading took us almost past my front door so I asked to be dropped off on the way and I would drive over to Reading in the morning. I could have stayed in the motorhome but after three weeks in a cramped bunk, all I wanted to do was sleep in my own bed.

Forty five minutes into the journey to my house, Mick remembered the other thing he was meant to collect from home, his mountain bike shoes. This was a fairly major oversight on his behalf as a rider's shoes clip to his pedals and the clip system on a mountain bike is completely different to a road bike. Mick only had his road shoes with him and therefore had no suitable shoes in which to race his mountain bike. Mick's race wasn't due to start until 12:30 pm so there was time to get someone to pick the right shoes up and bring them over in the morning. However there would be a chance for Mick to ride the course prior to this so that he could get a few practice laps in. Without his shoes, he wouldn't be able to ride the course and this would put him at a distinct disadvantage when it came to the actual race. The last thing any of us wanted to do was drive back to Mick and Sara's house. Mick asked if he could borrow my mountain bike shoes.

'You certainly can,' I laughed, 'what size shoes do you take again?'

Mick has weeny girl's feet, size 7 or some similarly ridiculous size. I need a size 12 to contain my massive plates. The crowd would think Coco the Clown had entered the race when they saw Mick riding with my shoes hanging off the end of his toes. But it was a better option than turning round and driving back, so when I got home I dug out my shoes and handed them over.

Sara laughed at how clean they were, saying, 'Don't expect to get them back looking anything like that.'

Mick has an innate ability to get anything he touches covered in mud, oil or grease. When he tells someone he has Diesel jeans on, it isn't because this is the brand, it is because they are covered in diesel. I suspected my shoes would never be the same again.

To fall back into a proper bed after three weeks in the motorhome bunk was incredible. To get up in the morning and have a long, hot shower was even better. To then be able to dress in clean clothes was the icing on the cake. I was so glad to be home. I could have happily lazed around the house all day but I had a race to attend.

I arrived at the race venue at 11:30 am and found Mick waddling about in my clowns shoes. He had managed to ride the course but was glad he wasn't going to be wearing them for the actual race. Sara's sister had delivered Mick's own shoes shortly before I arrived and she was now sitting in the motorhome with Sara catching up on the details of the One Day Ahead adventure. Sara poured me a cup of tea and I joined them. France already seemed like an age away and the bad experiences of the trip were slowly fading to leave just the highlights in my memory. The human mind is excellent at remembering the good bits of something and completely disregarding the bad bits. Not just when it comes to something like One Day Ahead but anything – jobs, relationships, whole periods of life. It's no wonder that people make the same mistakes over and over again.

Mick was called to the start line for the old duffers' race or Grand Veterans as they have to call it so as to be politically correct. Thirty one of the UK's top amateur mountain bike riders lined up next to Mick. The commentator had been tipped off and when introducing some of the riders to the crowd, mentioned in passing that Mick had done a quick circuit of the Tour de France route for his training ride. The race would consist of four laps of a cross-country circuit which would take the riders about an hour and twenty minutes to complete. There was one pit lane in which Sara positioned herself so that she could swap Mick's drinks bottles. There would be no stopping for sandwiches today.

As Mick came past after his first lap, we could see there was a problem. Blood which should have been inside Mick's arm was now very clearly on the outside. He had obviously fallen off. Mick had managed to ride the full route of the Tour de France without so much as a stumble but put him in a bit of woodland and he was off in the first couple of miles. A bit of blood wasn't going to stop him however and he pushed on, racing hard to the end. Unfortunately the time lost during his crash meant that he never regained his position at the front of the race and he ended up finishing in fourth place. A very respectable result though, especially as none of the other riders would have had over 3,500 km in their legs that afternoon. It was a fitting end to the One Day Ahead adventure.

Stage 20, the final stage of the 2012 Tour de France, was all about the sprinters. The ride to Paris was a tranquil one, with an average speed in the first hour of just 31.7 km/h. 153 riders had made it this far. The leaders of the respective competitions rode bicycles which had been coloured the same as their jerseys.

As the *peloton* reached the Champs-Élysées a few attacks were made. By this time in the race, any breaks for freedom are highly unlikely to result in anything more worthwhile for the rider than a bit of extra exposure for themselves and their sponsors.

Mark Cavendish had won the final stage of the Tour de France for the last three consecutive years and he wanted to add a fourth victory to his tally. We all knew how it was going to play out and the fairytale ending saw Wiggins, in yellow, leading out his teammate, the current World Road Racing Champion, for the final sprint. Cav took the stage and so ended a difficult Tour for the Manxman. He hadn't been a priority in the 2012 Tour as Team Sky were concentrating on winning the yellow jersey.

In 2011, Cavendish had won the green jersey points competition; in 2012 he was never really in contention. It was no surprise when he left Sky the following year to join a team who would make winning the green jersey their priority.

Tour positions at end of STAGE 20

Stage winner: Mark Cavendish/Sky Procycling

Yellow: Bradley Wiggins/Sky Procycling
Green: Peter Sagan/Liquigas-Cannondale
Polka Dot: Thomas Voeckler/Team Europcar
White: Tejay Van Garderen/BMC Racing Team

EPILOGUE

'That was $?*$%@ hard.'
Richard Grady - One Day Ahead driver talking about the
Isle of Man End to End

In September 2013 I had the opportunity to race across
an entire country on a bike myself. This would be an
unsupported ride and would be off-road, a much harder
prospect than road riding. A proper man's ride, none of
your girlie smooth tarmac nonsense, this was hardcore.
Admittedly the country in question was tiny but it was a
country nonetheless.

Sitting in the middle of the Irish Sea you will find the
Isle of Man. Although it is commonly thought to be part
of the United Kingdom, it actually isn't. The Isle of Man
is a self-governing British Crown Dependency and each
year the End to End Mountain Bike Challenge takes
place, racing from the most northerly point to the most
southerly. The race is roughly 75 km long with the vast
majority of the route being off-road and passing through
fields, woods and along single-track. There is also over
1500 metres of climbing just to keep you awake.

Standing in the starting area with almost 1700 other
competitors, I did wonder what on earth I was doing. It
was 10:00 am and not particularly warm; it had also just
started to drizzle. By 10:15 am I was on my way. The
first 20 km are pleasant enough as they are all on the
road. I had started somewhere near the back so as not to
get caught up with the fast riders, I wanted to ride at my
pace. I broke away from a few stragglers and as I passed
some spectators at the side of the road, they called out to

me, 'Are you the last one?'

Seriously? Did I look that bad? I'd bought a new bike for this event; I definitely had all the gear and looked the part. I clarified that there were at least 200 riders behind me and rode on, pride intact. I managed to pass a number of riders on the road. Although this was a mountain bike race, good form dictated that if you took advantage of other riders by riding in their slipstream, you should take a turn on the front to give them a break. I was going to be lucky to get to the end so I am afraid etiquette went by the wayside, it was every man for himself as I jumped from one wheel to another.

The road turned sharply onto a gravel track and started to head upwards. It had been raining for the week leading up to the event and I had my first indication of what conditions were going to be like on the off-road section. The standing water and mud were bad enough but after over a thousand riders had passed through each section before me, conditions were horrendous. My poor shiny new bike, it would be ruined!

I pushed on, sticking religiously to the instructions on my energy gels and bars, four gels an hour plus a bar plus 500 ml of energy drink. I knew the importance of eating and keeping fluid levels up. The first checkpoint was situated 30 km into the race. The cut-off time to get here was 1:00 pm. I arrived at 12:30 pm with plenty of time to stop for a five minute break. A nice lady filled up my water bottles and I munched on a tasteless energy bar. I was already covered in mud from head to toe, as was my bike. It started to rain, at least that might wash some of the mud off, I thought.

By the time I made it to the second checkpoint at 42 km, it was 1:45 pm. I made it with minutes to spare – the checkpoint closed at 2:00 pm. I was over halfway now. Another rider started to chat to me, he was supposed to meet a friend at the second checkpoint but he hadn't turned up. His friend had his energy gels and drinks. I offered him some of mine, confident that I had more than enough to get to the end. He looked knackered. He was probably thinking the same about me.

I suppose the real suffering started shortly after leaving the second checkpoint. A quick spurt along a road and then a gruelling climb. Many riders were walking but I pushed on as far as I could. In the end I had no choice but to walk too as the pathway was littered with bikes and people pushing them. I was secretly grateful for the opportunity to get off, my legs were burning and my whole body wanted to give up.

More mud, more climbs and then some downhill runs through fields, all I had to do was hang on but even that was hard now as my hands and arms were aching from the effort. I had lost all sense of where I was, all I could see around me were trees, hills, fields and mud. I must be close to the final checkpoint surely?

51 km into the race and the last checkpoint appears. I was cutting it fine but arrived just before the cut-off at 3:30 pm. A marshal informed me it was easy from this point on. His expanding waistline told me that he hadn't been on a bike for years and would have no idea whether it was easy or not. I thanked him regardless and then checked myself for feeling superior when I realised that he was the smart one in this situation, not me.

The final kilometres counted down slowly. At least two marshals told me I only had 10 km to go and they were standing at least 5 km apart. The final bit of off-road is over a large hill. It's mostly single-track along the side of the hill which makes it a technical ride. Standing on your pedals trying to balance the bike along a path maybe a metre wide, which has already been ridden over by hundreds of other bikes, is not an easy thing to do at this stage. My legs were crying out every time I tried to stand, they were screaming when I asked them to pedal. Keep going, I'm not giving up this close to the end. I thought of Adnan, riding for 222 km feeling sick as a dog. How did he do it? Maybe I should have packed a Snickers bar instead of all the energy gels. For the last 20 km, I felt pretty sick myself; I think it was a mixture of the effort and all the gels. They contain caffeine and all sorts of who knows what. They weren't sitting well with me.

Down off the final hill and a marshal tried his best to encourage me, 'Only the last bit of road to go, well done!'

Yes but I knew that the last 2 km were up a brutal climb, everyone had been talking about it before the race, a real killer after so long in the saddle. They weren't wrong and I was reminded of Mick grovelling up the Col du Granier and did some grovelling of my own. On the other side of the road riders were descending the climb having finished their race. Many would ride back to the main town on the island, Douglas, 30 km away. I didn't need to ask my legs if they fancied a bonus return journey, I already knew the answer.

Towards the top I could hear music and a loudspeaker announcing the finishers' names; the pain would soon be over. Motivated by this thought, I stood up on the pedals and pushed as hard as I could (which wasn't very hard). I overtook someone towards the top of the hill.

'Why does everyone keep going past me?' he joked,

'Because you aren't pedalling hard enough!' I shouted back. Mick would have been proud.

Round the corner and into a field and there was the finishing line. A rider a few metres in front of me sat up and I knew I could beat him. He didn't even see me coming as I flew past him on the line, safely securing that coveted 1010th place!

At least I wasn't last – several hundred riders failed to complete the challenge and plenty more trailed in behind me. I had done what I had set out to do; I'd made it to the end but I was glad I wouldn't have to do it all over again the next day.

I have mixed feelings when I look back on my One Day Ahead experience. On one hand there was a lot of the journey which I didn't enjoy but on the other, I wouldn't have missed it for anything. To help support the team round such a challenging route as '*la grande boucle*' (the big loop) was something to be proud of. If nothing else, we managed to raise over £11,000 for our supported charities, Leukaemia and Lymphoma Research UK and the Ben Trend Foundation. The team also made it into the Independent on Sunday 2013 'Happy List.' Published annually, the Happy List names 100 outstanding people whose volunteering, caring, fundraising, mentoring, charity founding or selflessness makes Britain a more contented, supportive, better adjusted and happier place.

The day we left for France, I would have told you that the riders were the ones who were going to struggle and I would genuinely have believed it. As it was, our cycling team did amazingly well and if anyone was struggling with the whole thing, it was me. Admittedly our riders were above average in the pedalling department but they weren't professional cyclists and none had ever ridden multiple long distance stages day after day for three weeks. I expected the boys to get tired as time went on but the opposite occurred and they got stronger as their bodies adjusted to riding such great distances. In the end, it became normal for them and this was perfectly illustrated by Adnan who managed to ride over 220 km despite feeling like death warmed up. Adnan has told me he would love to ride the Tour route again and Mick wouldn't have a problem with doing it, but he is more of the 'done that, let's find something else to do' brigade.

As for me, would I do it again? I have to say, almost certainly not. Sara and I had the rough end of the deal for sure. Looking after people is nowhere near as much fun as doing the event yourself. Sara jokingly commented recently that maybe we should cycle the route and let Mick and Adnan follow us round in a motorhome but then we remembered the mountains. I told Mick shortly after One Day Ahead that he should stick to endurance events which last a maximum of twenty four hours in the future or count me out.

So far he has adhered to my request.

If you enjoyed this book I would really appreciate it if you could take a moment to leave me a review on Amazon. You don't need to write a long essay (unless you want to!); a couple of lines to say what you liked about it would be great. Thank you.

Contact me:
Twitter: @mr_richardgrady